MODERN STUDIES IN PROPERTY LAW: VOLUME 13

This collection is based on papers presented at the well-established Modern Studies in Property Law biennial conference.

It contains cutting-edge research relating to property law broadly conceived, covering land law, equity and trusts, and the interaction between property law and the environment.

Part 1 of Volume 13 in the Modern Studies in Property Law series examines a diverse range of topics in property law and uses a wide range of methodological approaches to reflect on a variety of current and emerging issues that have been overlooked, offering new analysis and insights that will be valuable for property lawyers, academics and students.

The contributors are leading academics and practitioners from several common law jurisdictions, which expands the book's focus and enhances its value to the reader.

Previous volumes in this series:

Modern Studies in Property Law: Volume 1
Edited by Elizabeth Cooke

Modern Studies in Property Law: Volume 2
Edited by Elizabeth Cooke

Modern Studies in Property Law: Volume 3
Edited by Elizabeth Cooke

Modern Studies in Property Law: Volume 4
Edited by Elizabeth Cooke

Modern Studies in Property Law: Volume 5
Edited by Martin Dixon

Modern Studies in Property Law: Volume 6
Edited by Susan Bright

Modern Studies in Property Law: Volume 7
Edited by Nicholas Hopkins

Modern Studies in Property Law: Volume 8
Edited by Warren Barr

Modern Studies in Property Law: Volume 9
Edited by Heather Conway and Robin Hickey

Modern Studies in Property Law: Volume 10
Edited by Ben McFarlane and Sinéad Agnew

Modern Studies in Property Law: Volume 11
Edited by Sue Farran, Russell Hewitson and Adam Ramshaw

Modern Studies in Property Law: Volume 12
Edited by Natalie Mrockova, Aruna Nair and Luke Rostill

Modern Studies in Property Law: Volume 13,
Part 1: Use, Abandonment, and Protection of Land
Edited by Martin Dixon and Emma Lees

Modern Studies in Property Law: Volume 13,
Part 2: Doctrinal Problems for Modern Property Law
Edited by Martin Dixon and Emma Lees

Modern Studies in Property Law

Volume 13

Part 1: Use, Abandonment, and Protection of Land

Edited by
Martin Dixon
and
Emma Lees

•HART•
OXFORD • LONDON • NEW YORK • NEW DELHI • SYDNEY

HART PUBLISHING

Bloomsbury Publishing Plc

Kemp House, Chawley Park, Cumnor Hill, Oxford, OX2 9PH, UK

1385 Broadway, New York, NY 10018, USA

Bloomsbury Publishing Ireland Limited, 29 Earlsfort Terrace, Dublin 2, D02 AY28, Ireland

HART PUBLISHING, the Hart/Stag logo, BLOOMSBURY and the Diana logo are trademarks of Bloomsbury Publishing Plc

First published in Great Britain 2026

A catalogue record for this book is available from the British Library.

A catalogue record for this book is available from the Library of Congress.

ISBN: HB: 978-1-50999-020-7
ePDF: 978-1-50999-018-4
ePub: 978-1-50999-019-1

Typeset by Compuscript Ltd, Shannon

For product safety related questions contact productsafety@bloomsbury.com

To find out more about our authors and books visit www.hartpublishing.co.uk. Here you will find extracts, author information, details of forthcoming events and the option to sign up for our newsletters.

Contents

List of Contributors

Vanessa Casado-Pérez is Professor at Texas A&M School of Law, US.

Heather Conway is Professor of Property Law and Death Studies at Queen's University Belfast, UK.

Catherine de Contreras is Lecturer at the Dickson Poon School of Law at King's College London, UK.

Martin Dixon is Professor of the Law of Real Property at the University of Cambridge, UK.

Victoria Evans (née Ball) is Lecturer at the Dickson Poon School of Law at King's College London, UK.

Sheena Grattan is Visiting Professor at Ulster University.

Russell Hewitson is Solicitor and Associate Professor of Law at Northumbria Law School, Northumbria University, UK.

Emma Lees is Professor of Environmental and Property Law at the University of Cambridge, UK.

Yael R Lifshitz is Reader at King's College London, UK.

John Page is Professor of Law at Southern Cross University, Australia.

Susan Pascoe is Associate Professor of Law at Middlesex University, UK.

Michael W Poulsom is Senior Lecturer at Manchester Metropolitan University, UK.

Teresa Sutton is Associate Professor in Law at the University of Sussex, UK.

John Tribe is Senior Lecturer in Law, University of Liverpool and Academic Associate, Exchange Chambers.

1

Introduction

MARTIN DIXON AND EMMA LEES

THE FIFTEENTH BIENNIAL *Modern Studies in Property Law Conference* took place at Queens' College, Cambridge in March 2024. This two-volume set contains the final versions of the papers presented there. Each paper has been peer reviewed and the authors have responded warmly to the suggestions and comments of the peer reviewers. We are grateful to all of those who contributed to the fascinating scholarship on display in these volumes. Once again, the *Conference* has demonstrated both the depth and breadth of property law scholarship being undertaken in the UK and beyond. For those who argue – and, unbelievably, there are such idealogues – that 'property law' is one-dimensional, mechanical or 'merely' practical, we suggest you open these volumes so that you can see what you have been missing. The essays in this collection cover the practical, the theoretical, the abstract and the concrete. They talk about land, nature, the environment and people. They ask fundamental questions about our relationship with the world around us, with our legal neighbours and with society. They investigate the intricacies of statute law, the role of judges in private law property disputes and, most of all, remind the reader that all of us have a relationship to 'property' that is complex and important.

So it is, then, that the *Conference* takes a broad view of what 'property' is. For sure, there is an emphasis on private law, and a large proportion of the essays presented in the two volumes swirl around the nitty gritty of land law and trusts or the resolution of private law disputes. This is important. All of us working in the more traditional areas of private law – land, trusts, torts, contract and criminal law – know that both resources and opportunities for private law scholars are rare, and in some cases are wearing an invisibility cloak. While few would deny (at least we hope!) that the study, elucidation and advancement of private law is a key skill in the legal universe, the ability to deliver quality research and effective teaching in this broad field is diminishing at an alarming rate. How many of us work in institutions where recruitment in these areas is exceptionally difficult (and Cambridge is not an exception) and where this 'nuts and bolts stuff' (not always meant kindly) takes a back seat to other legal scholarship? More than once, and far too often, we have been told that a colleague's application for resources or professional advancement has been declined because these opportunities have been offered for 'more impactful', 'more relevant' or even 'more interesting' work. Of course, we do not for one moment seek to argue that private law scholarship deserves *more* recognition, or *more* status or *more* resources or *more* opportunities than any other type of legal discourse, and no one reading this should think that we regard the work of non-private law scholars as any less valid or distinguished than ours. That would be the very essence of hypocrisy. But we do want to remind those running law schools, and funding bodies and promotion panels that simply because something has been done for a long time does not mean it is out of date or irrelevant in the modern world. Just ask those dealing with the HM Land Registry how they are getting on after the 'efficiency drive' that saw the legal teams replaced with much less expensive customer service agents, or the law student whose lectures in contract are being delivered by a junior lecturer whose real (and laudable) passion is public law or the socio-economic analysis of the law on domestic violence, but who is forced to deliver a course on contract formation because 'somebody has to do it'. Perhaps we should all move away from driving cars with petrol or diesel engines and embrace the exciting world of electric vehicles, but those vehicles will be going precisely nowhere without roads and traffic lights.

These realities are why the *MSPL Conferences* are so important. Not only do they provide an opportunity for the publication (the 'research output' or 'impact case study') of high-quality property law scholarship, they also give property scholars from all heritages the opportunity to meet, to discuss and to learn. It is good to know that we are not, in fact, ploughing a lone furrow and that there is a richness and an enthusiasm that is infectious. We hope that others felt as energised after the Conference as we did and we look forward to the *16th Conference* in Southampton in 2026.

That there are two volumes for the *15th Conference*, instead of the usual large single volume, does not indicate a cunning plan. It is more a reflection of how the world of print publishing has changed. We are grateful that we are able to continue the *Conference*'s long association with Hart Publishing/Bloomsbury and once again their practical and professional support has been invaluable. The change has, however, given us the opportunity to think about how we should group the essays. As you read them, you may think that we have not put much thought into it(!), but we have tried to collate the essays in such a way that no piece feels out of place or disconnected.

This volume, Volume 1, might be said to have essays grouped around three broad themes. First, we have three essays shedding new light on old concepts. Here is a perfect example of why we should never assume that there is nothing to say about familiar ideas, especially as the world changes. Russell Hewitson ('*Caveat Emptor*: Is it Time for a Change?') brings a fresh perspective to the principle of *caveat emptor*, the 'well-established legal doctrine in conveyancing'.[1] If you see the word 'conveyancing' and conclude that this 'practitioner stuff' is

[1] Chapter 2 of this Volume, page 5.

not for you, you will miss a persuasive re-assessment of this critical doctrine in property law and contract law, analysed in the light of its history and its modern purpose. Likewise with John Tribe's 'The Dangers of Feudal Escheat' and Teresa Sutton's 'Ecclesiastical Easements'. Property law and legal history have always been siblings, but there is more to these than a jolly historical romp. John's title hints at why escheat still matters and why it still lays traps for the unwary, and Teresa reframes her analysis of the practical, modern importance of ecclesiastical land, especially in rural communities, in a unique way. Thinking about church land in terms of changing conceptions of easements was for us a novel and intriguing idea. Everyone should have a pew easement, or more practically understand the role that ecclesiastical land plays in the lives of communities across the Kingdom.

The second broad theme reminds us of why empirical property research matters. Heather Conway and Sheena Grattan ('Dicta and Dissent; Doubt and Indecision') take a hard look at the role of the Supreme Court in settling estate disputes in the 15 or so years since the Court's inception. The results were surprising, at least to us, because we would have expected more homogeneity and consistency than Heather and Sheena discovered. After all, the 1966 Practice Direction has rarely, if ever, been invoked in a property law dispute[2] because (as we all *know*) consistency and certainty are key in property law. Crystals not mud! Perhaps, however, we are just fooling ourselves because, as this analysis shows, it's not that simple. Similarly, in their chapter, Victoria Evans and Catherine de Contreras consider, from, a socio-legal perspective, 'how the Supreme Court has shaped the concept of "property"'[3] in the last 15 years. For those of us whose work focuses more on rules and doctrine, this piece provides the context we need to understand the law in action. Together, these two essays shine a light on the role of our apex court in shaping the concepts and ideas that we sometimes take for granted. It is easy to forget, when mining the depths of the Land Registration 2002 or the Landlord and Tenant Act 1954, that these are living legal instruments whose application can change people's lives.

The third set of essays in Volume 1 examine what 'property' means in the modern world and how different conceptions of property can have a uniqueness that we might sometimes ignore. They remind us that we do not, in fact, have to have a unifying concept of 'property'. Thus, while we do not necessarily mean to take sides in the Great Crypto Property War, we were already on board with the idea that 'property' as an abstract concept is not one-dimensional. In 'The Doctrine of Abandonment: Lost Cause or Chimera?', Susan Pascoe undertakes a thematic analysis of the idea of abandonment across planning law (a holiday destination not usually visited by property scholars),

[2] As the Practice Direction ([1996] 3 All ER 77) states: 'In this connection they will bear in mind the danger of disturbing retrospectively the basis on which contracts, settlements of property and fiscal arrangements have been entered into …'.

[3] Chapter 6 of this Volume, page 89.

easements, adverse possession and the enjoyment of other interests in land (as opposed to titles and easements). We see, again, just how *connected* our different approaches to property can be. Mike Poulsom ('Conservation Covenants: A New Opportunity?'), and Vanessa Casado-Pérez and Yael Lifshitz ('Registering Nature') take ideas which are largely alien to real property law in the UK jurisdictions and demonstrate powerfully that this ignorance might be a mistake, or at least a mistake in the twenty-first century. Here are two essays that build on traditional concepts with which we are all familiar and then drive us in new directions. They epitomise why it is so important for property lawyers to be involved in policy conversations about the things that matter today. And so, if you were not by this stage persuaded, John Page finishes with an essay that says all of this in a sentence: '[o]ur relations with land are complex, multivalent, and multilayered'.[4] 'The Metaphysicality of Real Property' is not only a great title, it is a punchy, sweeping analysis that brings together many of the themes addressed in the other essays in this volume. It's not about theory, it's about law. We will not pretend that we had planned it this way, but John's piece is the perfect end to this first volume.

[4] Chapter 10 of this Volume, page 177.

2

Caveat Emptor
Is it Time for a Change?

RUSSELL HEWITSON

I. INTRODUCTION

A WELL-ESTABLISHED LEGAL doctrine in conveyancing is the principle of *caveat emptor*, or let the buyer beware. As Hamilton observed in his excellent history of the doctrine:

> An adage was never fitted more neatly to the part than caveat emptor; it is, among many excellent examples, the ideal legal maxim. It is brief, concise, of meaning all compact. Its terms are too broad to be pent up within the narrow confines of rules of law; they are an easy focus for judicial thought, a principle to be invoked when the going is difficult, a guide to be followed amid the baffling uncertainties of litigation. The phrase seems to epitomise centuries of experience; it is written in the language of Rome, the great law-giver; it comes with the repute of the classics and with the prestige of authority.[1]

However, the doctrine is not without its critics. The Conveyancing Standing Committee of the Law Commission called it 'an unjustifiably ramshackle principle' and provisionally proposed that it should be reversed,[2] whilst according to McKendrick and Gleeson, the conventional wisdom that *caveat emptor* is the rule in relation to the sale or letting of land has come under some challenge.[3] Mark Thompson has noted that 'in recent times … a strong blast of protectionism has blown into conveyancing law',[4] whilst it seems that the debate over its place in the law has not always been settled.[5]

[1] WH Hamilton, 'The Ancient Maxim Caveat Emptor' (1931) 40(8) *Yale Law Journal* 1133, 1156.

[2] Law Commission, *Caveat Emptor in Sales of Land: A Consultation Paper from the Conveyancing Standing Committee of the Law Commission* (1988).

[3] E McKendrick and L Gleeson, 'The Rotting Away of Caveat Emptor?' [1987] *Conveyancer and Property Lawyer* 121.

[4] MP Thompson, 'Must a Purchaser Buy a Charred Ruin?' [1984] *Conveyancer and Property Lawyer* 43.

[5] See, for example, C Harpum, 'Selling without Title: A Vendor's Duty of Disclosure?' (1992) 108 *LQR* 280, 331.

A current criticism is that it creates a pinch point in the conveyancing process as it places the onus on a purchaser to find out if there are any physical defects or legal issues relating to the property they are purchasing. As a result, the conveyancing process is slowed down whilst information is gathered about the property. Such information will usually consist of an inspection of the property, a survey of the physical condition of the property, the raising of enquiries with the vendor through their conveyancer, an investigation of the legal title, and the carrying out of property searches, such as a local authority search together with any necessary location specific searches. Additional checks will also be needed where the property is leasehold, such as making sure that any ground rent and service charge have been paid. All this due diligence must be carried out before the purchaser is in a position to exchange contracts and invariably increases the time involved.

The home selling and buying process in England and Wales has been criticised as being notoriously slow, inefficient and not consumer-friendly,[6] and along with relationship break-ups and the loss of a spouse or partner, moving house is frequently cited as one of life's most stressful events.[7] The growth of home ownership since the end of the Second World War has been one of the most fundamental social changes to have taken place in England and Wales,[8] and it is arguable that the conveyancing process has not kept pace with this. In the financial year 2022/23, there were an estimated 1,034,020 residential property transactions in England and 53,450 in Wales,[9] with the average time to complete the sale of a property from its initial listing being approximately 18 weeks.[10] A government study in 2017 on the consumer experience of buying and selling a home found over half of buyers and sellers thought the process of buying and selling a home took longer than they expected, whilst around one in four found it much longer than expected.[11] The conveyancing process is not mandated by law; rather the law provides a broad framework within which the parties to a transaction can decide how to proceed and in practice most transactions follow a standard industry protocol[12] and are completed through a private contract,[13] though such a protocol falls short of creating

[6] See, for example, Department for Levelling Up, Housing & Communities, *How to Sell a Home*, available at www.gov.uk/government/publications/how-to-sell-a-home.

[7] See, for example, www.legalandgeneral.com/insurance/life-insurance/moving-house-stress-signs.

[8] C Hamnett, *Winners and Losers: Home Ownership in Modern Britain* (London, Taylor & Francis, 1999).

[9] HMRC – see www.gov.uk/government/statistics/monthly-property-transactions-completed-in-the-uk-with-value-40000-or-above.

[10] RICS, 'December 2023 UK Residential Market Survey', available at www.rics.org/news-insights/market-surveys/uk-residential-market-survey.

[11] Department for Business, Energy & Industrial Strategy, 'Research on Buying and Selling Homes', Research Paper Number BIS/283, October 2017, available at www.gov.uk/government/publications/buying-and-selling-homes-consumer-experience-study.

[12] The Law Society Conveyancing Protocol provides a framework for the sale and purchase of a home for an owner occupier – see www.lawsociety.org.uk/topics/property/conveyancing-protocol.

[13] *Hansard*, HC (series 6) vol 611, col 61WH (7 June 2016).

a regulatory framework unlike, say, the Association of British Travel Agents (ABTA) Code of Conduct.[14] So, might it be possible to ameliorate the effect of *caveat emptor* to reduce the time that the conveyancing process takes and thus improve consumer experience?

Carol Rose has argued that in property law, there are crystals and mud.[15] According to her theory, a 'crystal rule' is one which signals, in a clear and distinct language, precisely what our obligations are and how we may take care of our interests. For her, these hard-edged rules are what property is all about. They are the very stuff of property. On the other hand, a 'mud rule' is quite the opposite. Over time, she argues, some of the crystal rules have been so muddied by exceptions and judicial opinions that they are now difficult to interpret and apply, and she characterises these as 'fuzzy, ambiguous rules of decision'. It is into this latter category that she places the doctrine of *caveat emptor*.[16] Johnson agreed with Rose that the simple and easy-to-apply rule of *caveat emptor* had been muddied as she hypothesised.[17] This chapter uniquely uses Rose's theory as a prism to examine the mud attached to *caveat emptor* and how it might be washed off so that its effect on the conveyancing process is reduced and it returns to a crystal, and whether alternatives to the principle or its complete reversal might improve the conveyancing process.

II. THE ORIGINS AND DEVELOPMENT OF *CAVEAT EMPTOR*

Stetson and McGlynn traced the concept of protecting purchasers from defects back to the works of St Thomas Aquinas in the thirteenth century.[18] Over time, Aquinas' principles gave way to the doctrine of *caveat emptor* and Hamilton found the phrase used as early as 1534,[19] in the context of a horse trade about which the judge, scholar and legal author Sir Anthony Fitzherbert wrote 'if he be tame and have ben rydden upon, then *caveat emptor*'.[20] Pearce suggested that the use of Latin in the maxim may suggest that it was drawn from Roman law, but like Hamilton he concluded that it instead owed its origins to the trading practices of the Middle Ages.[21]

[14] www.abta.com/about-us/code-of-conduct.

[15] CM Rose, 'Crystals and Mud in Property Law' (1988) 40 *Stanford Law Review* 577.

[16] ibid 580–83.

[17] AM Johnson, 'An Economic Analysis of the Duty to Disclose Information: Lessons Learned from the Caveat Emptor Doctrine' (2008) 45 *San Diego Law Review* 79.

[18] RW Stetson and PB McGlynn, 'Buyer Beware: The Return of Caveat Emptor: Sullivan v. Five Acres Realty Trust, 487 Mass. 64 (2020)' (2022) 103 *Massachusetts Law Review* 74.

[19] Hamilton (n 1) 1164.

[20] WW Skeat (ed), *The Book of Husbandry by Master Fitzherbert* (reprinted from the edition of 1534, Trübner & Co, 1882) § 118.

[21] C Pearce, 'Caveat Emptor or Caveat Venditor? Stigmatised Properties and Obligations of Disclosure' in S Farran, R Hewitson and A Ramshaw (eds), *Modern Studies in Property Law*, volume 11 (Oxford, Hart Publishing, 2021).

The maxim then started to make appearances in the law reports from the seventeenth century onwards, reflecting a laissez-faire economic model facilitated by a non-interventionist policy.[22] As King observed, it developed in response to the dramatic decline in the power of the church during this time, with rapid trade growth creating an attitude of self-fulfilment within merchants and tradespeople.[23] The case of *Chandelor v Lopus*[24] is credited with creating the doctrine as we now know it. A goldsmith who sold a bezar stone for £100 was held not liable to the purchaser as he had not expressly warranted that it was a bezar stone.[25] A few years later, in *Moore v Hussey*,[26] a case which involved the valuation of a married woman's estate, the maxim was expressed as 'caveat emptor, qui ignorare non debuit quod jus alienum emit',[27] which translates as 'let a purchaser, who ought not be ignorant of the amount and nature of the interest which he is about to buy, exercise proper caution'.[28]

The relationship between morality and *caveat emptor* was considered by the House of Lords in the nineteenth century in *Peek v Gurney*,[29] where Lord Cairns said: 'Mere non-disclosure of material facts, however morally censurable … would in my opinion form no ground for an action in the nature of an action for misrepresentation.'[30] As Craine has remarked, it seemed that complete honesty in business transactions was not as important as the certainty which arose from following *caveat emptor*.[31] Thus, each person was expected to watch out for themselves as the courts deemed themselves dispensers of law, not morality.[32] As Hamilton stated: 'Not until the nineteenth century, did judges discover that caveat emptor sharpened wits, taught self-reliance, made a man – an economic man – out of the buyer, and served well its two masters, business and justice.'[33] This created a market dynamic where all purchasers needed to be on their guard and Atiyah regarded the doctrine as representing the apotheosis of nineteenth-century individualism.[34]

[22] T Naggar, 'Adam Smith's Laissez Faire' (1977) 21 *The American Economist* 35.

[23] JM King, 'Broker Liability after Easton v. Strassburger: Let the Buyer Be Aware' (1985) 25 *Santa Clara Law Review* 651.

[24] *Chandelor v Lopus* (1603) Cro Jac 4, 79 ER 3.

[25] A bezar or bezoar stone was a stone found in the stomach or intestines of some animals, such as a goat, and was believed to have magical powers.

[26] *Moore v Hussey* (1609) Hob 93, 80 ER 243.

[27] ibid 99.

[28] H Broom and RH Kersley, *A Selection of Legal Maxims, Classified and Illustrated*, 10th edn (Pakistan Law House, 1939) 528.

[29] *Peek v Gurney* (1873) LR 6 HL 377.

[30] ibid 403.

[31] B Craine, 'Real Property – Sellers' Liability for Nondisclosure of Real Property Defects – Johnson v. Davis' (1986) 14 *Florida State University Law Review* 359, 360.

[32] R Basso, 'Reed v. King: Fraudulent Nondisclosure of a Multiple Murder in a Real Estate Transaction' (1984) 45 *University of Pittsburgh Law Review* 877, 879.

[33] Hamilton (n 1) 1186.

[34] PS Atiyah, *The Rise and Fall of Freedom of Contract* (Oxford, Clarendon Press, 1979) 464.

Whilst *caveat emptor* originally applied to all commercial transactions of both personal and real property, by the start of the twentieth century it was moving away from transactions involving personal property.[35] The Industrial Revolution led to the mass production of goods and concerns from purchasers about quality.[36] The Sale of Goods Act 1893 and its introduction of implied terms represented an important step towards the death of *caveat emptor* in relation to personal property.[37] As a consequence, the law began to reflect purchasers' expectations and *caveat emptor* has now been rejected in relation to contracts of sale when the seller sells the goods in the course of a business in favour of a consumer protection-orientated system.[38] This transition culminated with the Consumer Rights Act 2015. However, *caveat emptor* is still alive in relation to real property, leading to Bright remarking that a purchaser has more rights when buying a toaster than when buying a home.[39]

Rose noted that Atiyah regarded the preference for crystal over mud and vice versa as taking place in long historical cycles, and that he saw the eighteenth century as largely a mud era, full of ambiguity and judicial discretion, whereas the period between 1770 and 1870 was an era in which crystal rules came to be important.[40] The next section of this chapter will examine how we are now in a mud era of *caveat emptor*.

III. THE MUDDYING OF *CAVEAT EMPTOR*

It is well established under *caveat emptor* that 'failure to disclose a material fact which might influence the mind of a prudent contractor does not give the right to avoid the contract'.[41] Over many years, this has been muddied by various common law and statutory exceptions, including the duty of the vendor to disclose latent defects in title, contracts induced by fraud and, potentially, the impact of consumer protection regulations.[42]

Three of these muddying exceptions are well-known general exceptions in the law of contract. The first is where a contract requires *uberrima fidei*, such

[35] Hamilton (n 1) 1156-1176.

[36] L Bearman Jr, 'Caveat Emptor in Sales of Realty: Recent Assaults upon the Rule' (1961) 14 *Vanderbilt Law Review* 541, 542–43.

[37] C Twigg-Flesner and R Canavan, *Atiyah and Adams' Sale of Goods*, 14th edn (Harlow, Pearson, 2021) 113.

[38] J de Lacy, 'Business Sellers' Liability for the Implied Terms under the Sale of Goods Act 1979' (2000) 1 *Insolvency Lawyer* 27, 29.

[39] See S Bright, 'Resilient High-Rise Property? Grenfell Tower and Beyond' (2023) 8 *Journal of Law, Property, and Society* 9.

[40] Rose (n 15) 595.

[41] Per Lord Atkin in *Bell v Lever Bros Ltd* [1932] AC 161 (HL), 227.

[42] See further Law Commission (n 2); J Farrand, 'Disclosure by Vendors' (1986) 280 *Estates Gazette* 961; J Farrand, *Contract and Conveyance*, 4th edn (London, Oyez Longman, 1983) 62–75; Anon, 'Would You Buy a Used Car …?' [1989] *Conveyancer and Property Lawyer* 69.

as where the contract relates to insurance.[43] It was settled by Lord Mansfield in *Carter v Boehm*[44] that there is a duty of the utmost good faith and so an obligation to disclose to an insurer all known material facts which were not within the insurer's knowledge or means of knowledge. The second is where a fiduciary relationship exists between the parties, for example, where the parties are solicitor and client, or trustee and beneficiary. The third exception is where a positive representation would become distorted by silence, such as happened in *Laurence v Lexcourt Holdings Ltd*,[45] where a property described in the agent's sales particulars as 'offices' only had planning permission to use part of it for offices.

The vendor's silence is only golden provided the purchaser does not ask the vendor any questions. So, the next muddy exception is that, where the purchaser seeks specific information from the vendor, the purchaser must be given it accurately to the best of the vendor's ability.[46] As part of the purchaser's due diligence, they will usually seek information for the vendor using industry-standard forms, such as the Law Society's Property Information Form (TA6):

> In the ordinary case, a purchaser has to go for his information to the vendor, but, bearing in mind the principle of *caveat emptor*, he is bound to make proper inquiries for himself. But he must, in almost every case, in the first instance, at any rate, seek his information from the vendor, who knows the facts, whereas the purchaser probably does not know them. When a purchaser, with a possible view of making an offer for the property, seeks information from the vendor, the vendor, of course, is bound to the best of his ability to supply him with accurate information.[47]

In most residential conveyancing transactions, the Law Society Conveyancing Protocol[48] will be used. On receipt of instructions, the vendor's solicitor should send the TA6 form to the vendor to complete. The completed form should then be sent to the purchaser's solicitor as part of the contract bundle. The purchaser's solicitor may raise additional enquiries, but the Protocol permits this only in limited circumstances.

The next mud to be thrown on the doctrine is, according to the Law Commission, somewhat esoteric and peculiar to sales of land.[49] It has also been described as a half-exception to *caveat emptor*,[50] as well as being obscure and not

[43] This can be compared with *Livesey v Jenkins* [1985] AC 424 (HL), where an infringement of the duty of full and frank disclosure in a matrimonial dispute led to the consent order – which, inter alia, provided for the transfer of an equitable interest in land – being set aside.

[44] *Carter v Boehm* (1766) 3 Burr 1905, 97 ER 1162.

[45] *Laurence v Lexcourt Holdings Ltd* [1978] 1 WLR 1128 (Ch). See also *Mustafa v Baptist Union Corp Ltd* (1983) 266 EG 812.

[46] *Terrene Ltd v Nelson* [1937] 3 All ER 739 (Ch).

[47] ibid 744.

[48] The Law Society Conveyancing Protocol provides a framework for the sale and purchase of a home for an owner occupier; see www.lawsociety.org.uk/topics/property/conveyancing-protocol.

[49] Law Commission (n 2) para 2.4.

[50] Farrand, *Contract and Conveyance* (n 42) 63.

to be regarded as finally settled.[51] It requires a vendor to disclose latent defects in title to a purchaser, except for those which the purchaser already knows about.[52] A latent defect is one which a purchaser could not have discovered by a reasonable inspection of the property.[53] This obligation also applies to latent defects in title that the vendor does not know of but ought to have known might exist.[54] A vendor can exclude their liability for defects in title, but only if they are ones of which they neither know nor ought to have known.[55] The precise nature of the seller's obligation to disclose irremovable latent defects in title should be regarded as an open contract obligation that the property is either free of such defects, or that they have been disclosed.[56] A vendor is under no duty to disclose remediable defects in title as they should be able to remove them before completion. However, if a vendor fails to disclose such a defect and is unable to remedy it before completion, the vendor may be in breach of either the contract, any warranties given or the implied covenants for title. The vendor is under no duty to disclose latent defects other than in title.[57]

A defect in title 'which arises either to the eye, or by necessary implication from something which is visible to the eye' will be patent[58] and 'it is undoubted that on the case of a patent defect the rule *caveat emptor* applies', so will be one that the vendor is not obliged to disclose.[59] In practice, the distinction between a latent and a patent defect may be unclear – for example, a right of way that was apparent on an inspection of a property has been held to be a latent defect.[60] Consequently, a prudent vendor should take a cautious approach and make full disclosure of all third-party rights and defects in title. This exception has been further muddied by the decision in *SPS Groundworks and Building Ltd v Mahil*,[61] where references in an auction brochure and by the auctioneer to the need to read the legal pack were insufficient for a vendor to have complied with their duty to disclose a defect in title. Full and frank discourse required an

[51] S Bridge, E Cooke and M Dixon, *Megarry & Wade: The Law of Real Property*, 9th edn (London, Sweet & Maxwell, 2019) para 14-069.

[52] The purchaser must have actual knowledge and constructive notice will not be enough (*Caballero v Henty* (1873–74) LR 9 Ch App 477).

[53] Latent defects include a tenancy (*Pagebar Properties Ltd v Derby Investment Holdings Ltd* [1972] 1 WLR 1500 (Ch)) and a restrictive covenant (*Re Stone and Saville's Contract* [1963] 1 WLR 163 (CA)).

[54] *Becker v Partridge* [1966] 2 QB 155 (CA), 171–72.

[55] ibid; *Rignall Developments Ltd v Halil* [1988] Ch 190 (Ch). For a study of judicial attitudes to exclusion clauses in contracts for the sale of land, see C Harpum, 'Exclusion Clauses and Contracts for the Sale of Land' [1992] *CLJ* 263.

[56] Law Commission, *Land Registration for the Twenty-First Century. A Consultative Document* (Law Com No 254, 1998) para 11.32. *cf* Harpum (n 5) 332.

[57] In *Sykes v Taylor-Rose* [2004] EWCA Civ 299, [2004] 2 P & CR 30, there was no breach of the duty to disclose latent defects where the vendor failed to disclose that the property had, before the vendor bought the property, been the scene of a gruesome child murder.

[58] *Yandle v Sutton* [1922] 2 Ch 199 (Ch), per Sargant J at 210.

[59] ibid 204.

[60] *Yandle v Sutton* (n 58).

[61] *SPS Groundworks and Building Ltd v Mahil* [2022] EWHC 371 (QB).

overage clause to be specifically brought to the attention of a potential purchaser by description in the property particulars, an addendum notice or specific reference by the auctioneer. The purchaser was not put on notice of any unusual feature of the property that they intended bidding for and could not have been put on notice by inspection. According to Harpum, in such a situation, the case for pre-contractual duty of disclosure will be a strong one.[62]

The next mud thrown at the doctrine is only relevant to unregistered land. Where a defect in title is registered under the Land Charges Act,[63] it was said obiter in *Re Forsey and Hollebone's Contract*[64] that registration was deemed to give the purchaser notice and so they could not repudiate on account of a registered entry, even if the vendor did not disclose it to them. However, section 24 of the Law of Property Act 1969 provides that, so far as registered land charges are concerned, the purchaser's knowledge is to be determined by reference to their actual knowledge and not according to imputed knowledge. Section 24 does not apply to registered title and so registered conveyancing seems to remain subject to the latent defects in title exception.[65]

A further exception applies in relation to local land charges. Millet J, as he then was, considered the position of entries under the Local Land Charges Act 1975 in *Rignall Developments Ltd v Halil*[66] and concluded that a vendor had a duty to disclose removable local land charges as the vendor would be liable to discharge them, even if the purchaser did not make a local land charges search and even if the contract expressly put the liability for them onto the purchaser. The vendor must also disclose local land charges that they know and this knowledge may be from something such as the local search made when they purchased the property and which they were never shown by the solicitor who acted for them on their purchase.[67]

An express term in a contract which implies a term as to physical quality equivalent to that for latent defects in title will displace *caveat emptor* and the vendor will then have a duty of disclosure.[68]

Caveat emptor has no application where there is fraud on the part of the vendor,[69] such as where the vendor has concealed physical defects, such as by papering over cracks in the wall,[70] or by the vendor removing flagstones from the garden, without having told the purchaser what they were doing.[71] Such conduct would also now be caught by the Fraud Act 2006, which introduced a general criminal offence of fraud that can be committed by false

[62] Harpum (n 5) 331.
[63] Now the Land Charges Act 1972.
[64] *Re Forsey and Hollebone's Contract* [1927] 2 Ch 379 (CA) 387.
[65] Law Commission (n 2) para 2.7.
[66] *Rignall Developments Ltd v Halil* (n 55).
[67] ibid 198.
[68] *Shepherd v Croft* [1911] 1 Ch 521 (Ch).
[69] *Gordon v Selico Ltd* (1986) 18 HLR 219 (CA); *Rignall Developments Ltd v Halil* (n 55); *Taylor v Hamer* [2002] EWCA Civ 1130, [2003] 1 EGLR 103.
[70] *Gordon v Selico Ltd* (n 69).
[71] *Taylor v Hamer* (n 69).

representation or by failing to disclose information. So, a vendor may be guilty of fraud if they dishonestly make a false representation with the intention to either make a gain for themselves or someone else, or cause a loss to another, or expose another to a risk of loss.[72] They may also be guilty if they dishonestly fail to disclose to another person information they are under a legal duty to disclose with the intention to either make a gain for themselves or someone else, or cause a loss to another, or expose another to a risk of loss.[73] A legal duty to disclose information may derive from statute, the fact that the contract requires *uberrima fidei*, the express or implied terms of the contract, the custom of a particular trade or market, or the existence of a fiduciary relationship between the parties.[74]

Another exception to *caveat emptor* is where the vendor has done something dangerous, such as carrying out incompetent do-it-yourself work on the property, and they can then be liable to the purchaser in negligence.[75]

In relation to physical defects, the orthodox view is that in the absence of an express provision in the contract, a collateral warranty or an actionable misrepresentation, they are within *caveat emptor*.[76] However, the Law Commission felt that there may be a duty to reveal a physical defect known to the vendor which would endanger the life of a purchaser, though there seems little judicial authority for any such proposition.[77] They felt that this exception was somewhat speculative, but may well be thought patently indefensible. In reaching this conclusion, they relied on what they said was a 'most persuasive' article by Newsome, who argued that the way was open to impose a duty of care on a vendor for known latent and dangerous or potentially dangerous defects, whether created by work done, neglect or otherwise.[78]

The purchase of a 'new build' house may fall within an exception to *caveat emptor*. A builder, as a supplier of services in the course of a business, is subject to implied terms as to reasonable care and skill, completion within a reasonable time and payment of a reasonable charge.[79] However, these terms may be excluded and do not prejudice any 'rule of law' which imposes a stricter duty or which implies other not inconsistent terms.[80] When a purchaser buys a house from a builder who contracts to build it, a threefold contractual warranty is implied at common law: first, that the builder will carry out their work in a good and workmanlike manner; second, that they will use good and proper materials; and third, that it

[72] Fraud Act 2006, s 2.
[73] ibid s 3.
[74] Law Commission, *Fraud* (Law Com No 276, 2002) para 7.28.
[75] *Hone v Benson* (1978) 248 EG 1013.
[76] Condition 3.2.1 of the Standard Conditions of Sale (fifth edition – 2018 revision) provides that a purchaser accepts the property in the physical state it is in at the date of the contract unless the vendor is building or converting it.
[77] Law Commission (n 2) para 2.9.
[78] EL Newsome, 'Pre-contractual Disclosure of Dangerous Defects' [1980] *Conveyancer and Property Lawyer* 287.
[79] Supply of Goods and Services Act 1982, ss 13, 14 and 15.
[80] ibid s 16.

will be reasonably fit for human habitation.[81] This warranty is not implied where the sale is of an already built house, even if it is on a building estate and was finished just before the contract was made,[82] nor is it implied where an existing dwelling is extended or refurbished.[83] But it will be implied where the house is sold during the course of construction.[84] Whilst this implied warranty only protects the original purchaser of a house to be built, any purchaser may seek protection in either tort or by statute or both. Independently of any remedies in tort, liability may be incurred by a builder under section 1 of the Defective Premises Act 1972, which imposes a duty to build dwellings properly. This duty is limited to works regarding the 'provision' of a dwelling by erecting, converting or enlarging it, and does not apply to other works, such as works of improvement to an existing dwelling by way of a major refurbishment.[85]

Finally, there may be an obligation on a vendor to disclose planning restrictions.[86] Thus, a vendor has been held to be under a duty to disclose to a purchaser that the locality in which the house was situated had been zoned as a public space.[87]

So these exceptions have coated on *caveat emptor* in mud. However, more mud has recently been thrown at it by consumer protection regulations, which will be explored in the next section.

IV. FURTHER MUDDYING: THE POTENTIAL EFFECT OF CONSUMER PROTECTION LAWS ON *CAVEAT EMPTOR*

Consumer protection laws started to have an influence on *caveat emptor* in the twentieth century, with a divergence appearing between personal and real property. The Property Misdescriptions Act 1991 created an offence of providing false or misleading information in relation to certain specified matters. But it was only an offence if estate agents disclosed information that was false or misleading. Some agents therefore felt it was safer not to disclose anything at all rather than run the risk of stating something that might be inaccurate. Greater security for consumers including homebuyers was subsequently introduced by the Consumer Protection from Unfair Trading Regulations 2008[88]

[81] Per Lord Denning MR in *Hancock v BW Brazier (Anerley) Ltd* [1966] 1 WLR 1317 (CA) 1332.
[82] *Hoskins v Woodham* [1938] 1 All ER 692 (KB).
[83] *Jenson v Faux* [2011] EWCA Civ 423, [2011] 1 WLR 3038.
[84] *Perry v Sharon Development Co Ltd* [1937] 4 All ER 390 (CA).
[85] This gap has been filled by a new duty in s 2A of the Defective Premises Act 1972, which applies to 'work in relation to' any part of a 'building consisting of or containing one or more dwellings'.
[86] *Sidney v Buddery* (1949–51) 1 P & CR 34 (Ch).
[87] *Sakkas v Donford Ltd* (1983) 46 P & CR 290 (Ch); Anon, 'Cross My Heart – Disclosure by Vendors' [1987] *Conveyancer and Property Lawyer* 153.
[88] Consumer Protection from Unfair Trading Regulations 2008, SI 2008/1277, as extended by the Consumer Protection (Amendment) Regulations 2014, SI 2014/870. These regulations will be revoked and replaced by the Digital Markets, Competition and Traders Act 2024 on a date to be appointed.

(hereinafter 'the regulations'). The regulations aim to prohibit trading practices that are unfair to consumers[89] and as a consequence the 1991 Act was repealed in October 2013.

The regulations apply to immoveable property and, according to the Law Society of England and Wales, may reduce the application of *caveat emptor* in transactions where the purchaser is a consumer.[90] The regulations implemented Directive 2005/29/EC of the European Parliament and of the Council of 11 May 2005, the overarching EU legislation on unfair commercial practices. Following the UK's departure from the EU, the regulations remain in force as 'assimilated law'.[91]

The regulations apply to services provided by a 'trader'[92] and so apply to estate agents selling a property to a consumer and, in the opinion of the Law Society of England and Wales, also to solicitors acting for a vendor on a sale of property to a consumer for personal use or private investment, even where the vendor is supplying it in a non-business capacity, such as in the case of residential conveyancing.[93] They do not apply where an individual[94] sells their house without using an estate agent, though they would subsequently apply to the solicitor who then carries out the conveyancing work for them. Despite the Law Society's view, the application of the regulations is uncertain. Until the courts are asked to provide a definitive interpretation, there is no clear statement on the impact of the regulations on *caveat emptor*.

The regulations created an offence of omitting or hiding material information or providing material information in a manner which is unintelligible, ambiguous or untimely, or which fails to identify its commercial intent and, as a result, causes or is likely to cause the average consumer to take a transactional decision that they would not otherwise have taken. It is also an offence to provide false information or present information in a way which deceives or is likely to deceive the average consumer and, as a result, causes or is likely to cause the average consumer[95] to take a transactional decision that they would not otherwise have taken.

Material information is information which the average consumer needs in order to make an informed decision. However, the regulations do not contain a definition of what this information should be and this lack of clarity caused uncertainty over what should be disclosed. This has been clarified

[89] 'Consumer' is defined in reg 2(1) of the Consumer Protection from Unfair Trading Regulations 2008, SI 2008/1277, as 'any individual who in relation to a commercial practice is acting for purposes which are outside his business'.

[90] See the Law Society practice note *Consumer Protection Regulations in Conveyancing* (3 June 2024), available at www.lawsociety.org.uk.

[91] Under the Retained EU Law (Revocation and Reform) Act 2023.

[92] See Consumer Protection from Unfair Trading Regulations 2008, SI 2008/1277, reg 2(1).

[93] See Law Society (n 90).

[94] Though the regulations would apply to a corporate body selling property.

[95] For these purposes, an 'average consumer' is reasonably well informed, reasonably observant and circumspect; see *Office of Fair Trading v Purely Creative Ltd* [2011] EWHC 106 (Ch).

by National Trading Standards, which in November 2023 published guidance for estate agents setting out a view as to what matters could be considered material information. This is split into Parts A, B and C, and now forms the minimum information that should be contained by an estate agent in a property listing.[96] National Trading Standards had previously announced that a property's council tax band, the property price and tenure information must be included on all property listings by the end of May 2022.[97] This information now forms Part A of the material information. Part B information is information which must be shown for all properties and is considered material information generally where the information may involve maintenance or repair costs, affect the availability of a mortgage or insurance, or affect the use or enjoyment of the property. This includes property type, property construction, number and types of rooms in the property, electricity supply, water supply sewerage, heating, broadband, mobile signal/coverage and parking. Part C information may or may not need to be established depending on whether the property is affected or impacted by the issue. This includes building safety, restrictions, rights and easements, flood risk, coastal erosion risk, planning permission, accessibility/adaptions and coalfield or mining area.

The material information requirements do not amount to a true mandatory disclosure law, nor do they require disclosure of everything which a vendor knows about their property. So, for example, they do not require disclosure of what Christopher Pearce discusses as stigmas on the property.[98] Warner calls such stigmatised properties as being psychologically impacted[99] and, in the environmental context, Hierlmeier says that stigma constitutes a mark or label that attaches to contaminated property, which results in a diminution in property value.[100] As Pearce discusses, a stigma could be the prevalence of crime within the neighbourhood,[101] the presence of a sex offender in the neighbourhood,[102] the

[96] www.nationaltradingstandards.uk/news/full-material-information-guidance-published.

[97] www.nationaltradingstandards.uk/news/material-information-for-property-listings-announced.

[98] Pearce (n 21). For a comparison between stigmatised properties in the US and those in Australia, see E Webb, 'Houses with a History: Disclosure Obligations and "Psychologically Stigmatised" Property' (2006) 13 *Australian Property Law Journal* 67; and L Griggs, 'The Duty of Disclosure by Vendors in a Conveyance: If Caveat Emptor, Are We Allowing the Camel's Nose of Unrestrained Irrationality Admission to the Tent' (1999) 7 *Australian Property Law Journal* 76.

[99] DM Warner, 'Caveat Spiritus: A Jurisprudential Reflection upon the Law of Haunted Houses and Ghosts' (1993) 28 *Valparaiso University Law Review* 207.

[100] J Hierlmeier, 'The Enigma of Stigma: A New Environmental Contamination Challenge Facing Canada's Judiciary' (2002) 11 *Dalhousie Journal of Legal Studies* 179. See also R Roddewig, 'Stigma, Environmental Risk and Property Value: 10 Critical Enquiries' (1996) 64 *Appraisal Journal* 375.

[101] TD Larson, 'To Disclose or Not to Disclose: The Dilemma of Homeowners and Real Estate Brokers under Wisconsin's "Megan's Law"' (1998) 81 *Marquette Law Review* 1161.

[102] S Ross Saxer, '"Am I My Brother's Keeper?": Requiring Landowner Disclosure of the Presence of Sex Offenders and Other Criminal Activity' (2001) 80(3) *Nebraska Law Review* 522; Lori A Polonchak, 'Surprise! You Just Moved Next to a Sexual Predator: The Duty of Residential Sellers and Real Estate Brokers to Disclose the Presence of Sexual Predators to Prospective Purchasers' (1997) 102 *Dickinson Law Review* 169.

general quality of the neighbourhood,[103] a prior owner's HIV/AIDS status,[104] the effects of pollution or waste on the condition of the property,[105] whether the property has been the site of an unnatural death[106] or the alleged presence of ghosts or poltergeists.[107] There is no requirement in English law to disclose these stigmas as they do not fall within an exception to *caveat emptor*. An example of this is *Sykes v Taylor-Rose*,[108] where the court took the view that to require disclosure of a murder in the property would amount to a 'great leap forward in the development of the law' which would mean that 'the principle of caveat emptor, hallowed though it may have been in the past, is nearing the end of its useful life'.[109]

The introduction of the material information requirements does not really help the conveyancing process or wash any mud off *caveat emptor*; instead, it raises a risk of duplication. Estate agents are required to assemble some, but not all, of the information that is usually required by a purchaser, but vendors will still be expected to provide answers to all of the purchaser's enquiries, subject to the requirements of the Law Society Conveyancing Protocol,[110] and these will include matters not covered by material information. It would appear that the requirement to provide material information, rather than cleaning off some of the mud, has instead added more by failing to require a vendor to either make full disclosure of defects in the property they are selling or provide a prospective purchaser with full upfront information, and this will be considered in the next section.

V. WASHING OFF THE MUD: UPFRONT INFORMATION

If the material information requirements have added more mud to *caveat emptor*, might it be possible to wash off some of this mud by expanding the

[103] PC Murray, 'AIDS, Ghosts, Murder: Must Real Estate Brokers and Sellers Disclose' (1992) 27 *Wake Forest Law Review* 689.

[104] ibid; SA McEvoy, 'Stigmatized Property: What a Buyer Should Know' (1992) 48 *Missouri Bar Journal* 57; RR Hartog, 'The Psychological Impact of AIDS on Real Property and a Real Estate Broker's Duty to Disclose' (1994) 36 *Arizona Law Review* 757.

[105] J Hierlmeier, 'The Enigma of Stigma: A New Environmental Contamination Challenge Facing Canada's Judiciary' (2002) 11 *Dalhousie Journal of Legal Studies* 179; TA Reuschel, 'Caveat Vendor: Sellers of Real Estate Now Need to Beware of Misrepresentations about the Condition of Property' (1999) 64(3) *Missouri Law Review* 661.

[106] *Reed v King* 193 Cal Rptr 130 (1983), where the seller's failure to disclose that the property had been the site of a multiple murder was held to be a misrepresentation. See Basso (n 32).

[107] *Stambovsky v Ackley* 572 NYS 2d 672 at 677 (App Div 1991); Anon, 'Poltergeist Visitation as a Defect in Title in USA' [1992] *Conveyancer and Property Lawyer* 8; M Pawlowski, 'No Place Like Home …' (2023) 173 *New Law Journal* 22.

[108] *Sykes v Taylor-Rose* (n 57); DM Collins, 'The Disclosure of Stigma Events in Property Transactions' [2008] *Conveyancer and Property Lawyer* 50; Pawlowski (n 107) 22.

[109] *Sykes v Taylor-Rose* (n 57), per Sir William Aldous at para 15, citing the judgment of His Honour Judge Langan QC.

[110] The Law Society Conveyancing Protocol is a framework for the sale and purchase of a home for an owner occupier; see www.lawsociety.org.uk/topics/property/conveyancing-protocol.

information which is provided to a purchaser at the start of a conveyancing transaction and requiring that this be provided by all vendors unlike the material information discussed above? The effect of this might then be to reduce the time from a purchaser making an offer to purchase a property to completion. Currently, vendors are only encouraged to collect together relevant information, such as planning permissions, building regulation completion certificates and builder's guarantee certificates for any alterations or additions to their property so that they are 'sale ready' before they market their home.[111] The government has also proposed that, in the longer term, most of the information purchasers need to know about a property should be available 'upfront' when the property is marketed.[112] This could be facilitated through the development of proptech commercial models such as a 'property passport' or 'property logbook' which would reduce siloed information leading to reduced transaction times. These would consist of an online or digital set of documents which records major events during a property's lifetime, such as maintenance, refurbishment and other changes to the fabric of the property. This would then ensure that the vendor has copies of significant documentation and certification relating to these events, and it could also include links to where information is held about those events on public and government repositories. If relevant information were gathered upfront, then a vendor would be able to identify and sort out issues early on in the process and the information would be ready to be shared with a purchaser when they make an initial enquiry about a property. This would reduce the burden on a purchaser and be more effective in aiding speed and certainty.

This call for upfront information is not new. In its Second Report published in 1985, the Conveyancing Committee appointed by the government under the chairmanship of Professor Farrand strongly recommended that there would be substantial advantages in requiring vendors, either in practice or by statute, to supply replies to local searches and enquiries and to standard preliminary enquiries when sending the draft contract to a purchaser.[113] The Law Commission in 1988 also provisionally proposed that a vendor should be under a positive duty to disclose all material facts about the property being sold.[114]

These proposals were later taken forward by the government in 1997 with the introduction of Home Information Packs, which were arguably the most ambitious attempt to reform *caveat emptor* and moved the point at which information about a property was collated and presented to potential purchasers.

[111] Department for Levelling Up, Housing & Communities (n 6).

[112] Ministry of Housing, Communities and Local Government, *Improving the Home Buying and Selling Process: Summary of Responses to the Call for Evidence and Government Response*, available at www.gov.uk/government/calls-for-evidence/improving-the-home-buying-and-selling-process-call-for-evidence.

[113] The Second Report of the Conveyancing Committee (1985) *Conveyancing Simplifications*, para 9.4.

[114] Law Commission (n 2) para 4.1.

The aim was to try to speed up the home-buying process, lead to fewer sales falling through and reduce the opportunity for gazumping or gazundering.

Originally, a Home Information Pack was to consist of various compulsory documents together with authorised optional documents. These documents included standard searches, evidence of title, a Home Condition Report (a type of survey carried out by a certified home inspector), an Energy Performance Certificate and, in the case of a leasehold property, a copy of the lease. A vendor would then compile the pack before putting their property on the market. Most of these documents have always been part of the conveyancing process, but the introduction of Home Information Packs brought forward the point at which they were provided and changed the requirement to provide them from the buyer to the seller, which in turn moved the cost burden to the seller. After a long gestation period and a phased implementation, Home Information Packs were fully introduced in April 2009, although the Home Condition Report was made a voluntary component. Not all properties were required to have a pack, such as properties which were not marketed through an agent but were instead sold privately by the homeowner and properties not sold with vacant possession. Following myopic criticism[115] that the additional upfront cost to vendors of providing a Home Information Pack might deter them from marketing their properties and that delays in obtaining searches would reduce the rate at which properties were coming on the market, the incoming Coalition government in 2010 suspended the requirement to have a Home Information Pack when marketing a property and subsequently repealed the legislative basis for them via the Localism Act 2011. There was also felt to be a lack of confidence in the Home Condition Report, despite an Office of Fair Trading survey in 2009 finding that a large majority (78 per cent) of buyers felt that a survey at the outset would be helpful or very helpful.[116] However, one element – the Energy Performance Certificate – was retained on the grounds of environmental benefit.[117]

This unsuccessful attempt at providing upfront information through the use of Home Information Packs can be contrasted with the successful introduction in 2008 of a similar scheme in Scotland. Subject to a few exceptions, residential properties in Scotland must be marketed with a Home Report, which is put together by the vendor.[118] The Home Report contains a survey of the property and an energy report setting out the energy efficiency of the property, both of which are prepared by a chartered surveyor, together with a property questionnaire completed by the vendor which contains additional information about the property. Unlike the Home Information Pack, a Home Report must be provided by a vendor even if they are selling the property themselves and not through a

[115] See, for example, L Bachelor, 'Home Information Packs Scrapped' *The Guardian* (20 May 2010), www.theguardian.com/money/2010/may/20/home-information-packs-scrapped-hips.

[116] Office of Fair Trading, 'Home Buying and Selling: A Market Study' (OFT1186, 2010) para 7.55.

[117] Energy Performance of Buildings (England and Wales) Regulations 2012, SI 2012/3118.

[118] See Housing (Scotland) Act 2006 (Prescribed Documents) Regulations 2008, SSI 2008/76.

solicitor or an estate agent. For the Home Report to work, a purchaser must be able to rely on it, so legislation provides that if a purchaser suffers a material loss due to a mistake in the Home Report, the surveyor will be liable to pay them damages and a vendor can also hold a surveyor responsible for any problems with the survey.[119] In addition to the Home Report, the vendor will also provide a purchaser with a legal report disclosing, among other things, who owns property and whether there are any legal proceedings against the seller relating to unpaid debts, and a Property Enquiry Certificate which provides information on matters that are within the control of the local authority. This immediate information deflects speculative sellers and buyers from participating and removes much of the back-and-forth between agents and solicitors. It also helps that solicitors are involved far earlier in the home-buying and selling process to handle the bids and the making and receiving of offers. Whilst this has speeded up the home-buying and selling process in Scotland, with transactions being routinely capable of being completed within 12 weeks,[120] *caveat emptor* remains and whilst Brymer and Rennie have proposed that there should be legislation abolishing *caveat emptor*,[121] Clapham in response did not think *caveat emptor* such a bad concept.[122] So it may be argued that a modified doctrine, which Johnson calls '*caveat emptor* light', has started to emerge in Scotland.[123]

VI. MANDATORY VENDOR DISCLOSURE AND *CAVEAT VENDITOR*

If mandatory upfront information does not wash the mud off *caveat emptor*, then perhaps mandatory vendor disclosure may do so. This could shift *caveat emptor* to a model requiring greater transparency, as is the case in various states in both the US and Australia, so we have *caveat venditor* or, if that is too far to go, Johnson's '*caveat emptor* light'.[124]

In the US, most states have moved away from *caveat emptor* and have enacted legislation requiring a vendor to provide a purchaser with a written disclosure report. The doctrine of *caveat emptor* now only remains in a handful of states, including Alabama, where it has been said to remain remarkably robust,[125] though the courts have carved out three exceptions based on the state's fraud statute.[126] So, a vendor must disclose defects to a purchaser if there is a fiduciary

[119] Housing (Scotland) Act 2006 (Consequential Provisions) Order 2008, SSI 2008/1889.
[120] Email from Professor S Brymer to the author (5 February 2024).
[121] S Brymer and R Rennie, 'Missives: Can We Conclude More Quickly?' (2017) 62 *Journal of the Law Society of Scotland* 34.
[122] D Clapham, 'Standard Missives: an Unachievable Dream?' (2017) 62 *Journal of the Law Society of Scotland* 32.
[123] Johnson (n 17).
[124] ibid.
[125] E Murphy, 'The Current State of Caveat Emptor in Alabama Real Estate Sales' (2009) 60 *Alabama Law Review* 499.
[126] Ala Code § 6-5-102 (1975).

relationship between the vendor and the purchaser; if the vendor knows that the property contains a material defect which is not readily visible and which could pose a health or safety risk to the purchaser; or if the purchaser directly asks the vendor about something. In addition, US federal law mandates that vendors in all states must disclose whether their property, if built prior to 1978, has been affected by lead-based paints, and there is a standard disclosure form for vendors to complete.[127] Otherwise, the overall format of disclosure statements varies across states.

The catalyst for the introduction of these disclosure laws across the US can be traced back to the California Court of Appeal's decision in *Easton v Strassburger*,[128] which has been described as the birth of negligence in real estate broker–purchaser relationships.[129] In this case, the Court held that a real estate broker must carry out a reasonable, competent and diligent inspection of a residential property they are selling and disclose to a purchaser everything which is revealed by the inspection that materially affects the value or desirability of the property. Consequently, the California state legislature was the first to introduce laws specifying the type of inspection that must be carried out, together with a requirement that a vendor must complete a Real Estate Transfer Disclosure Statement.[130]

As well as protecting the parties to a transaction, disclosure statements shift the risk from purchasers and real estate brokers to the vendors. As Nanda notes, they can also be viewed as a tool to avoid lawsuits.[131] Using the works of Kiefer[132] and de Figueiredo and Vanden Bergh,[133] Nanda formulated a discrete time proportional hazard model to ascertain which factors led to the introduction of disclosure laws.[134] This empirical analysis supported two key inferences: a higher level of consumer and real estate board dissatisfaction, as indicated by a higher level of complaints and disciplinary actions against real estate licensees, and a lower level of broker supervision. Nanda found that both of these increased the likelihood of a state adopting disclosure laws, whereas greater broker supervision had a negative impact. The difficulty with comparing

[127] See Residential Lead-Based Paint Hazard Reduction Act (42 US Code §4852d), commonly referred to as Title X.

[128] *Easton v Strassburger* 152 Cal App 3d 90, 199 Cal Rptr 383 (Cal Ct App 1984).

[129] GA Partida, 'Easton: The Birth of Negligence in Real Estate Broker-Purchaser Relationships' (1987) 14 *Pepperdine Law Review* 3. See also King (n 23); JB Hicks III, 'Easton v. Strassburger: Judicial Imposition of a Duty to Inspect on California Real Estate Brokers' (1985) 18 *Loyola of Los Angeles Law Review* 809.

[130] Available at dre.ca.gov/files/pdf/re6.pdf.

[131] A Nanda, 'Property Condition Disclosure Law: Why Did States Mandate 'Seller Tell All'?' (2008) 37 *The Journal of Real Estate Finance and Economics* 131.

[132] NM Kiefer, 'Economic Duration Data and Hazard Functions' (1988) 26 *Journal of Economic Literature* 646.

[133] RJP de Figueiredo, Jr and RG Vanden Bergh, 'The Political Economy of State-Level Administrative Procedure Acts' (2004) 47 *Journal of Law & Economics* 569.

[134] A Nanda, 'Property Condition Disclosure Law: Why Did States Mandate "Seller Tell All"?' (2008) 37 *Journal of Real Estate Finance and Economics* 131.

Nanda's model to England and Wales is that estate agents, unlike real estate brokers in the US, are not required to be licensed by a regulatory body. In California, for example, the California Department of Real Estate examines and licenses real estate agents, and also provides a mechanism to investigate written complaints made against real estate brokers accused of misleading or defrauding consumers.[135] The only requirement in England and Wales in relation to complaints against estate agents is that the Consumers, Estate Agents and Redress Act 2007 requires that estate agents who engage in residential work must belong to an approved redress scheme.[136] If a consumer wishes to make a formal complaint against an estate agent, they must first raise it with the estate agent. If the complaint remains unresolved, the matter can then be directed to the appropriate redress scheme. Whilst there is a national regulator for estate agency, the National Trading Standards Estate and Letting Agency Team,[137] its remit is to assess whether an individual or business is fit to carry out estate agency work within the terms of the Estate Agents Act 1979 and so it does not directly investigate individual complaints. If an estate agent is found to be in breach of the Estate Agents Act 1979 – for example, by engaging an undesirable practice[138] – the National Trading Standards Estate Agency Team can consider making either a banning order or a warning order,[139] which are then published on the Estate Agents Public Register.[140]

Mandatory disclosure requirements also operate in other jurisdictions, for example, New South Wales, Australia,[141] where section 52A(2) of the Conveyancing Act 1919 requires a vendor to provide certain information in the contract as prescribed by Schedule 1 of the Act.[142] As this information is not provided when the property is marketed, but later when the contract is issued to the purchaser's solicitor, it may not go so far as to solve the mischief of delay in the conveyancing process.

If a positive duty were imposed on a vendor to disclose all material facts relevant to the property, then mud would certainly be washed off *caveat emptor*, but it would only be fully washed off if there was also a reversal of *caveat emptor* to

[135] See dre.ca.gov.

[136] There are two redress schemes: the Property Ombudsman (www.tpos.co.uk) and the Property Redress Scheme (www.theprs.co.uk).

[137] See www.bristol.gov.uk/ntselat. Powys County Council is the lead enforcement authority for the purposes of the Estate Agents Act 1979.

[138] See Estate Agents (Undesirable Practices) (No 2) Order 1991, SI 1991/1032.

[139] See Estate Agents Act 1979, ss 3 and 4.

[140] See en.powys.gov.uk/article/3992/Estate-Agents-Public-Register.

[141] For an analysis of the requirements, see L Griggs, 'A Draft Vendor Disclosure Statement: Consideration and Comparison' (2001) 9 *Australian Property Law Journal* 143; and E Miller et al, 'Is Mandatory Disclosure an Effective Consumer Protection Mechanism in Australian Real Estate Markets? The Perspective of Queensland Industry Experts' in C Hall and C Hopkinson (eds), *Social Change in the 21st Century 2006 Conference Proceedings* (Queensland University of Technology, 2006), available at eprints.qut.edu.au/10255.

[142] See www.lawsociety.com.au/for-the-public/know-your-rights/selling-a-home/before-you-sell for the information and documents which must be provided.

caveat venditor. This was provisionally proposed in 1988 by the Conveyancing Standing Committee of the Law Commission, which put forward that a vendor should have a positive duty to disclose all material facts about the property they are selling, provided the seller is aware of those facts or ought reasonably to be aware of them, and to that significant extent, they proposed that *caveat emptor* should be reversed.[143] The overwhelming response to this proposal, however, was opposition to *caveat emptor* being reversed.[144] It was felt that the principle gave certainty and was well known, so that a fundamental change required justification by demonstrating material advantages. The Committee felt that the near-unanimous reaction to their proposal underlined the wisdom of the Conveyancing Committee, which said in 1985:

> The suggestion of a general duty of disclosure being imposed upon vendors may well be thought by practitioners to be too radical an alteration of a well understood relationship between the parties to a sale of land.[145]

As the Conveyancing Committee suggested, *caveat emptor* could be changed by a statute implying terms as to title, quality and description of the property, or alternatively they suggested that a general duty of disclosure could be imposed on a vendor by amending the conditions of sale.[146] Whilst the current conditions of sale already contain a duty to disclose certain matters, this does not extend to the physical condition of the property.[147] A reversal of the principle might also lead to an increase in litigation. As the Law Commission said, 'a buyer wants to buy a house not a law suit'.[148] The only recourse for a purchaser who having completed their purchase discovers a problem would be to sue the vendor for damages. This is likely to be unsatisfactory as a purchaser might consider that damages would not be adequate compensation, or the vendor may not be traceable or might not have any assets. The Law Commission concluded that it is clearly better to avoid a purchaser being left with a problem than merely to provide them with remedies when a problem occurs.[149]

VII. CONCLUSION

This chapter has explored the principle of *caveat emptor* and demonstrated that the crystal has now become so muddied that it contributes to delays in

[143] Law Commission (n 2) para 4.1.
[144] Law Commission, *Let the Buyer Be Well Informed – Recommendations of the Conveyancing Standing Committee of the Law Commission* (1989).
[145] The Second Report of the Conveyancing Committee (n 113) para 2.19.
[146] ibid para 2.16.
[147] Condition 3.2.1 of the Standard Conditions of Sale (fifth edition – 2018 revision) provides that a purchaser accepts the property in the physical state it is in at the date of the contract unless the vendor is building or converting it.
[148] Law Commission (n 144).
[149] ibid.

the home-buying and selling process. The development of consumer protection laws and their cultural impact present a significant challenge to the place of *caveat emptor* in modern conveyancing practice. There have also been significant improvements in technology since the Law Commission last considered *caveat emptor*. Whilst there are alternatives to *caveat emptor*, it is clear that these will require government intervention and political will, as in Scotland, the US and Australia, in order to make them work. The unanswered question is whether there would be any appetite from either government or stakeholders for a reversal of *caveat emptor*, though intervention in the form of mandatory upfront property information or disclosure taken together with technology solutions and processes could lead to a re-engineering of the conveyancing process so that the mud could certainly be washed off *caveat emptor* perhaps not fully, but maybe enough so that a '*caveat emptor* light' emerges.

3

The Dangers of Feudal Escheat, Being the Two Pipe Problem of the Baglan Operations Ltd Liquidation and Post-disclaimer Responsibility

JOHN TRIBE*

I. INTRODUCTION

NATIONAL INTEREST LIQUIDATIONS give rise to a number of interesting questions. The 2021 liquidation of Baglan Operations Ltd in the Cardiff Bay area of South Wales has given rise to a number of points.[1] These include issues around public interest insolvency, where stakeholders in the local community are affected by the consequences of the liquidation,[2] director behaviour leading up to the liquidation where a hazardous industrial facility is left to be dealt with by various government agencies, broader environmental

* This chapter was read on three separate occasions in front of separate insolvency law and property law audiences, first at the *Liverpool Business and Property Court Forum* in March 2023 and second as a paper entitled 'What is Meant by "Subject to Escheat" in the Context of Disclaimer of Onerous Property in the Realm of Company Liquidation? A Critical Discussion of the Crown Estate's Ownership of Ownerless Land' at the Exchange Chambers Annual Insolvency Conference 2023 (Leeds and Manchester, 2023). Finally, it was delivered at the 2024 MSPL conference at Queen's College, Cambridge. I would like to thank Justin Dionne, Chief Technical Officer, Insolvency Service, UK and Jag Saroe, Head of Special Operations, Insolvency Service, UK, for the countless discussions on the subject addressed in this chapter. I would also like to thank the various audience members for their interesting comments at all three events, as well as Professor Emma Lees, Professor Martin Dixon KC (Hon), Dr Lorren Eldridge and the anonymous reviewer for their helpful and constructive feedback. Any errors or omissions are the author's sole responsibility.

[1] *In the Matter of Baglan Operations Limited (Baglan Norris)* [2022] EWHC 647 (Ch).

[2] For a discussion of stakeholders and public interest insolvency, see J Tribe, 'Communitarianism and the Public Interest in Large Corporate Insolvencies: Future Directions for Value and Potential in Commonweal Undertakings' in J Harris (ed), *A Research Agenda for Insolvency Law* (Edward Elgar, 2025). See also J Tribe, 'Communitarianism Bankruptcy Law & Policy as a Bulwark against Neo-liberalism: Forging a Humane Future with Stakeholder Insolvency Responses to Public Interest and Sports Club Insolvency' (2022) 15 *Corporate Rescue and Insolvency* 183.

concerns regarding the safe disposal of hazardous materials,[3] social issues including community schooling and safety, continuity of electricity supply and so on. In short, the Baglan Operations Ltd liquidation provides a fascinating case study and there is much to consider ranging over various aspects of insolvency law and related subjects.[4]

This chapter concentrates on the most important issue arising from the Baglan Operations Ltd liquidation, namely, disclaimer of onerous property in a liquidation and questions around subsequent responsibility for that property following the liquidator's decision to disclaim. It is well known that the disclaimer operates to absolve a liquidator of responsibility for that onerous property. However, the property which has been disclaimed still exists, including any hazardous material which is situated upon it, or there may be ongoing maintenance obligations. The land and any property on it must be dealt with and cannot simply be allowed to fester, particularly when the property is physically dangerous, contains toxins or for some other reason is dangerous to trespassers and other individuals that might enter the land and expose the land owner to tortious liability through occupiers' liability.

The question this chapter seeks to address is: who is responsible for real property when the liquidator has disclaimed that freehold property and it escheats to the Crown Estate, but where the Crown Estate refuses to manage that property? Put another way, how does the medieval doctrine of escheat work,[5] why is it relevant in modern practice and does escheat encumber the Crown Estate with responsibility for property, even if that property is onerous and the Crown Estate has refused to manage the property? In relation to this type of property, the Crown Estate has noted:

> Properties that may be subject to escheat are frequently onerous in nature, and many have little or no monetary value. The total cost of all potential past, present and future liabilities connected to such properties, of which there are many, would be enormous. As The Crown Estate accounts to the Treasury for its operating surplus, such a cost would end up as a burden on the public purse.[6]

This post-disclaimer escheat tension arises in the Baglan Operations Ltd case. An answer to the question is required because of ongoing potential liability,

[3] On environmental tensions in insolvency law, see A Jones, 'For the Greater Good? Directors' Duties to Manage Environmental Liabilities during Insolvency Proceedings' (2021) 34 *Insolvency Intelligence* 108.

[4] Or as Sir Alistair Norris observed, 'The applications raised fundamental issues of potentially wide import': *Baglan Norris* (n 1) para 1. See also P Hertz et al, '*In the Matter of Baglan Operations Limited* [2022] EWHC 647 (Ch): The Future of Trading Liquidations?', Clifford Chance, Insolvency Service Research Day, Nottingham, 2022.

[5] On arcane points of legal history as applied in modern litigation, see J Roche, 'Legal History in Court: Lessons from Mexfield and Southward' [2016] *Conveyancer and Property Lawyer* 286. See also E Nugee, 'The Feudal System and the Land Registration Acts' (2008) 124 *LQR* 586. See also C Harpum, 'Does Feudalism Have a Role in 21st Century Land Law?' (2000) 23 *Amicus Curiae* 21.

[6] See the Crown Estate website FAQs, where there are a number of interesting and informative paragraphs on ownership and escheat: www.thecrownestate.co.uk/en-gb/resources/faqs.

eg, by tort claimants hurting themselves on the land, or other hazardous consequences flowing from the state of the land and hazardous materials on it.

This chapter is divided into three sections.

In section II, the Baglan Operations Ltd liquidation is examined in order to show how the disclaimer issue arose and how the escheat issue becomes operative. This section of the chapter examines Sir Alistair Norris' March 2022 judgment in *In the Matter of Baglan Operations Limited (in Compulsory Liquidation)*.[7] In this case the liquidator continued to manage and run Baglan Operations Ltd and the problematic site of a £350 million power plant to try and deal with the most problematic aspects of the property and its disposal.

In section III, disclaimer of onerous property rules are examined in order to demonstrate why, in policy terms, disclaimer is permitted by insolvency legislation. However, as this chapter demonstrates, disclaimer can give rise to 'ownerless' property. It is argued that this is not satisfactory when that property is hazardous by its own nature or by what is stored on it.

In section IV, the relatively unexplored and contested doctrine of escheat is examined.[8] It is argued that once property has escheated to the Crown Estate, the Crown Estate should be responsible for that property in all circumstances. This liability arises as a result of the operation of escheat and the return of what was freehold land back into the Crown Estate.[9] It is argued that it is no defence to say that the Crown Estate is a passive actor with no responsibility. Once escheat reclaims or reverts the land for the Crown Estate, the Crown Estate must be responsible for that land, even if they do not want to be responsible. This is how escheat and tenure operates. Land cannot be ownerless, hence the doctrine of escheat. As Lord Loughborough argued when Attorney-General in *Middleton v Spicer*[10] in 1783, the Crown is owner of everything which has no other owner. Once it is (re)'owned' by the Crown Estate via escheat, ie, the land is no longer encumbered by an estate and passes back to the Crown Estate, the Crown Commissioners should be responsible.

A conclusion then follows, which argues that legislative intervention[11] is required to update the area of escheat as disclaimer of onerous property becomes more prominent, particularly through both large-scale public interest insolvencies and also the strategic parcelling of land by insolvency practitioners (IPs) seeking to rid insolvent estates of liability. Finally, it is suggested that the

[7] See *Baglan Norris* (n 1). On the case, see also Clifford Chance, 'Liquidation: Continuation of Electricity Supply' (2022) 33 *PLC Magazine* 75.

[8] The distinction between escheat and how it differs from *bona vacantia* is also discussed – see section IV.A below.

[9] Escheats occur around 300–500 times each year according to the *Land Registration Act, Explanatory Notes*, para 133.

[10] *Middleton v Spicer* (1783) 1 BroChRep 201.

[11] There is precedent for the reform of feudal land law in recent times. See, for example, the Abolition of Feudal Tenure, etc (Scotland) Act 2000 and the Scottish Law Commission, *Report on Abolition of the Feudal System*, (1999, Scot Law Com No.168). See also Harpum (n 5).

Crown Estate should cross-subsidise escheat issues and liabilities from *bona vacantia* income.

II. BAGLAN BAY AND BAGLAN OPERATIONS LIMITED

Baglan Bay (Bae Baglan) is part of the Swansea Bay coastline. The area has a long and proud industrial heritage stretching back to the nineteenth century.[12] This included British Petroleum (BP)'s Llandarcy Oil Refinery in Port Talbot, which was operational between 1919 and 1998.[13] It was for a time one of Europe's largest petrochemical factories.

The Baglan factory was also situated in a 'highly visible location'[14] with close proximity to residential areas and schools in Baglan village. Sandfields and Baglan Moors also make up the area. In environmental terms, the site was problematic.

Leading up to the 2004 closure of the BP isopropanol chemicals plant in Baglan Bay, there was a period of re-development and regeneration.[15] There was 'a genuine desire to avoid leaving an economic vacuum in the local community in its exit from Baglan Bay'[16] and 'BP Chemicals had formulated the concept of the Baglan Energy Park in the mid 1990s and in alliance with the Welsh Development Agency and Neath Port Talbot County Borough Council the concept developed into substantive form'.[17] At the time, this was the single largest re-development site in the UK at 500 hectares. The re-development included the construction of a £350 million gas turbine power plant on Baglan Moors, west of Port Talbot. General Electric (GE) Power Systems built the power plant on the site of the former BP plant.[18] The power plant was served by a 12 km gas pipeline connecting it to the gas network. Electricity generated by the Baglan Bay power station was fed into the National Grid. A proportion of the output was also distributed via a private wire network. There was an electricity sub-station on the site for this purpose.

The Baglan Bay power station sits alongside the Baglan Energy Park, which is a 180-acre site populated by numerous businesses. The principal

[12] See Royal Commission on the Ancient and Historical Monuments of Wales, 'Copperopolis: Landscapes of the Early Industrial Period in Swansea', 2–11. See also AH John, *The Industrial Development of South Wales 1750–1850* (Cardiff, University of Wales Press, 1950). Some of this industrial activity led to litigation; see *Re Baglan Hall Colliery Co* (1869–70) LR 5 Ch App 346.

[13] See further D Strawbridge and P Thomas, *Baglan Bay: Past, Present and Future* (Baglan Bay, BP Chemicals Ltd, 2001). See also R W Ferrier, *The History of the British Petroleum Company Volume 1: The Developing Years, 1901–1932* (Cambridge, Cambridge University Press, 1984).

[14] Strawbridge and Thomas (n 13) 237.

[15] The re-development included a demolition phase which has been saved for posterity in video form. See https://youtu.be/r5OaDzNLF6w.

[16] Strawbridge and Thomas (n 13) 264.

[17] ibid.

[18] An interesting General Electric (GE) health and safety video providing a tour of the new Baglan Bay power station, GE Baglan, is available here: https://youtu.be/UBmDB57zrpE.

unique selling point of the Baglan Energy Park was the close proximity and availability of cheap electrical energy from the GE plant.[19] As well as the industrial park, there were also schools and homes that were supplied by the Baglan Bay power station.

Over time, the ownership of the power station changed on a number of occasions. Following BP's ownership, the power station site was acquired by GE. GE sold the plant in October 2012 to Macquarie, who were acting on behalf of a group of investors.[20] In 2019 the power plant was transferred along with its staff to Calon Energy.

A. The Insolvency of Baglan Operations Limited

In June 2020, an administration order was made which placed Baglan Group into administration. The administration order was made with a view to rescue, but this was scuppered by the secured creditor. The pre-pack administration had been supported by tenants on the Baglan Energy Park and the Mardon Business Park. A month later in July 2020, the power station stopped generating electricity. Instead, electricity was sourced from Western Power Distribution and the power station became a conduit for electricity being supplied to premises on the Baglan Enterprise Park. The administration was caused by a Calon group reconstruction as part of a 'cost-cutting exercise cause by the financial distress of the group'[21] and the fact that the power plant was reaching the end of its useful life.

On 24 March 2021, winding-up orders were made against a number of companies in the Calon group.[22] The Calon group owned three gas turbine power stations. No private-sector liquidator was appointed due to the risks related to decommissioning the power plant, including the gas pipeline and water pipeline which fed the power station, as well as the electricity conduit element of the power station. The health and safety risks were substantial. These included flammable chemicals and turbine lubricant oil and a high-pressure gas pipeline.

The court appointed the Official Receiver, Gareth Jonathan Allen, as Liquidator. David Pike and Michael Pink from KPMG were appointed as Special Managers of the estate and business of Baglan Operations Ltd by the court.[23] The Official Receiver received an indemnity from the Department for Business, Energy, Industrial Strategy (BEIS) for the costs of the liquidation. This was

[19] Strawbridge and Thomas (n 13) 265.

[20] R Morison, 'Macquarie Buys UK Gas-Fed Power Plants in Bet Profits to Rise' (Bloomberg, 16 January 2013).

[21] *Baglan Norris* (n 1).

[22] 'Calon' means 'Heart' in the Welsh language.

[23] On Special Managers, see IF Fletcher, *The Law of Insolvency*, 5th edn (London, Sweet & Maxwell, 2017), [22-100].

followed by an indemnity from the Welsh government for liabilities arising from continuing to run the Baglan site.[24]

The purpose of the liquidation was to work towards a disclaimer of onerous property and an orderly winding up of the operations of Baglan Operations Ltd.[25] However, the ramifications of the liquidation were far-reaching because of the nature of the land and continuity of supply issues. Some of the customers provided vital functions. These included four pumping stations operated by Welsh Water, including sewage pumps. These serviced approximately 40 local commercial enterprises and approximately 69,000 non-commercial customers. If these pumps were inactive for more than four hours during heavy rainfall, there would be 'severe environmental damage'[26] in the wider Swansea Bay area, including to its protected shellfish beds, due to sewage discharge. The environmental damage was viewed as 'potentially catastrophic'.[27]

This was a problematic liquidation for multiple reasons, including obsolete technology at the plant, a high-pressure gas pipeline, a lack of funding resources, local school safety concerns with the 1,400 pupils at Ysgol Bae Baglan and street lighting for their safety, and the need for continued electricity supply to local businesses.

Applications were made in 2022 pursuant to section 168(5) of the Insolvency Act 1986 (IA 1986) before Sir Alistair Norris to prevent the Official Receiver from finalising the liquidation.[28] These were successful in part. The applicants (the Welsh government, Welsh Water, Neath Port Talbot Council and Sofidel) argued that 'no reasonable Official Receiver who was in possession of all the facts would act in the way proposed and the decision to terminate the Connection was a perverse one'.[29] The Official Receiver did not want to continue to run the site and be liable for the associated costs of doing so. Before the judge, the appellants also argued that the Official Receiver did have the power to continue supply.

As Sir Alistair Norris' judgment makes clear, the Official Receiver was appointed 'so that health and safety and environmental concerns relating to the Baglan Plant could be addressed, not for the financial benefit of creditors'.[30] He continued to note that the purpose of the liquidation was for the 'benefit and well-being of those in the locality expose to those hazards. These hazards

[24] As is noted in *Baglan Norris* (n 1), the indemnity was 'an indemnity against all liabilities, costs, expenses, damages, and losses arising out of any delay in the termination of the provision of electricity to Welsh Water and the Council … and against any other costs or liabilities arising from the continued occupation of the Baglan Plant which would not otherwise have been incurred had termination of the Connection occurred on 14 January 2022' (para 36).

[25] Sir Alastair Norris states in this regard: 'The liquidation of the Company is therefore not focused on realisation of value for creditors, but upon the safe, efficient and orderly winding down of the Company leading to a disclaimer of its burdensome assets under s.178 IA 1986.' ibid [17].

[26] ibid [5].

[27] ibid.

[28] ibid.

[29] ibid [41].

[30] ibid [55].

principally arose from toxic materials and hazardous structures on the site of the Baglan Plant itself'.[31] These hazards could carry both criminal and civil liability. In addition to the hazards, the Official Receiver should also pay attention to wider flooding issues which would flow from the closure of the power plant.

The result of the application hearing was a modification of the Official Receiver's decision. The judge ordered that the Official Receiver was to continue to supply facilities to Welsh Water and the Neath Port Talbot Council until 18 April 2022.

Ultimately the property was disclaimed by the liquidator. The property therefore still subsists and must be dealt with. It is to that vexed question that we now turn.

III. DISCLAIMER OF ONEROUS PROPERTY

Liquidators, Trustees in Bankruptcy[32] and the Official Receiver have the power to disclaim onerous property. As HHJ Davis-White QC has noted, 'the power of the trustee in bankruptcy to disclaim goes well back into bankruptcy legislation in the nineteenth century'.[33] In the early nineteenth century, bankruptcy assignees had to elect to accept a leasehold interest.[34] The Bankruptcy Act 1869 introduced the first disclaimer provisions which enabled the disclaimer of leases and other onerous property.[35] The Bankruptcy Act 1883[36] and the Bankruptcy Act 1914[37] both included disclaimer provisions.[38]

For liquidation, the pertinent provisions on disclaimer of onerous property are located in sections 178–82 IA 1986.[39] The corporate side of the subject largely

[31] ibid. Some locals argued that cancer clusters were present around Baglan Bay, causing research to be undertaken to test the claims: see S Sans et al, 'Cancer Incidence and Mortality Near the Baglan Bay Petrochemical Works, South Wales (1995) 52 *Occupational and Environmental Medicine* 217.

[32] On disclaimer in personal insolvency, see further Fletcher (n 23) [8-124] to [8-136]. See also Cork Report, Cmnd 8558, ch 27.

[33] *James Sleight (as Trustee of the State of Jillian Paula Mascall Deceased) v The Crown Estate Commissioners* [2018] EWHC 3489 (Ch), [9] (*Re Mascall*). For a nineteenth-century case in disclaimer, see *Hill v East and West India Dock Company* (1884) 9 App Cas 448 (HL), which also involved a lease.

[34] 49 Geo 3, c 121, s 19. See further *Inglis v MacDougal* (1817) 1 Moo Rep 196. See also *Tuck v Fyson* (1829) 6 Bong 321.

[35] See s 23 of the Bankruptcy Act 1869; and *Smyth v North* (1872) LR 7 Ex 242. See also *Ex parte Walton; In re Levy* (1881) 17 Ch D 746.

[36] Bankruptcy Act 1883, s 55. See further *Harding v Preece* (1882) 9 QBD 281; *Hill v East and West India Dock* (n 33).

[37] Bankruptcy Act 1914, s 54.

[38] On pre-IA 1986 approaches to disclaimer under the Bankruptcy Act 1914, see Fletcher (n 23) 192–97.

[39] On s 178, see further Fletcher (n 23) [24-003]. See also K van Zwieten, *Goode on Principles of Corporate Insolvency Law*, 5th edn (London, Sweet & Maxwell, 2018) [6-26]. The previous provisions on disclaimer were contained in ss 618, 619 and 620 of the Companies Act 1985 before they were repealed. These were discussed in *Re Potters Oil (in Liquidation)* [1985] PCC 148 by Harman J.

mirrors the personal in terms of the disclaimer provisions. The case law discussion that follows touches on both corporate and personal insolvency authorities on disclaimer and escheat. As Fletcher has opined, the purpose of the disclaimer provisions in terms of policy objectives is, 'to enable … liquidators to put an end to ongoing costs and outgoings from the estate'.[40]

Under the modern disclaimer provisions in the IA 1986, the Official Receiver may, by the giving of the prescribed notice,[41] disclaim any onerous property and may do so notwithstanding that he has taken possession of it, endeavoured to sell it or otherwise exercised rights of ownership in relation to it.[42]

In terms of what constitutes onerous property, the statute notes that this includes any unprofitable contract,[43] any other property of the company which is unsaleable or not readily saleable, or is such that it may give rise to a liability to pay money or perform any other onerous act.[44] The property must also be property as defined by section 436 IA 1986.[45] As has been noted, 'property disclaimed is not likely to prove a very valuable acquisition'.[46]

The effect of the disclaimer by the liquidator is to determine the rights, interests and liabilities of the company in respect of the property that has been disclaimed.[47] This occurs from the date of the disclaimer. There are limits to disclaimer. Its effect is not meant to affect the rights or liabilities of any other person, except as is necessary for the purpose of releasing the company from any liability.[48]

A. Why Might an Officeholder Disclaim?

In essence, the officeholder is after a 'clean break'. As Fletcher notes, the act of disclaimer permits 'a crystalisation of the debtor's liabilities, thereby assisting the trustee … to complete his administration and to close his files and accounts within a reasonable time span'.[49] The case law contains a number of examples of drivers leading to a decision by the Trustee in Bankruptcy to disclaim. Property being in negative equity has driven the decision to disclaim in at least one case. Where 20 or so properties were worth less than the sums secured by way of charge, the Trustee in Bankruptcy disclaimed the properties.[50] Disclaimer was

[40] Fletcher (n 23) [24-003].
[41] IA 1986, s 178(2).
[42] ibid s 178(1).
[43] ibid s 178(3)(a). On unprofitable contracts and disclaimer see *Re SSSL Realisations (2002) Ltd* [2006] EWCA Civ 7, [2006] Ch 610.
[44] IA 1986, s 178(3)(b).
[45] For a discussion of what constitutes property in the context of disclaimer, see *Official Receiver v Environment Agency* [2001] Ch 475 (CA). See also *Re Celtic Extraction Ltd* [2001] Ch 475 (CA).
[46] FW Hardman, 'The Law of Escheat' (1888) 4 *LQR* 318, 322 and 327.
[47] IA 1986, s 178(4)(a).
[48] ibid s 178(4)(b).
[49] Fletcher (n 32) [24-003].
[50] *Re Mascall* (n 33) [4].

also used where it was felt that the costs of realising the property outweighed any benefits to the bankruptcy estate.[51] In the famous disclaimer decision of *Hindcastle Ltd v Barbara Attenborough Associates Ltd*,[52] Lord Nicholls of Birkenhead stated in the context of disclaimer that 'unprofitable contracts can be ended, and property burdened with onerous obligations disowned'.[53] In *Hindcastle* itself, the rent payable under a lease exceeded the rental value of the property in the open market which was in recession.[54]

IV. POST-DISCLAIMER RESPONSIBILITY AND ESCHEAT

What happens to property once it has been disclaimed by the officeholder? Who is responsible for the property? The answer lies in some vestiges of feudal land law, and it is to those that we now turn.[55]

A. *Bona Vacantia* or Escheat?

Ownerless property can be subject to the rules on *bona vacantia*[56] or the doctrine of escheat. Escheat is the relevant doctrine in the area of tenure, particularly where that tenure has become extinct.[57] Different conditions apply to freehold property and leasehold property. That distinction is discussed below, but first we must differentiate between *bona vacantia* and escheat. It has been noted that escheat applies to real property, whereas *bona vacantia* applies to personal property[58] – so escheat for realty and *bona vacantia* for personalty.[59] The Crown claims ownerless goods via *bona vacantia* as a result of the royal prerogative,[60] not as lord paramount as occurs with escheat

[51] *Lee v Lee* [1999] BPIR 926.

[52] *Hindcastle Ltd v Barbara Attenborough Associates Ltd* [1997] AC 70 (HL).

[53] ibid 87 (per Lord Nicholls).

[54] ibid 83(B) (per Lord Nicholls).

[55] For a fascinating discussion of land law history, see M Wonnacott, *Forgotten Land Law* (Clark, NJ, Talbot Publishing, 2022) 24 (escheat).

[56] On *bona vacantia*, see ND Ing, *Bona Vacantia* (London, LexisNexis, 1999). See also FA Enever, *Bona Vacantia under the Law of England* (London, HMSO, 1927), which discusses escheat at 15–16: 'In the case of the Crown's title by way of escheat in respect of the real estate of inheritance of a person dying before 1926 intestate and without an heir at law the Crown did not acquire any right or interest of the deceased, *but continued to be the owner of the land, freed from the estate previously carved out of the Crown's interest in the land*'. *(author's italicised emphasis).*

[57] See further Ed, 'Do You Know the Difference between Escheat and Bona Vacantia?' (1998) 1 *Comm Prop* 22.

[58] Anon, 'Origins and Development of Modern Escheat' (1961) 61 *Columbia Law Review* 1319, 1326.

[59] RH Garrison, 'Escheats, Abandoned Property Acts and Their Revenue Aspects' (1947) 35 *Kentucky Law Journal* 302, 303.

[60] W Blackstone, *Commentaries on the Laws of England*, vol 1 (Oxford, Clarendon Press, 1765) 298.

(see below).[61] As one commentator has observed, *bona vacantia* is 'predicated on the absence of any owner, rather than on its status as ultimate owner'.[62] This is because the Crown can claim in a more equitable manner than permitting an unseemly contest between strangers as private parties litigating over the spoils.

B. *In Re Fivestar*

An instructive case highlighting the difference between *bona vacantia* and escheat is *In Re Fivestar Properties Ltd*.[63] This case involved a property re-development company, Fivestar Properties Ltd, which had been dissolved following an administration.[64] The company was incorporated in 2003. It took out several loans secured against its properties. By 2011, the company had encountered financial difficulties, owing at least £3.15 million to creditors. Following a Law of Property Act (LPA) 1925 receivership, the company was put into administration in July 2012 to investigate various links with third-party companies (eg, North Salford Estates Ltd) utilising the administrator's broader powers.

Subsequently the company was dissolved. As a consequence of the dissolution, the estates that the company owned were held to be *bona vacantia* and vest in the Crown by virtue of the operation of the Companies Act 2006 (CA 2006 – see below).[65] These company assets included freehold property which had been charged by way of legal mortgage for a loan from a bank, West Bromwich Commercial Ltd. The Crown then disclaimed the freehold property[66] following the tenant's request for a new lease. By its application, the bank wanted the company to be restored to the companies register.[67] This would enable it to enforce the mortgage and realise the value in the property. The court also had to consider whether the Crown disposition constituted a disposition of property.

HHJ Cooke (sitting as a High Court judge) granted the application. His judgment provides a very useful summary of escheat and its interaction with *bona vacantia*. This is expanded upon below, but it provides a useful starting

[61] See also *Attorney General v Kohler* (1861) 9 HLC 654, 11 Eng Rep 885. See also *Middleton v Spicer* (1867) 1 Bro CC 201, 28 Eng Rep 1083.

[62] Anon (n 58) 1326.

[63] *In Re Fivestar Properties Ltd* [2015] EWHC 2782 (Ch). See further D Gray and J Williams, *Dissolution: Practical Advice to Mortgagees on Asset Realisation* (2016) 2 *Corporate Rescue and Insolvency* 43. See also S Leslie, 'Escheating Bona Vacantia: Re Fivestar Properties Ltd' (2015), www.lexisnexis.co.uk/blog/restructuring-and-insolvency/escheating-bona-vacantia-re-fivestar-properties-ltd.

[64] Pursuant to IA 1986, s 84(1) of sched B1.

[65] Pursuant to Companies Act 2006, s 1012.

[66] Pursuant to ibid s 1013.

[67] Pursuant to ibid s 1029.

point to consider the qualities of escheat. HHJ Cooke stated that following dissolution of a company:[68]

> [T]hat the effect is that the land escheats to the Crown. Escheat is an ancient term, denoting the principle that if the interest of an inferior tenant determines or is extinguished, the land reverts to the tenant's immediate feudal lord. All land is ultimately held of the Crown, and a freehold interest (otherwise called a 'tenancy in fee simple') is a tenancy for these purposes, so that if the freehold interest is extinguished the land reverts to the immediate lord, in practice nowadays being the Crown.[69]

Perhaps the most interesting point emanating from the judgment for the responsibility thesis being tested in this chapter is not the comments of HHJ Cooke in relation to escheat, but what he tells us about the Deputy Judge's comments in their first instance judgment. In summarising the judgment, HHJ Cooke notes 'that the escheat operated *automatically* without need for an election by the Crown'.[70] By reference to *Megarry & Wade*, the judge continued: 'The disclaimer may nevertheless serve a purpose for the Crown in that it may not come under liability as owner of the land unless it takes some step to asset ownership.'[71] This election point is central to this chapter.

Returning to the judgment in *Fivestar*, as well as demonstrating the difference between *bona vacantia* and escheat, the case also highlights the fact that there are a number of statutory provisions that relate to company property and *bona vacantia* specifically, as opposed to escheat. These provisions are contained in the CA 2006.[72] Section 1012 CA 2006 states that the property of a dissolved company is to be *bona vacantia*. The provision notes that:

> When a company is dissolved, all property and rights whatsoever vested in the company immediately before its dissolution are deemed to be *bona vacantia* and (a) accordingly belong to the Crown, and (b) vest and may be dealt with in the same manner as other *bona vacantia* accruing to the Crown.

The section therefore says nothing about adoption, acts of management and the like. *Bona vacantia* vesting is automatic and immediate. There appear to be no issues around a decision to not manage. The property is now vested in the Crown. The Crown may disclaim pursuant to section 1012 CA 2006, as it did in the instant case. At this point, the property escheats to the Crown and this takes us to the circumlocution point mentioned above. The Crown is able to disclaim

[68] Which is obviously different from disclaimer of a company's property by a liquidator.

[69] *In Re Fivestar Properties Ltd* [2016] 1 WLR 1104, 1109[F].

[70] ibid (emphasis added).

[71] ibid 1109[G], citing C Harpum and M Dixon, *Megarry & Wade: The Law of Real Property*, 8th edn (London, Sweet & Maxwell, 2012) [2-024].

[72] The Company Law Review Steering Group (CLRSG) documents are perhaps unsurprisingly quiet on the issue, bearing in mind it is at the intersection of land law, insolvency law and company law. This may be another area where points have fallen between 'regulators'.

property which vests in it *bona vacantia* pursuant to section 1013 CA 2006.[73] As HHJ Cooke notes, 'this has the curious result in the case of freeholds that on such a disclaimer the land ultimately came back to the Crown in any event as an escheat'. The judge also noted the 'apparent illogicality'[74] of this situation.[75]

An explanation for this circuitous activity might be that the different departments of government have responsibility for each route to the Crown. The Treasury Solicitor deals with *bona vacantia* cases to protect the Crown's interests. The Crown Estate deals with escheat cases to protect the Crown's interests. Another explanation, provided by Harpum, is that 'the liability of the Crown for land that it receives as *bona vacantia* may be much more stringent than its liability for property that passes to it by way of escheat'.[76] This is because the Crown can be liable for covenants to a lease over land which has come to the Crown via *bona vacantia*.[77]

V. ESCHEAT

A. Freehold Property: Disclaimer and Responsibility

In *Mascall v The Crown Estate Commissioners*,[78] HHJ Davis-White QC made reference to a Government Legal Department letter which stated that '[f]reehold property which has been disclaimed by a trustee in bankruptcy does not vest in the Crown as bona vacantia, but rather becomes subject to escheat to the Crown and may be dealt with thereafter by the Crown Estate'.[79]

This raises the important question of what exactly is escheat and what it means in terms of responsibility, particularly for the Crown Estate Commissioners. HHJ Davis-White QC visits this point, again by reference to correspondence which stated that: 'Land may be deemed subject to escheat to the Crown … Longstanding legal advice to the Crown Estate Commissioners is that if they undertake no act of possession, entry or management, no liability or responsibility in respect of the property arises in the circumstances of escheat.'[80] This

[73] Formerly Companies Act 1985, s 654 – on the operation of which, see *Allied Dunbar Assurance plc v Fowle* [1994] BCC 422.

[74] *In Re Fivestar Properties* (n 69) 1109[H].

[75] A similar trajectory occurred – ie, dissolution, *bona vacantia*, disclaimer, then escheat – in *Pall Mall 3 Ltd v Network Rail* [2021] EWHC 1835 (Ch); [2022] 2 P & CR 11. See further P Dollar, 'The Final Curtain' (2021) 2137 *Estates Gazette* 76–78. See also *Re Buzzlines Coaches Ltd* [2020] EWHC 3027 (Ch); [2021] BCC 239, where HHJ Halliwell notes that: 'At common law, land was never entirely ownerless … the freehold would historically return or escheat to the Crown' (at [6]). However, as we have seen, the freehold is extinguished, the estate disappears and the land reverts to the Crown.

[76] Harpum (n 5) 23.

[77] See *Toff v McDowell* (1993) 69 P & CR 535.

[78] *Re Mascall* (n 33).

[79] ibid [11].

[80] *Re Mascall* (n 33) [12].

might then mean that the Crown Estate Commissioners would not be liable for making good any issues caused by hazardous materials at a property that has escheated. However, it that really the case, particularly if escheat applies only to freehold land? Can it also apply to leasehold, and if it does not, what does? This point is taken up below.

Figure 3.1 Escheat frequency from 2013 to 2023

Year	(1) Notifications	(2) Completed and no longer "StE"	(X) Unresolved?? (in limbo/"blinking first" position?)
2013	1079	43	1036
2014	794	30	764
2015	774	31	743
2016	750	48	702
2017	711	45	666
2018	693	49	644
2019	680	33	647
2020	523	43	480
2021	634	25	609
2022	515	14	501
2023 (mid-Jan)	17	No data supplied	*
TOTAL(S):	7170	361	6792

Source: Crown Estate – Freedom of Information Request One, 2023.[81]

Scmlla Properties Ltd v Gesso Properties (BCI) Ltd[82] is a decision of Stanley Burnton QC.[83] The case involved the disclaimer of a freehold on insolvency of a landlord and a discussion of escheat. Escheat, as noted above, is an interesting process which has long historical roots.[84] Escheat operates in relation to freehold land. When land becomes subject to escheat, the freehold title determines. The Crown becomes the owner of the land in question. The Crown is freed from the previous freehold estate interest. The Crown need not do anything to bring

[81] Crown Estate – Freedom of Information Request One, 2023. Contains public sector information licensed under the Open Government Licence v3.0.

[82] *Scmlla Properties Ltd v Gesso Properties (BCI) Ltd* [1995] BCC 794. See also the judgment of HHJ Wethered in *British General Insurance Co Ltd v Attorney-General* [1945] 12 LJNCCR 113.

[83] Sitting as a deputy judge of the Chancery Division, later a Lord Justice of Appeal.

[84] W Holdsworth, *A History of English Law*, vol 3 (London, Sweet & Maxwell, 1977) 67–73. See also TFT Plucknett, *A Concise History of the Common Law*, 5th edn (Boston, Little Brown & Co, 1956) 177, 536 and 442, with lords and their reaping the 'harvest of escheats' following felonies. See also Note, 'Origins and Development of Modern Escheat' (1961) 61 *Columbia Law Review* 1319–40; DC Auten, 'Modern Rationales of Escheat' (1963) 112 *University of Pennsylvania Law Review* 95.

about this result.[85] Escheat is based on the fundamental principle that 'land is still the object of feudal tenure; the Sovereign remains the lord paramount of all the land within the realm; every parcel of land is still held of some lord'.[86] This point was made in 1628 by Sir Edward Coke, sometime Chief Justice of the Common Pleas, when he stated that 'all lands within the realm were originally derived from the crown, and therefore, the King in sovereign, or lord paramount, either mediate or immediate, of all and every parcel of land with the realm'.[87]

As tenure requires a tenant where none exists due to disclaimer of onerous property, the land escheats to the Crown as lord paramount. *Megarry & Wade* made this point when they stated: 'Escheat is a principle inseparable from tenure which ensures that land can never be without an owner, for if there is no tenant and no mesne lord it will return to the Crown.'[88] A similar point was made by Hardman writing in 1888 when he observed that:

> The conception of escheat is inseparably connected with the idea of tenure. It proceeds upon the assumption that all lands in the occupation of a tenant are held of some superior under certain conditions, by virtue of an original grant. The tenant is not the owner of the land, but only of an estate in the land, and upon the determination of this estate, the feud falls back into the lord's hands by a termination of the tenure.[89]

Commonwealth case law supports this view. In *Attorney-General of Ontario v Mercer*,[90] it was stated that: 'When there is no longer any tenant, the land returns, by reason of tenure, to the lord by whom or by whose predecessors in title, the tenure was created.'

These commentators are discussing the 'feudal pyramid',[91] namely the process of infeudation, so disposing of land in exchange for service,[92] and subsequent sub-infeudation by tenants. At the top of the feudal pyramid sits the Crown, now the Crown Estate. Parcels of land were disposed of through the process of infeudation.[93] In the modern context, the Crown, as lord paramount, can grant 'a fee simple by way of infeudatory grant from its paramount ownership'.[94] It is from this understanding of how land is held that we can

[85] See further *Scmlla Properties* (n 82); and *Hunt v Withinshaw* [2015] EWHC 3072.

[86] R Megarry and HH Wade, *The Law of Real Property*, 5th edn (London, Sweet & Maxwell, 1984) 36. See also *Attorney-General of Ontario v Mercer* [1883] 8 App Cas 76, per the Earl of Selborne LC at 771–72. See also *In Re Mercer & Moore* [1880] 14 ChD 287, 295.

[87] E Coke, *Commentary on Littleton's Tenures* (1628) 65a.

[88] Megarry and Wade (n 86) 34. See also AWB Simpson, *A History of the Land Law*, 2nd edn (Oxford, Oxford University Press, 1986) 47–48.

[89] Hardman (n 46) 322.

[90] *Attorney-General of Ontario v Mercer (1883)* 8 App Cas 772.

[91] Harpum (n 5) 21.

[92] On which see E Wambaugh (ed), *Littleton's Tenures in English* (John Byrne & Co, Ltd, 1903) 49. See also G C Cheshire, *The Modern Law of Real Property*, 7th edn (London, Butterworth & Co (Publishers) Ltd, 1954) 18–19.

[93] But see the abolition provisions in the Tenants Abolition Act 1660.

[94] Harpum (n 5) 21.

more closely understand escheat, namely, the process where 'land reverts to the tenant's lord'.[95] Where there are no mesne lordships (which is usually the case, save for the Dukedoms of Cornwall and Lancaster), the land passes back into the Crown as 'absolute property',[96] which has also been called 'dominium directum'.[97] Blackstone also took the view that all land in England and Wales emanates from the sovereign. In his famous commentaries, he observed: 'The grand and fundamental maxim of all feudal tenure is this: that all lands were originally granted out by the sovereign, and are therefore holden, either mediately or immediately, of the crown.'[98]

Historically there were two versions of escheat.[99] The first was escheat *proper defectum sanguinis*, which operated where a tenant died without heirs and the land reverted to the lord.[100] The second type was escheat *proper delictum tenentis* and this operated to return the land to the lord where the tenant had committed a felony 'in the original sense of that term'.[101] Baker has stated that this second type of escheat was later called 'forfeiture'.[102] Potter has made a similar point,[103] also noting that '"to revert" and "to escheat" were practically synonymous terms'.[104] The term escheat is derived from 'eschier, to fall'.[105]

Escheat therefore operated where the freehold had no tenant because of death or because the tenant had committed a felony and was no longer capable of giving service.[106] Escheat operated as a tenurial right which permitted the lord to take the fee simple. In this sense escheat was 'a fruit of signiory, the Crown

[95] ibid 21.

[96] Real Property Commissioners, Third Report on Real Property, 1832, p 3, cited in Harpum (n 5) 22.

[97] *Attorney-General of Ontario v Mercer (1883)* 8 App Cas 772, citing Co Litt 1a and 1b. It could be argued that this terminology is not helpful in English and Welsh law. It is much more useful in Scots law, where the idea of two dominiums was adopted, but has never been the terminology or concept used to understand feudal tenure in England.

[98] Blackstone (n 60) vol II, 53.

[99] For a discussion of 'modern escheat' and its use in America, see TJ Gregory, 'Unclaimed Property and Due Process: Justifying "Revenue-Raising" Modern Escheat' (2011) 110 *Michigan Law Review* 319, where the author discusses states' ability to take custody of presumably abandoned property through the doctrine of escheat. Gregory suggests (by reference to James Story) that escheat has Roman roots, arguing that under Roman law, an officer would be appointed 'to assert the right of the emperor to a decedent's estate when that decendent left no heirs to claim it' (at 322).

[100] See Glanvill, Book VII, ch 17. See further JO Orth, 'Escheat: Is the State the Last Heir?' (2009) 13 *Green Bag 2d* 73, 75. See also *Dyke v Walford* (1846) 5 Moo PC 434, 13 Eng.Rep 557(PC). See also *Escheat to the Crown* (21 October 1916), 141 *LT* 424.

[101] Holdsworth (n 84) 67.

[102] JH Baker, *An Introduction to English Legal History*, 3rd edn (London, Butterworths, 1990) 274.

[103] H Potter, *A Short Outline of English Legal History*, 4th edn (London, Sweet & Maxwell, 1945) 182.

[104] H Potter, *An Historical Introduction to English Law and its Institutions*, 2nd edn (London, Sweet & Maxwell, 1943) 422.

[105] See Baker (n 102) 274. The term is derived from Norman French (eschete, eschet, escheoir, eschoir), 'meaning to happen to fall as a windfall'. See W Jowitt (ed), *The Dictionary of English Law*, vol 1 (London, Sweet & Maxwell, 1959) 731.

[106] See further AWB Simpson, *An Introduction to the History of the Land Law* (Oxford, Oxford University Press, 1961) 19–20.

or lord of the fee, from whom or from whose ancestor or predecessor the estate was originally delivered, taking it as *ultimus haeres* upon the failure, natural or legal, of the intestate tenant's family'.[107] Because of this, Jenks has noted that 'escheat is rather an inevitable consequence, than an incident, of the principle of tenure'.[108] Hargrave took a more nuanced view, noting that 'the lord's title to take possession commences immediately on the want of a tenant and is vested in him by mere act of law'.[109] Yet, critically, he continued 'though he must do some act to put himself into the *actual possession*'.[110] In essence, the tenant's estate has come to an end. The lord takes the land by his own right. This demonstrates that 'escheat is in its nature an incident of tenure'.[111]

Escheat could be a source of profit. An Escheator was an officer who was appointed to look to escheats.[112] As Jenks noted, 'escheats were a valuable source of revenue; and the Crown employed regular officials and held periodical enquiries, or "inquests", to discover and enforce them'.[113]

Escheat was heavily reformed by the Administration of Estates Act 1925 in relation to certain elements of the doctrine. Holdsworth, perhaps overstating the effect of the Act, observed:

> The last class of bona vacantia is the most important; and its importance has been increased by the Property Legislation of 1925. In the first place, the law of escheat is abolished by the Administration of Estates Act 1925, and freeholds now devolve as bona vacantia.[114]

Williams has stated that: 'However, escheat does still arise, principally in two contexts. The first is insolvency. If an individual's trustee in bankruptcy or a company's liquidator exercises his statutory power to disclaim the land, the land will escheat.'[115] In *James Sleight (as Trustee of the State of Jillian Paula Mascall*

[107] Jowitt (n 105) 731. Jowitt's use of *ultimus haeres* could be queried here. The Crown does not take as ultimate heir in England. There is no scope for ultimate heirs because the land will fall back to the Crown. As such, there is the same outcome, but a different mechanism is used.

[108] E Jenks, *A Short History of English Law* (London, Metheun & Co, 1912) 36.

[109] *Hargrave*, Co Litt 18b.n, cited in Hardman (n 46) 322. Hardman continues: 'the Crown is commonly entitled as the immediate lord. The title of the Crown to escheats is entirely based upon the feudal idea that all land is held of some superior, and that, where no badge of tenure can be traced, the land is to be considered as held immediately, as well as ultimately, of the Crown. The king is lord paramount, and where no intermediate lord appears to claim, all tenants are assumed to hold of him directly by service of mere fealty' (at 323).

[110] Hardman (n 46) 323.

[111] Hardman (n 46) 322.

[112] Co Litt 13b and Co Inst 225.

[113] Jenks (n 108) 36.

[114] Holdsworth (n 84) 350 and 251, citing 15 George V, c 23, s 45(1)(d). This section states: 'With regard to the real estate and personal inheritance of every person dying after the commencement of this Act, there shall be abolished … Escheat to the Crown or the Duchy of Lancaster or the Duke of Cornwall or to a mesne lord for want of heirs.'

[115] I Williams, 'The Certainty of Term Requirement in Leases: Nothing Lasts Forever' (2015) 74 *CLJ* 592, 600. Williams also notes: 'Escheat remains possible when a trustee in bankruptcy or liquidator disclaims the land, when a foreign company is dissolved or when the Crown obtains land as *bona vacantia* from a dissolved company and then itself disclaims the land' (at 607).

Deceased) v The Crown Estate Commissioners,[116] HHJ Davis-White QC relied on a Burges Salmond advice letter for the continued existence of escheat. In addition to *Mascall*, other modern authorities have also referred to escheat, including mostly famously Stanley Burnton QC's judgment in *Scmlla Properties Ltd v Gesso Properties (BVI) Ltd*.[117] As noted above, the case involved the insolvency of a landlord and some engagement with medieval land law. The judge noted:

> I have to say that I was initially amused, but ultimately dismayed, that the rights of the parties under a modern statute reforming the law of landlord and tenant should depend on the vestiges of feudal land law. My dismay grew as it became apparent that my decision in this case involved an examination of fundamental concepts of our land law, and an examination of concepts and authorities dating back several centuries. It was with some relief that I noted that the last authority to be cited in this case was a textbook dating from as recent a date as 1794; but even that referred me back to medieval writs of escheat.[118]

The case concerned Grantborough Ltd, a landlord company that went into insolvent liquidation on 20 April 1993. Pursuant to section 178 IA 1986, the Official Receiver, as liquidator of Grantborough Ltd, disclaimed the freeholds of 1–90 Southwold Mansions and 1–60 Cleveland Mansions in Maida Vale, London. Grantborough Ltd had been the freeholder. The case raised a number of interesting, 'important and potentially far-reaching'[119] questions, including: whether or not escheat to the Crown on disclaimer of a freehold is automatic; whether or not escheat to the Crown is at its option; whether or not a freehold interest in land is determined on disclaimer of the freehold under section 178 IA 1986; and whether, if the freehold interest is determined, derivative interests such as charges, mortgages and leases are similarly determined.

As part of his extensive discussion of the history of escheat, Stanley Burnton QC stated that: 'Escheat was applicable only to freehold land; and it follows that on escheat the freehold interest came to an end.'[120]

B. Management and Possession: Is Escheat at the Crown Estates' Option?

Who is responsible for any ongoing liability for property following the liquidator's disclaimer? This is the critical point being examined in this chapter. The question of whether or not the Crown Estate takes possession automatically or, in the alternative, if they have to elect to take the property or manage

[116] *Re Mascall* (n 33) [12].
[117] *Scmlla Properties* (n 82).
[118] ibid [1].
[119] ibid.
[120] ibid. This statement is correct where land is held tenurially, ie, if leasehold is a tenure, which it must be after 1925 if not earlier, it applies there too.

the property before they become liable is at the crux of this potential ongoing responsibility.

Ongoing liability could take a number of forms. It could be hazardous materials still left on the site or it could be defective cladding that needs to be replaced. Buildings clad in defective material simply cannot be left; it is a fundamental fire risk. There is therefore an obligation on the relevant parties to make good any problems with the property. Liability could also arise from tort claimants suing through the rules of occupiers' liability.[121]

This might then move us from the idea of the Crown Estate Commissioners as passive escheat recipients who are non-committed recipients of property on the face of it to a more serious position. Because of the need to remedy the defective state of the cladding, the Crown Estate Commissioners must be compelled to act. This would then move them from passive recipients to active managers of the relevant property.

This is where liability arises on the property for those who start to deal with the property. This management point was discussed by Knox J in *London Borough of Hackney v Crown Estate Commissioners*.[122] Referring to this case, HHJ Davis-White QC noted that 'only upon an act of management would the properties fall within the Crown Estate and that such properties could be burdened with significant liabilities'.[123] Those liabilities in the modern sense must include replacement cladding costs, or making good issues with the Baglan power station.

Sir Stanley Burnton QC (sitting as a Deputy Judge of the Chancery Division) examined escheat in *Scmlla* and observed that: 'The Crown becomes the owner of the land in question freed from the previous freehold interest.'[124] He also noted that the questions before him included 'whether escheat to the Crown on disclaimer of a freehold is automatic or whether escheat to the Crown is at its option'.[125]

Harpum's view, as one of the most learned commentators on land law of the past half-century, is that: 'Escheat is only completed when the lord to whom it reverts either enters on the land or takes proceedings to recover it.'[126] As authority on this point, Harpum refers to the obsolete practice of inquisitions prior to escheat and the Crown's employment of escheators in the counties to enforce the Crown's rights. This authority highlights different kinds of possession: possession in law and possession in fact.

Escheat can then be viewed as a process. One commentator made this clear when they observed: 'Escheat at common law was the process by which tenurial

[121] On which see further MA Jones et al, *Clerk & Lindsell on Torts*, 23rd edn (London, Sweet & Maxwell, 2020) ch 11.

[122] *London Borough of Hackney v Crown Estate Commissioners* [1996] BPIR 428.

[123] *Re Mascall* (n 33) [14].

[124] *Scmlla Properties Ltd v Gesso Properties (BVI) Ltd* [1995] BCC 794, 805.

[125] ibid.

[126] Harpum (n 5) 22.

land returned to the lord of the fee upon the occurrence of an event obstructing the normal course of descent'.[127]

Viewed from this process perspective escheat does seem to need to have a number of steps to be undertaken to be fulfilled. Historically this process manifested itself by either (1) entry, or (2) a writ of escheat. Either of these approaches was needed to confirm the lord's title.[128] Coke said that the title was to vest in the lord immediately upon escheat.[129] As Eldridge has observed this process is contested. The extra process was evidential, not substantiating the right.[130]

Figure 3.2 The process and steps of escheat

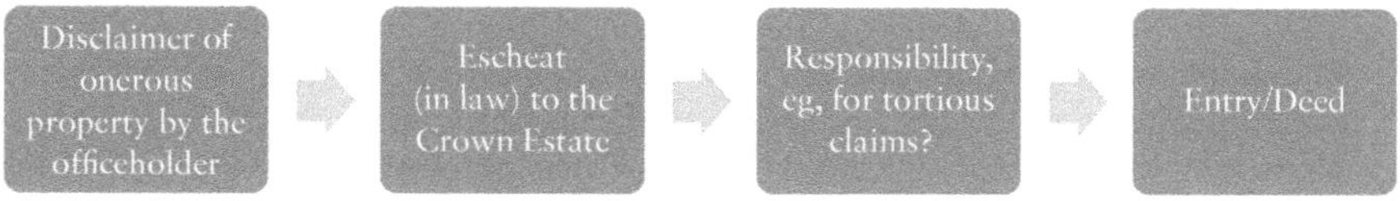

Section 40(4) of the Crown Proceedings Act 1947[131] protects the Crown from any proceedings in tort where property vests in the Crown by rule of law. This section does not apply where the Crown takes possession of the property or enters into it.

Re Nottingham General Cemetery Co[132] was an interesting liquidation and disclaimer case dating from 1955. Nottingham General Cemetery Company ran a cemetery in Nottingham. Following liquidity issues, the company was placed into compulsory liquidation in May 1953. The liquidator (the Official Receiver) successfully sought an order that he could disclaim the land constituting the company's cemetery because the land was burdened with onerous covenants within the meaning of section 323 of the Companies Act 1948. Twelve acres of freehold land constituting the cemetery in Nottingham was disclaimed. In terms of management and entry, the case is of note because counsel for the Commissioners of Crown Lands argued that:

> Notwithstanding, however, that the cemetery will thereupon vest in the Crown as bona vacantia, the Crown will not be in possession thereof until re-entry, and by virtue of the Queen's Remembrancer's Act 1859 (22 & 23 Vict, c.22), a right of

[127] *Note Origins*, 1319, citing Blackstone, W. *Commentaries on the Laws of England*. vol. p.245.
[128] E Coke, *Coke's Institutes*, vol 1 (1628) 18bn2.
[129] ibid.
[130] L Eldridge, 'What Happened to Tenure?' [2024] *Conveyancer and Property Lawyer* 251.
[131] 'Where any property vests in the Crown by virtue of any rule of law which operates independently of the acts or the intentions of the Crown, **the Crown shall not by virtue of this Act be subject to any liabilities in tort by reason only of the property being so vested**; but the provisions of this subsection shall be without prejudice to the liabilities of the Crown under this Act in respect of any period after the Crown or any person acting for the Crown **has in fact taken possession or control of any such property, or entered into occupation thereof**'. (authors' bold and underlined emphasis).
[132] *Re Nottingham General Cemetery Co* [1953] Ch 683.

> re-entry accruing to the Crown may be exercised or enforced without any actual re-entry being made on the land. Nevertheless, until re-entry, the Crown has by seisin in law as distinct from seisin in deed.[133]

On this point, Wynn-Parry J swerved the bullet. He observed:

> Mr Waite, for the Commissioners of Crown Lands, intimated that while he was prepared to admit that upon disclaimer by the liquidator the land would vest in the Crown, he would contend that the Crown would only become involved in any liability if and when it entered into possession a step which it was not intended should be take. Mr Shawcross [the liquidator] invited me to resolve this dispute in dealing with this summons, but I propose to decline this invitation.[134]

The judge continued:

> If I were to accede to the liquidator's application, the question might well have to be debated between the Crown and the Nottingham Corporation, as the local authority within whose area the cemetery lies, but that question does not arise on this summons.[135]

This is a critical passage in terms of the Baglan Operations Ltd disclaimer and post-disclaimer responsibility.

VI. CONCLUSION

This chapter has explored the doctrine of escheat against the backdrop of the Baglan Operations Ltd liquidation and modern disclaimer practice. It has been argued that once property has escheated to the Crown Estate, the Crown Estate will be responsible for that property in certain circumstances, if not all circumstances.[136] Such specific circumstances could include liability for any tortious claims arising from contact with that property, even if the Crown Estate have not elected to manage the property. This liability arises as a result of the operation of escheat and the return of what was freehold land back to the Crown Estate.[137] It is argued that it is no defence to say that the Crown Estate is a passive actor with no responsibility. Once escheat reclaims or reverts the land for the Crown Estate, the Crown Estate must be responsible for that land, even if they do not want to be responsible. This is how escheat and tenure operates. Land cannot be ownerless, hence the doctrine of escheat. As Lord Loughborough argued when Attorney-General

[133] ibid 685–86.
[134] ibid 689.
[135] ibid.
[136] Responsibility can also arise in other areas due to escheat, eg, in the area of cladding and exposure to make good buildings.
[137] Escheats occur around 300–500 times each year according to the *Land Registration Act, Explanatory Notes*, para.133.

in *Middleton v Spicer*[138] in 1783, the Crown is owner of everything which has no other owner. Once it is owned by the Crown Estate via escheat, the Crown Commissioners are responsible.

Writing in the *Law Quarterly Review* in 1888, Frederic William Hardman drew readers' attention to escheat legislation which had recently been introduced into the House of Lords by the Lord Chancellor.[139] The reforms eventually led to the Escheat (Procedure) Act 1887.[140] Hardman stated that 'it is believed that a revision of the whole subject, with a view to legislation, is desirable, for the improvement of the form, as well as the substance, of the law'.[141] A similar point was made by Charles Harpum KC in 2000 when he was then a Law Commissioner:[142] 'legislation is needed for England and Wales ... what remains of feudalism does no good and a great deal of harm'.[143] This disquiet was caused by the fact that when land escheats, it is no longer registered land, as the land reverts to the Crown as lord paramount. The land is removed from the Land Register. A principal motivation of the Land Registration Act 2002, for which Harpum was responsible, was to bring as much land on to the Land Register as possible. This removal via escheat was clearly a major lacuna, although it was not so problematic as to demand reform at the time. Harpum referred to this removal as 'galling'[144] and 'nonsensical'[145] before concluding that 'the time has come to sweep away both escheat and the Crown's paramount lordship'.

What these two great authorities called for in 1888 and again in 2000 is true in 2025. It is again time to re-visit legislative intervention and escheat to clarify post-disclaimer responsibility. Until that occurs, we might share similar dismay to that expressed by Sir Stanley Burnton QC as far back at 1995[146] at the continued and uncertain relevance of the medieval doctrine of escheat and its operation in modern English and Welsh law.

[138] *Middleton v Spicer* (1783) 1 Bro Ch Rep 201.
[139] Hardman (n 46).
[140] 50 & 51 Vict, c 53. The statute repealed 11 escheat statutes enacted between 1300 and 1548 and tidied up escheat procedure. The repealed statutes included: 8 Hen VI c 16; 18 Hen VI c 6; 1 Hen VIII c 8; 1 Hen VIII c 10; 2&3 Edw VI c 8.
[141] Hardman (n 46) 344.
[142] See also Harpum (n 5) 21–25.
[143] ibid.
[144] ibid 24.
[145] ibid.
[146] *Scmlla Properties* (n 82) [1].

4

Ecclesiastical Easements

TERESA SUTTON*

I. INTRODUCTION

THIS CHAPTER FOCUSES on one aspect of land publicly set aside for religious use. Such land is rarely spoken of on a property law course bar an apologetic introductory reference to advowsons or chancel repairs. Nevertheless, the ecclesiastical context of land law has much to contribute to wider understandings of property law. Within communities, especially rural village communities, churches are normally one of the oldest buildings ('the one stone structure enduring through the centuries')[1] and their purpose and ownership hold a unique continuity. The surviving records and the archives pertaining to them often surpass that of other land in that community.

This chapter defines a category of rights as ecclesiastical easements and then uses those rights as an example of the value of ecclesiastical property to wider land law debates. Ecclesiastical easements include rights of way, rights to seats, rights to vaults and, possibly, rights to make noise for religious purposes. This chapter shows that ecclesiastical easements are significant for three reasons. First, the recent developments concerning recreational easements in *Regency Villas v Diamond Resorts*[2] suggest a need for a renewed concentration on the nature and character of the dominant and servient land. There is no other type of land with such a clearly designated purpose and character to test this against than land set aside for religious purposes. Second, ecclesiastical easements highlight the need for change in the current law of easements. As traditional religious activity has decreased, the maintenance of ageing religious buildings has become an increasing burden. In some communities, current stewards of such land are seeking additional

* I am grateful for the helpful comments on the first draft of this chapter from Dr Bonnie Holligan, Professor Lara McMurty, Oliver Radley-Gardner KC, Professor Thomas Glyn Watkin KC and participants at the Modern Studies in Property Law Conference, Queens' College, Cambridge, 2024. Any errors and omissions that remain are my own

[1] J Morris, *A People's Church: A History of the Church of England* (London, Profile, 2022) 16.

[2] *Regency Villas Title Ltd and Others v Diamond Resorts (Europe) Ltd and Others* [2018] UKSC 57.

or alternative community uses.[3] Covenants on land may be modified or discharged to facilitate change, but in the continuing absence of progress on the recommendations of the Law Commission, alterations to easements remain a greater challenge.[4] Third, many modern types of easements are recent creations in the context of the history of land law. Ecclesiastical easements are amongst the oldest examples of easements, and they allow us to look behind Cheshire's four characteristics of easements recognised in *Re Ellenborough Park*[5] and followed in *Regency Villas*.[6]

The chapter is divided into three main sections. Section II defines the type of cases and religious property to be considered, and situates this work within the wider legal history of easements. It includes analysis of the legal privilege given by society to land set aside for religious purposes. Section III uses doctrinal and legal history methodologies to consider each type of right that can be shown to be part of the category of ecclesiastical easements, and explores the connections between land use and land right. Section IV considers the changing use of ecclesiastical land and draws together arguments about the value of the category of ecclesiastical easements to wider modern land law debates about easements.

II. THE SCOPE OF ECCLESIASTICAL EASEMENTS

A. The Religious Diversity of Cases

All the cases considered in this chapter, aside from *Regency Villas*, concern land that is or has been or is adjacent to land set aside for religious purposes. There is a lack of diversity in the religious use because of the limited case law available. Cases are drawn from both ecclesiastical courts and secular courts. Sometimes they show individual courts wrestling to work with a mix of property law and ecclesiastical law. Davie has observed that whilst the Church of England, as the Established Church, has 'quite rightly' 'lost any sense of dominance' it 'retains its constitutional privilege'.[7] This extends to certain bodies within it performing some public functions.[8] The outworking of that historic constitutional privilege

[3] Department of Culture, Media and Sport, *The Taylor Review: The Sustainability of English Churches and Cathedrals* (2017).

[4] Law Commission, *Making Land Work: Easements, Covenants and Profits a Prendre* (Law Com No 327, 2011) paras 3.230, 7.32.

[5] *Re Ellenborough Park* [1956] Ch 131, 1.

[6] GC Cheshire, *The Modern Law of Real Property* (London, Butterworths, 1925) 225.

[7] G Davie, *Religion in Britain, A Persistence Paradox*, 2nd edn (Chichester, Wiley Blackwell, 2015) 223–24.

[8] *Aston Cantlow and Wilmcote with Billesley Parochial Church Council v Wallbank* [2004] 1 AC 546 [13], [86]. See also M Hill, '*Aston Cantlow v Wallbank*: A Twenty-Year Retrospective' (2024) 26 *Ecclesiastical Law Journal* 6; M Hill, 'Change and Decay: The Twilight Years of the Established Church 1994– 2023' in N Doe and S Coleman (eds), *The Legal History of the Church of England: From the Reformation to the Present* (Oxford, Hart Publishing. 2024) 213–32.

in this easements context is that most cases considered in this chapter concern land held or previously held by the Church of England. Some relate to the faculty jurisdiction that the ecclesiastical courts of the Church of England hold with respect to its churches.[9] There are some twentieth-century cases concerning discharge and modification of covenants that connect to use in other Christian denominations and religions, but these are limited.[10]

B. Identifying Ecclesiastical Land

The four *Re Ellenborough* characteristics of an easement are that there must be a dominant and servient tenement, the right must accommodate the dominant tenement, the tenements must be owned by different persons and the right must be capable of forming the subject matter of a grant.[11] This chapter concentrates on the second *Re Ellenborough* characteristic of an easement, that the right must accommodate the dominant land. Bevan explains that 'the utility of the land is increased' in the context of the 'normal use to which the dominant land is put (eg. agricultural, commercial, residential etc.)'.[12] In *Regency Villas* the timeshare owners were recognised as having easements to use the extensive recreational facilities in the country club setting. Ecclesiastical easements are suitable for exploring this connection between land use and land right as they exist in the context of sacred use. Much of the land has been consecrated and thereby set aside for sacred use in perpetuity. Land is consecrated after transfer of title. For example, in *Collingwood King & Blair v Benefice of Newburn*[13] the land was consecrated nine days after the church and churchyard had been donated to the Church Commissioners.[14] A bishop's sentence of consecration, traditionally accompanied by perambulation of the land and an oral declaration, was recorded by the diocesan register and that changed the legal status of the land.[15] After consecration land together with what is on it falls within the jurisdiction of the bishop's consistory court.[16]

[9] For ecclesiastical courts and the faculty jurisdiction, see generally M Hill, *Ecclesiastical Law*, 4th edn (Oxford, Oxford University Press, 2018); C Mynors, *Changing Churches* (London, Bloomsbury, 2016).

[10] See, eg, *Re Cowdrey's Application* (1957) 7 P & CR 184; *Re Mahavir Foundation Ltd* [2007] WL 1685189; *Re Green Masjid and Madrasah Trustees* [2013] UKUT 355 LC.

[11] *Re Ellenborough Park* (n 5) 163.

[12] C Bevan, *Land Law*, 3rd edn (Oxford, Oxford University Press, 2022) 438. See also A Lawson, 'Easements' in L Tee (ed), *Land Law: Issues, Debates, Policy* (Cullompton, Willan, 2002), 72.

[13] *Collingwood King & Blair v Benefice of Newburn in the Diocese of Newcastle* [2019] UKUT 176 (LT).

[14] The 1837 conveyance kept back the paper title to the vault underneath the nave of the church for family burials. This became an adverse possession issue when the church was closed.

[15] Consecration has been pictured as freezing the land 'for ever by setting it aside *in sacros usus*': G Moore and T Briden, *Moore's Introduction to English Canon Law*, 2nd edn (London, Mowbray, 1985) 102.

[16] Hill (n 9) 203. See also *Re Tonbridge School Chapel (No 2)* [1993] Fam 281 [289]; N Orme, *Going to Church in Medieval England* (New Haven, Yale University Press, 2021) 85.

Land set aside as sacred has historically been afforded special privilege. The ancient practice of sanctuary recognised 'churches as islands of peace' with immunity for those accused of crime.[17] Ecclesiastical privilege still survives in the context of the ecclesiastical exemption. The Ecclesiastical Exemption (Listed Buildings and Conservation Areas) (England) Order 2010 made under Section 60(1) and (2) of the Planning (Listed Buildings and Conservation Areas) Act 1990 allows ecclesiastical buildings being used for ecclesiastical purposes to be exempted from listed building consent and conservation systems. This is conditional upon the existence of proper alternative internal procedures. In the case of the Church of England and the 16,000 parish churches that belong to it, the alternative oversight is provided by the faculty system of the consistory courts.[18] A faculty permission is needed for any alterations to a church including its interior and immediate surroundings and the granting of any rights over it.[19] This oversight allows heritage issues to be married with the needs of the congregation and the wider community in the context of the place of worship. This ecclesiastical exemption clearly identifies a category of ecclesiastical land with a definite purpose.

All the easements discussed will be implicitly linked to that sacred purpose. Qualification for the faculty jurisdiction does not change the nature or application of the general principles of property law with respect to easements. For example, when the Upper Tribunal recognised the descendants of a donor had the benefit of an easement to access a vault underneath a church in *Collingwood King*, it did so by way of an express right of access in the original conveyance or alternatively an implied right citing *Pwllbach Colliery v Woodman*.[20] When the Upper Tribunal recognised the right of access claimed by a parish church over adjacent land in *Hughes v Incumbent of the Benefice of Frampton-on-Severn et al*,[21] it did so by way of prescription by lost modern grant under *Dalton v Angus*[22] and *Tehidy Minerals Ltd v Norman*.[23]

The ecclesiastical easements set out in the following sections exist because of the underlying character of the land they serve and are served by. The potential rights to ring bells, to have access for worship as a parishioner, to occupy a seat in the church or use a vault are all tied to a furtherance of the utility of that land. They accommodate and serve that land and do not logically extend to other contexts. They evolved in the context of sacred

[17] S McSheffrey, *Seeking Sanctuary, Crime, Mercy, and Politics in English Courts, 1400–1550* (Oxford, Oxford University Press, 2017) 2.

[18] The Church of England's faculty system has been described as a 'paradigm' of internal regimes; see P Edge, 'The Construction of Sacred Spaces in English Law' (2002) 14 *Journal of Environmental Law* 161, 179.

[19] Hill (n 9) 202.

[20] *Collingwood King* (n 13) [30]. *Pwllbach Colliery Co Ltd v Woodman* [1915] AC 634.

[21] *Hughes v Incumbent of the Benefice of Frampton-on-Severn, Arlingham, Saul, Fretherne & Framilode* [2021] UKUT 184 (LC), [2022] 1 P & CR DG1.

[22] *Angus v Dalton* (1877) 3 QBD 85.

[23] *Tehidy Minerals v Norman* [1971] 2 QBD 528.

use and remain there. The existence of these ecclesiastical easements gives weight to the idea that specific easements can belong to specific types of land. This can in turn support arguments, discussed in some academic commentary on *Regency Villas*, that the recreational rights of *Regency Villas* should be confined to land with the same clear recreational character akin to the holiday timeshare arrangements in that case.[24] The consideration of ecclesiastical easements in this chapter thereby contributes to the wider debate on the context of the *Regency* judgment and favours limiting the extent of the impact that *Regency* will have in broadening the remit of easements as property rights.

C. The Early History of Ecclesiastical Easements

Some ecclesiastical rights have existed for such a length of time that they pre-date Gale and Cheshire, and pre-date any clear concept of what an easement was at all in English law. Rights to seats and vaults and access to places of worship all pre-date what Simpson described as the nineteenth-century 'settlement of the modern law of easements and profits' in the context of urbanisation and enclosure.[25] Writing on servitude doctrine in early law in the context of the history of water rights, Getzler refers to the 'slow and confused development of the law of easements' and a 'formulaic path of legal evolution', with a concentration on 'professional argument over forms of pleading, proof and remedy'.[26] Simpson describes Gale's 1839 volume *A Treatise on the Law of Easements* as 'the first written attempt' to 'knit together a body of principle' on easements since Bracton.[27] Gale was well aware of both the novelty and the tenuous nature of parts of his work. Gale acknowledged that aspects, especially on prescription, were 'in some degree unsupported by authority', but said that he preferred to 'open the law upon the doubts that presented themselves than to pass them over in silence'.[28] Legal historians agree on the importance of Gale's work to the development of easements

[24] See especially C Bevan, 'Opening Pandora's Box? Recreation Pure and Simple: Easements in the Supreme Court' (2019) 1 *Conveyancer and Property Lawyer* 55, 66. See also M Cardwell, 'Recreational Easements: A Right to Have Fun?' (2019) 78 *CLJ* 506; and G McLeod, 'The Traditional Concept Hits a Bunker: Easements after *Regency Villas v Diamond Resorts*' (2019) 3 *Conveyancer and Property Lawyer* 250.

[25] AWB Simpson, *A History of the Land Law*, 2nd edn (Oxford, Oxford University Press 1986) 261.

[26] J Getzler, *A History of Water Rights at Common Law* (Oxford, Oxford University Press, 2004) 44, 47. See also J Baker, *An Introduction to English Legal History*, 5th edn (Oxford, Oxford University Press, 2019) 456; W Holdsworth, *A History of English Law*, 2nd edn (London, Sweet & Maxwell, 1937) 321.

[27] CJ Gale and TD Whatley, *A Treatise on the Law of Easements* (Sweet, 1839); Simpson (n 25) 262. See also Getzler (n 26) 65.

[28] Gale (n 27) vii.

in nineteenth-century courts, but understandings of Gale's contemporary sources continue to evolve.[29]

In his first edition, Gale recorded that 'the number and variety of these rights is almost infinite, according to the exigencies of domestic convenience, or the different purposes to which land or buildings may be appropriated'.[30] A right to bury in a particular vault was listed in that first edition and a right to a pew in a church was subsequently added in later editions.[31] The first edition also recorded 'ways of necessity' 'to church or to market' and easements incident to the rights that accompany an office such as a right of entry for a parson to take away his tithes.[32] The current edition of Gale still lists a right to a pew in a church annexed to a house, but not a vault.[33] The Law Commission's Report referenced 'an easement entitling its owner to walk across the neighbouring field to church', which has some connotation to churchway discussed below.[34] Each ecclesiastical easement is considered in turn below. This is done by acknowledging the risks of misunderstanding and distorting earlier cases in the context of rights acquired through lapse of time identified by Anderson.[35] Anderson shows that the 'present approach' in the law of easements whereby 'one asks *first* whether the right claimed can exist at law, and *only then* whether it has been acquired in an approved way' can lead to difficulty in reading older cases where judges thought 'primarily in terms of the mode of acquisition of the right'.[36]

III. SPECIES OF ECCLESIASTICAL EASEMENTS

The following sections consider each potential ecclesiastical easement: rights for parishioners to sit in a particular pew, rights to bury in a vault, rights to use a path to or across ecclesiastical land, and rights to ring bells to call parishioners to worship. Doctrinal and legal history methodologies are used to explore

[29] Kennefick describes Gale as 'one of only a few writers on whom accolades were bestowed so markedly in court': C Kennefick, 'Looking Afresh at the French Roots of Continuous Easements in English Law' in W Eves et al (eds), *Common Law, Civil Law and Colonial Law: Comparative Legal History from the Twelfth Century to the Twentieth Centuries* (Cambridge, Cambridge University Press, 2021) 183. See also AWB Simpson, 'Wheeldon v Burrows', [1967] 83 *LQR* 240; and Getzler (n 26) 282.

[30] Gale (n 27) 15.

[31] See, eg, R Roope Reeve, *Gale's A Treatise on the Law of Easements*, 8th edn (London, Sweet & Maxwell, 1908) 23.

[32] Gale (n 27) 75.

[33] J Gaunt and P Morgan, *Gale on Easements*, 21st edn (London, Sweet & Maxwell, 2020) 54; MJ Dixon et al, *Megarry & Wade: The Law of Real Property*, 10th edn (London, Sweet & Maxwell, 2024) 26-009. Footnote 31 describes the easement as 'of an exceptional kind.

[34] Law Commission (n 4) 2.25.

[35] S Anderson, 'Easement and Prescription: Changing Perspectives in Classification' (1975) 38 *MLR* 641, 642: 'there is a tendency to look back at the early cases and try to fit their results, sometimes even their reasoning, into our conceptual framework of "easements and prescription" or, simply "easements"'.

[36] ibid 642, 641.

the extent of each right. In every case, a clear link is shown between the nature of the right established and the religious use of the land in that parish location. These sections demonstrate that ecclesiastical easements are a complex and context-driven category of rights pre-dating more recent general definitions and glosses of the concept of an easement.

A. A Seat in a Church and Pew Rights as Easements

The idea of sitting in a regular seat, be it in a pub or a bus, is an instinct people still have and attach social and economic value to. Historically, where a person sat in church was indicative of their place in the local social order.[37] Victorian judges understood this and, where a party lost their claim to a formal right to a particular pew, can be seen to ask churchwardens to ensure that the losing party would still be able to sit in the same area of the church.[38] Helmholz describes the haphazardness of the development of church seating in medieval times and the gradual control taken by the church authorities.[39] The reference Helmholz makes to individuals originally building and then repairing their own seats is helpful for property lawyers trying to understand some of the later prescriptive easement rights which seem to turn on evidence of maintenance. From the perspective of an historian, Byng has argued that '[t]he pew was kept in a state of suspense, never passing irrevocably into the world of chattels, never manifesting a single, unified philosophy of sacred space', with case law showing that 'it could snap suddenly from one imaginative state to another'.[40]

Pew rights do still exist, and some churches retain visible evidence of their past workings. For example, the pews in St George's Church, West Grinstead, Sussex, are painted with the names of the individual farms that they belonged to. When modern land law textbooks refer to pew rights, they normally do so in the context of the fourth *Re Ellenborough* characteristics as a permissible exception to extensive use, akin to the use of a toilet in *Miller v Emcer*.[41] Luther's work on easements and exclusive possession included pew rights. Luther used three nineteenth-century cases to demonstrate that the courts were seeking 'a clear limit' to what could be done on the land rather than whether the right excluded the owner.[42] Two of these cases were on the discrete point of trying to use pew

[37] Orme (n 16) 120; JC Bennett, 'How Formal Anglican Pew-Renting Worked in Practice, 1800–1950' (2017) 68 *Journal of Ecclesiastical History* 766, 776.

[38] See, eg, *Crisp v Martin (No 2)* 2 PD 15 (1876) 28.

[39] RH Helmholz, *The History of the Laws of England*, vol 1 (Oxford, Oxford University Press, 2004) 501. Helmholz notes the relevance of pew rights in the development of faculty jurisdiction in *The Profession of Ecclesiastical Lawyers* (Cambridge, Cambridge University Press, 2019) 85.

[40] G Byng, *Church Building and Society in the Later Middle Ages* (Cambridge University Press, 2017) 233.

[41] *Miller v Emcer Products* [1956] Ch 304.

[42] P Luther, 'Easements and Exclusive Possession' (1996) 16 *Legal Studies* 51, 53.

rights to secure a right to vote. In *Hinde v Chorlton*, the court declined to recognise 'freehold pew' 'no 33, centre aisle, Oldham parish church' as a qualifying registration and held that the right was to hear 'divine service' alone.[43] No vote was allowed in *Brumfitt v Roberts* either, where the voting qualification had been described as 'Freehold pews, 72 and 72 ½, St Mark's Church' in Liverpool.[44] The court pointed to the real source of the right, which was 'not an interest in land, but an interest of a peculiar nature created by Act of Parliament, and more in the nature of an easement', 'a special interest in the pews and seats not known to the common law' created by statute.[45] The nineteenth century saw great building, re-building of churches and renovating connected to wider theological change, and this was often financed by the further letting of pews.[46] For example, when St Paul's Church in Brighton was opened in 1873, 460 of the 1,200 seats were rented for financial reasons.[47] Seats in new church buildings were governed by the statutes that created them and so can be viewed separately from the older rights created by express grant and prescription.[48]

i. Non-statutory Pew Rights

Today canon law still provides that there must be seats in every church for those who attend, and technically churchwardens can still indicate where people should sit.[49] Historically, this would have been an important role and older records give more than a hint of the language of ownership.[50] Allocation by a churchwarden did not constitute an easement. An easement type right for ongoing occupancy of a seat was rooted in an express grant by faculty or more likely through prescription. These rights were and also are separate from those that flow from the private ownership of a side chapel or lesser chancel owned by an individual or resulting from lay rectorship.[51] The party claiming the easement had to be shown to live in the parish, and the case law suggests that, at least for

[43] *Hinde v Chorlton* (1866) LR 2 CP 104, 115 The trustees had the right 'to grant not the soil and freehold of the pew, but the right to the pew, that is to say, the right to use the pew for the purpose of hearing divine service whenever it was celebrated in the church'. Rights could only be held by inhabitants of the parish.

[44] *Brumfitt v Roberts* (1869–70) LR 5 CP 224, 232.

[45] ibid 233.

[46] See generally C Webster, 'Patterns of Church Seating from Waterloo to 1850, and the Role of the Cambridge Camden Society' in T Cooper and S Brown (eds), *Pews, Benches and Chairs: Church Seating in English Parish Churches* (Cambridge, Ecclesiological Society, 2011) 197; JC Bennett, *A History of Pew Renting in the Church of England* (London, Palgrave Macmillan, 2024).

[47] A Wagner and A Dale, *The Wagners of Brighton* (Bognor Regis, Phillimore, 1983). Renting pews had long been a source of income for churches. See also Doe and Coleman (n 8) 138, 149 and 169.

[48] H Cripps et al, *A Practical Treatise on the Law Relating to the Church and Clergy*, 7th edn (London, Sweet & Maxwell, 1921) 390.

[49] Canon F 7.2.

[50] See, eg, H Johnstone (ed), *Churchwardens' Presentments, Part 1, Archdeaconry of Chichester* (Chichester, Sussex Record Society, 1948) 134, 74.

[51] See, eg, *Chapman v Jones* (1868–69) LR 4 Ex 273, 280.

a claim based on prescription, the right had to be attached to a definite dwelling rather than mere land.[52] Reliance upon a lost faculty for prescription also required evidence that any repairs done were completed by the holder of the right or their predecessors.[53] This requirement was rooted in the assumption that any right to use pews had been granted to a house in return for them relieving the parish of their obligation to repair and was described as 'ancient possession and repair time out of mind' 'shown conjointly'.[54] A faculty or presumed faculty could be apportioned.[55] The case law is by no means clear, but rights look to be lost if the party moved out of the parish.[56] A prescriptive right could not be lost by abandonment or intermittent user where there was no intention to relinquish the right. The outworking of this area of easements can be seen in nineteenth-century newspaper advertisements for the sale of substantial country houses. For example, a lengthy description of attributes of a property for sale in Long Melford in 1805 concludes with the line that the 'whole' forms 'a most desirable situation for a genteel family' and that '[a] pew in the church belongs to the house'.[57] Some advertisements stress the advantages of a pew in terms of the distance from the aisle or the pulpit.[58]

ii. Pew Rights and Changes to Churches

A pew right also gave and still gives the holder some control over changes to the church building. In the context of the nineteenth-century theological debates over church buildings and the current fashion for re-ordering, this has significance. In 1875, Horace Crisp objected to the enlargement of St Andrews, Grantchester.[59] Crisp complained that his family pew was to be removed.[60] The Court of Arches was sympathetic to the need for more space in the church for the growing population. Crisp lost because he could not show occupation from time 'immemorial appurtenant to a certain messuage' with acts by that 'messuage' to

[52] See, eg, *Byerley v Windus* (1826) 5 B & C 1; *Hallack v Cambridge* (1841) 1 QB 593 (a 'town and gown' argument concerning use of St Mary's turning on parish residence); and *Fuller v Lane* (1825) 162 ER 348 (a dispute between descendants of a previous owner and a new owner over the best pew in the parish). See generally on dominant tenements AJ McClean, 'The Nature of an Easement' (1966) 5 *Western Law Review* 37.

[53] See, eg, *Philipps v Halliday* [1891] AC 228, where the pew had been occupied, kept locked and repaired.

[54] *Stileman-Gibbard v Wilkinson and Others* [1897] 1 QB 749 [758]. See also Cripps et al (n 48) 387.

[55] Cripps et al (n 48) 389.

[56] R Phillimore, *The Ecclesiastical Law of the Church of England*, vol 2 (Sweet, 1873) 1799 suggested wording for a faculty linking grant to inhabitancy of a certain house in the parish, but noted that the reference to house is often omitted.

[57] *Bury and Norwich Post*, 18 September 1805.

[58] See, eg, *Cheltenham Chronicle*, 30 May 1816.

[59] *Crisp* (n 38). See generally for local village context C Jennings, *Widnall: A Capital Contriver* (Malvern, Folly Press, 2003) 147.

[60] *Crisp* (n 38) 16.

maintain and uphold that right akin to both benefit and burden. Crisp failed to show that all repairs had been at his property's expense because when the church had been repaired and the pews rebuilt 20 years earlier, funds had come from the parish, Corpus Christi College, Cambridge and King's College, Cambridge.[61] Stileman-Gibbard was more fortunate in obtaining a writ of prohibition in 1896 which prevented a faculty for new seating at St Peter's Sharnbrook.[62] He claimed a right to occupy two pews by prescription from his family's ownership and occupation of Sharnbrook House, regardless of the fact that he had never exercised his right. The court recognised 'acts of ownership beyond occupancy' 'beyond mere undisturbed possession' as his family had previously switched the former pews for new seats.[63] As a result, Stileman-Gibbard was able to restrict change to that part of the church.

This same pattern can be seen in more modern cases too. In *Re St Mary's Banbury*,[64] the Court of Arches heard an appeal on the refusal of a faculty for the removal of pews and significant re-ordering inside the nave of the church. Changing the interior of any church can raise theological and liturgical as well as practical arguments. Two hundred years earlier, this church had been demolished and re-built, the project being financed through pew income. The faculty application was objected to by the current holders of those statutory pew rights. The court recognised the statutory right 'to the use on religious occasions of specific numbered pews', acknowledging that the originally purchasers 'would not have paid for uncertainly located seats'.[65] The pews could not be removed without the consent of the owners of those rights and no faculty could remove the statutory rights.[66] This meant that the change – which it seems may have been driven by liturgical reasons that were not shared by those with the pew rights – did not go ahead. Since *Greenwich NHS Trust v London & Quadrant Housing*,[67] where a right of way was re-aligned in the context of a hospital development, there may be more potential for an existing pew right to be changed to facilitate wider benefit.

B. A Right to Bury in a Vault as an Easement

In addition to his pew right, Horace Crisp also claimed and failed to establish a right to continue to use a family burial vault. This is another ecclesiastical easement serving the sacred nature of the land itself. Both Sparkes and

[61] ibid 27. There was no consideration of the patronal link with Corpus Christi College, Cambridge in the context of repair.
[62] *Stileman-Gibbard* (n 54). There was also a claim to a seat in the chancel as lay rector.
[63] ibid 759.
[64] *Re St Mary's Banbury* [1987] 1 All ER 247.
[65] ibid 253.
[66] ibid.
[67] *Greenwich NHS Trust v London & Quadrant Housing* [1998] 1 WLR 1749, 1755.

Dowling have considered the nature of burial rights more broadly in religious, commercial and government settings.[68] Both searched for the true classification of burial rights. Dowling begins his article with the observation that '[a]rrangements which do not behave according to the rules [of property law], by appearing to create one type of interest while possessing the attributes of another, either undermine the recognised rules or are exceptional cases which must be acknowledged as such'.[69] Dowling suggests that exclusive burial rights are an example of this. Dowling concludes that for the property lawyer, they are at 'best' to be 'accounted as oddities' or at 'worst' indicative that 'existing orthodoxy needs to be reconsidered'.[70] On burial rights in church settings, both authors point towards prescriptive rights to burial and link these to pew rights. Both authors are troubled by calling the right an easement when it exists in gross.[71]

Gale regards the only true form of easement for burial to be one which is attached to an 'ancient messuage' as in *Waring v Griffiths*.[72] In this case the owner of the 'ancient messuage' was found to have the right to bury anyone dying in the house in a particular church vault. The authority of the case is limited by the fact that the right was proved against another individual ('merely a wrong-doer') rather than the bishop, patron, incumbent or churchwarden. The fee payable for burial in this case may be linked to an ongoing repair obligation, as discussed above with relation to prescriptive rights and pews.[73] This prescription for a burial in a particular vault belonging to a certain residence is also set out by Cripps.[74] The lengths to which a court could go to satisfy the need for the 'messuage' to be in the parish are clear from *Lousley v Haywood*.[75] In *Lousely* there was a claim to a prescriptive right, but the house in question was outside the parish boundary. To avoid finding that the prescription was 'rotten and bad', it was speculated that as the boundaries of parishes had moved and changed since 'the foundation of the churches', whilst it was known that the house was not within the parish now, the court was willing to think it might have been before.[76]

These easements are quite separate from both a right to burial that arises from simply being resident in a parish (whether a churchgoer or not) and faculties that

[68] P Sparkes, 'Exclusive Burial Rights' (1991) 2 *Ecclesiastical Law Journal* (1991) 133; A Dowling, 'Exclusive Rights of Burial and the Law of Real Property' (1998) 18 *Legal Studies* (1998) 438; A Dowling, 'Exclusive Rights of Burial' (1992) 43 *Northern Ireland Legal Quarterly* 228.

[69] Dowling, 'Exclusive Rights of Burial and the Law of Real Property' (n 68) 438.

[70] ibid 452.

[71] ibid 441; Sparkes (n 68) 135.

[72] *Waring v Griffiths* (1757) 2 Keny 183; Gaunt and Morgan (n 33) 1–25. Gale (1839) (n 27) 16 lists a right to bury in a particular vault as an affirmative easement.

[73] The court was undecided on the fee. See also *Magnay v The Rector, Churchwardens and Parishioners of St Michael, Paternoster Royal and St Martin Vintry* (1827) 1 Hagg Ecc 48, 503.

[74] Cripps et al (n 48) 623.

[75] *Lousley v Griffiths* (1827) 1 Y & J 583.

[76] ibid 805.

are granted to allow those from within and outside a parish to reserve a burial plot in advance.[77] Those later rights cannot be seen as easements, but they continue to cause confusion today as they have done for centuries before.[78] In *Bryan v Whistler* in 1828, the rector of St Clement, Hastings, had been paid 20 pounds to allow the plaintiff to construct a burial vault (with 'sole and exclusive possession') and paid again to conduct the service. The rector later opened the vault and buried someone else inside. The court held that no exclusive right to burial had been created as the rector had 'no power to grant the privilege claimed' without a faculty.[79] Moreover, there had been no deed and writing. Then as now, a faculty can be granted for a reserved burial place, normally in a churchyard. There is no requirement of residence. Arguably, this creates a licence rather than an easement. Sparkes' alternative conclusion is that the right of burial by faculty is seen 'as a true incorporeal hereditament, capable of existing in gross', a conclusion that Dowling also reached in his earlier piece on burial rights.[80] Whichever argument is preferred, the prescriptive rights attached to a house in the parish appear to be the only true easement. They are again implicitly tied to the sacred use of the land and make no sense outside of that use context.

C. Churchway and Rights of Way to and Over Ecclesiastical Land

As religious buildings exist to allow people to attend services, facilitating access to them has always been a primary concern. The recent case of *Hughes* is a contemporary example of a church benefiting from a prescriptive right of way for access via lost modern grant.[81] The case relied on the use of a track which formerly belonged to the church school for access to parking next to the church. The church showed definite and continuous use for over 20 years. The use made of the track by incumbents and other visitors for services, weddings and funerals and to access graves was sufficient within this rural ecclesiastical setting.[82]

Aside from grants of rights of way, a customary right of access for the inhabitants of a parish to use a set path across private land to reach a church has been recognised as existing since time immemorial. Cripps describes it as a 'quasi-easement' for 'parishioners at large' rather than any limited group.[83] The earlier work of Rogers from 1849 notes that 'the inhabitants of a particular house, hamlet, village or parish' can each 'maintain an action for nuisance with respect

[77] Hill (n 9) 151.
[78] In December 2023, the Law Commission announced a new consultation on burial and cremation.
[79] *Bryan v Whistler* (1828) 8 B & C 292.
[80] Sparkes (n 68) 138; Dowling, 'Exclusive Rights of Burial' (n 68) 295.
[81] *Hughes* (n 21).
[82] See generally T Sutton, 'An Easement through the Legal Jungle: *Hughes v Incumbent of the Benefice of Frampton-on-Severn et al*' (2022) 86 *Conveyancer and Property Lawyer* 319.
[83] Cripps et al (n 48) 421.

to the right'.[84] The churchway includes the portion of the land on consecrated land and the landowner is required to maintain the path.[85] In both *Brocklebank v Thompson*[86] and *Farquhar v Newbury*,[87] the respective churches had been built on rural land belonging to manors, and access for parishioners to attend church was by churchway paths across those estates. In *Brocklebank*, the tenant farmer lived three miles from the church. The High Court refused an application for an injunction to prevent him using a churchway. It recognised 'by immemorial custom a churchway path for the inhabitants generally of the parish of Irton'.[88] It is the 'generally' point that prevents these rights from being true easements. There is no capable grantee.[89] In Cheshire's first edition of his *Modern Law of Real Property*, he classifies these rights as local customary rights.[90]

Church buildings were also previously used for church vestry meetings, the remit of which extended to some forms of local governance, including poor relief.[91] It has been suggested that as parish churches and their buildings are now being put to more additional community uses, remaining churchways could be used by parishioners for those purposes.[92] Most churchways have been lost or, as in *Farquhar v Newbury*, replaced with public rights, but the preponderance of public footpaths that converge on rural churches is a lasting reminder.

i. Rights of Way and Ecclesiastical Grantors

Whilst churchway fails to be recognised as an easement because of a lack of a capable grantee, the special nature of consecrated land means that many claims for a right of way across church land are destined to fail for want of a capable grantor.[93] In a traditional parish, the incumbent – the rector or vicar – will hold the ecclesiastical office of the benefice and as such will be a corporation sole with a freehold interest in the real property of the benefice.[94] Hill describes them as the 'temporary custodian'.[95] This means that no grant of an easement can be made without wider consent, including via an application for faculty permission

[84] F Newman Rogers, *A Practical Arrangement of Ecclesiastical Law* (William Benning, 1849) 263–64.

[85] Cripps et al (n 48) 421; Newman Rogers (n 84) 263; *Collingwood King* (n 13) [29].

[86] *Brocklebank v Thompson* [1903] 2 Ch 344.

[87] *Farquhar v Newbury District Council RDC* [1909] 1 Ch 12.

[88] *Brocklebank* (n 86) 356.

[89] Dixon et al (n 33) 26-025, 26-049. See also Gaunt and Morgan (n 33) 57–61; *Egerton v Harding* [1975] QB 62, 68; and Holdsworth (n 26) 324.

[90] Cheshire (n 6) 236, 283.

[91] See generally WE Tate, *The Parish Chest*, 3rd edn (Cambridge, Cambridge University Press, 1969) 13.

[92] Legal Advisory Commission of the General Synod of the Church of England, *Legal Opinions Concerning the Church of England*, 8th edn (Norwich, Church House, 2007) 167, 169.

[93] For public rights of way, see also Legal Advisory Commission of the General Synod of the Church of England, *Public Rights of Way over Land Forming Part of a Churchyard* (Norwich, Church House, 2006).

[94] Hill (n 9) 135.

[95] ibid 65.

from a consistory court.[96] Section 42 of the Church Property Measure 2018 sets out requirements for easements over 'part of the property of the benefice'.

These restrictions on grant make it difficult to claim prescriptive rights over ecclesiastical land held by an incumbent. Glebe land was historically part of a benefice's endowment, but was not consecrated. In *Oakley v Boston*,[97] no presumption of lost modern grant over former glebe land was recognised because of insufficient evidence of consent to the grant. The Court of Appeal held that the incumbent was only able to grant a right of way over the glebe land with consent, in this instance from the Ecclesiastical Commissioners.[98] It was impossible to assume that this consent had been granted and then lost under the fiction. While the incumbent might have acquiesced in acts of trespass, there was no evidence that the Ecclesiastical Commissioners knew of them in the context of their statutory duty to protect the property 'for all time'.[99] Goulding J stressed the difficulty in ever making such a presumption where consent was needed from a party in this sort of fiduciary relationship.[100] In a similar way, the special character of the land, reflected in the way in which it is held, prevented the recognition of an easement passing under section 62 of the Law of Property Act 1925 in *Re St Clement's, Leigh-on-Sea*[101] in a consistory court. Section 62 could not apply because the incumbent would have been incapable of making an express grant of the easement in question.[102]

Where the potential right is claimed over consecrated land, it has not normally been possible to grant any right of way for secular purposes across that land because of its sacred status. Exceptions have been made for utilities and the like, but in most circumstances a licence is used instead.[103] A faculty for a licence of indefinite duration terminable by faculty was granted in *Re St Martin le Grand York*.[104] At the time of the case in 1989, a printing works sat between the fifteenth-century church of St Martin and the River Ouse in the centre of York. The river had been used for some access to the printing works. Ahead of a likely development of the printing works, there was a petition for a faculty to confirm a presumed grant of a right of way (by foot and with trolleys and a limited right of way for vehicles) over the churchyard to reach the printing works. The churchyard was consecrated. As it was closed for burials, this gave a discretion to allow some limited secular use. The evidence that the churchyard had been used for some pedestrian access for over 100 years was incapable of

[96] See also *MacNally v Digby & Sherborne Urban DC* [1957] 1 WLUK 258; *Re St Andrew Great Durnford* [2021] ECC Sal 3.

[97] *Oakley and Another v Boston* [1976] QB 270.

[98] ibid 281.

[99] ibid 282.

[100] ibid 285.

[101] *Re St Clement's, Leigh-on-Sea* [1988] 1 WLR 720.

[102] ibid 728.

[103] See, eg, *Re St Luke Charlton* [2016] ECC Swk 1; *Re St Chad's Churchyard, Bishop Tachbrook* [2014] Fam 118; *St Barnabus Downham* (2011) 14 ECC LJ 137.

[104] *Re St Martin le Grand, York; Westminster Press Ltd v St Martin with St Helen, York* [1989] 2 All ER 711.

proving prescription under lost modern grant. Given the consecrated nature of the land, the court was only willing to recognise a lost modern grant for a licence with a short-term discretionary faculty for a licence for vehicles.[105] *St Martin le Grand* is good example of the constancy of consecrated land whilst change surrounds. The printing works subsequently became a cinema. Twenty-five years later, that area of York between Coney Street and the river now looks set for major re-development, but the church remains.

The general restrictions on secular use of consecrated land are weakening and adjusting to changing times, but easements continue to be restrained by the character of the land and the ecclesiastical courts still prefer to recognise licences. Section 68(2) of the Mission and Pastoral Measure 2011 precludes the sale or lease of a church or the site of any consecrated land, but under section 68(4), there is provision for the application for a faculty to create a lease of part where the whole building remains primarily a place of worship.[106] In *St Matthew's Church Camberwell*,[107] this was not applied to easements. The Consistory Court said that the fact there was no power to grant an easement over a churchyard extended to a grant of derogation from an easement of light enjoyed by the church. A faculty for an indefinite licence was granted instead as 'equivalent protection'.[108]

The previous sections of this chapter have shown that the character of the land, as ecclesiastical land, and frequently consecrated land, is implicitly linked to the type of easements that can and cannot exist. This presents in different ways in the context of pew rights, burial rights and rights of way, but the underlying point remains that the day-to-day sacred use of the land and the nature of the ownership are the reasons behind each existing right and the reasons why some rights are not allowed to be created. There is one further easement that is worthy of consideration and that is a possible right to transmit sound waves from a noise on the dominant land: a noise made to call people to worship on that land.

D. Church Bells

Noise from church bells has long been a source of complaint.[109] There is extensive guidance on current limitations.[110] Since *Lawrence v Fen Tigers*,[111] we can

[105] ibid 732.

[106] Code of Practice for the Mission and Pastoral Measure 2011 (as amended), 14.21.

[107] *Re Matter of St Matthew's Church, Camberwell* (Ecclesiastical Law Association Index of Consistory Court Judgments, 10 March 2014).

[108] ibid [14].

[109] See, eg, *Calvert v Gardiner* [2002] EWHC 1394 (QB) for an unsuccessful attempt to sue the Bishop of Exeter for nuisance through bell ringing.

[110] See generally Legal Advisory Commission of the General Synod of the Church of England, 'Church Building: Bells, Ringing of Church Bells: Canon Law and the Potential Liability for Nuisance at Common Law and under the Environmental Protection Act 1990' in Legal Advisory Commission of the General Synod of the Church of England (n 92) 153; ChurchCare, *Guidance Note on Church Bells and the Law* (undated).

[111] *Lawrence and Another v Fen Tigers and Others* [2014] UKSC 13.

be confident that easements to transmit sound waves across neighbouring land may in theory exist.[112] However, it has proved hard to establish a concrete example. Developers and planners are nevertheless writing easements for noise into conveyances.[113] Academic commentary has focused on the practical difficulties of proving this sort of easement. *Thompson's Modern Land Law* suggests that it 'is difficult to see as properly belonging to the law of easements' since 'the right to make a noise is likely to fall foul of the rule that it must be sufficiently definite, unless the noise itself is clearly defined in terms of how loud and frequent it will be'.[114] Dixon has also highlighted the practical challenges over certainty of scope and the difficulties of establishing a grant through prescription with 'user as of right'.[115]

A case may be made for church bells in the specific context of their religious use of calling people to worship on the land. The same argument might be extended to other religious contexts. Recreational bell ringing and traditional bell ringing for community time-keeping purposes are weaker cases. Years before Cheshire wrote his *Modern Law of Real Property*, he was an undergraduate at Merton College, Oxford. The bells in the Merton Chapel are known as the oldest complete ring of eight bells by one founder and were cast in 1681.[116] Today the bells are rung before services in the same way as they would have been in Cheshire's time. All eight bells are rung for the special occasions of the year. The bells serve the normal day-to-day purpose of the land that is the Chapel, and they emit noise in a regular pattern. The academic commentary on bells predates *Lawrence* and is focused on tort law and private nuisance.[117] Thomas and Watkin explain that bell ringing can be a private or a statutory nuisance where it affects 'the reasonable comfort and convenience of the occupiers of neighbouring premises'.[118] Post-*Lawrence*, the noise of the bells accommodating the use of the ecclesiastical land might be suggested as a basis for an easement.[119] The pattern of the bells will meet the need for steadiness in 'intensity and frequency

[112] ibid [32]–[41]. On noise, nuisance and property rights, see generally E Lees, 'Lawrence v Fen Tigers: Where Now for Nuisance?' (2021) 5 *Conveyancer and Property Lawyer Conveyancer and Property Lawyer* 449; MJ Dixon, 'The Sound of Silence' (2014) 2 *Conveyancer and Property Lawyer* 79.

[113] L McDonnell, 'Live Music: the Housing Conundrum' [2020] *Property Law Journal* 14.

[114] M George and A Layard, *Thompson's Modern Land Law*, 8th edn (Oxford, Oxford University Press, 2022) 437.

[115] Dixon (n 112) 81.

[116] GH Martin and JRL Highfield, *A History of Merton College, Oxford* (Oxford, Oxford University Press, 1997) 218.

[117] See generally TG Watkin, 'A Happy Noise to Hear? Church Bells and the Law of Nuisance', (1996) 4 *Ecclesiastical Law Journal* 545, S Thomas and TG Watkin, 'Oh, Noisy Bells Be Dumb: Church Bells, Statutory Nuisance and Ecclesiastical Duties' (1995) *Journal of Planning Law* 1097; RH Bloor, 'Clocks, Bells and Cockerels' (1995) 3 *Ecclesiastical Law Journal* 393.

[118] Thomas and Watkin (n 117) 1105.

[119] But see ibid 1101. Thomas and Watkin argue that where a bell is being rung by a cleric in fulfilment of their duty under the Canons of the Church of England which require a bell to be tolled to give 'warning' of services and call people to prayer, that duty can be a defence to claim of nuisance.

(in the sense of timing and pitch)'.[120] As well as being clear in extent and duration, in most cases the sound will have been of long duration as of right and it shows a clear benefit to the religious purposes of the dominant land. Bells themselves are consecrated in that place and on some measures are taken to be part of the land dedicated.[121] Any potential right exists because of the sacred nature of the land. In the recent case of *Re St James, Kirk*,[122] a faculty to move church bells away from a closed church to a different church was granted because that would allow those bells to be used once again to call people to services.

IV. THE FUTURE OF ECCLESIASTICAL EASEMENTS

A. Changing Churches and Changing Easements

The modern cases discussed in this chapter all occurred in the context of a change of use of ecclesiastical land. For example, in *Re St James, Kirk*, the church had closed for public worship six years before the bells were moved, while in *Hughes*, the case occurred where there had been an amalgamation of benefices. This section of the chapter uses the category of ecclesiastical easements and changing land use to press the argument for implementing the Law Commission's recommendations for reform. When the *Taylor Review* was published in 2017 by the Department for Culture, Media and Sport, it provided a consideration of both funding and sustainability of listed Church of England buildings.[123] The Report emphasised the importance of seeking a 'cultural shift' and broadening use; '[t]o survive a church building must be both valued by, and useful to its community'.[124] Removing legal barriers was identified as one necessary step. Widening community use allows more buildings to remain in use, but it is inevitable that some will close. There are about 16,000 Church of England churches and 8,600 are Grade I and II* and another 4,000 Grade II.[125] The Closed Churches Database shows that between 1969 and 2019, there were 1,972 church closures.[126] Alternative use was found for 57 per cent of these churches and 18 per cent were preserved (normally by the Churches Conservation Trust).[127] The remaining churches were demolished because no alternative use could be found. The Church Commissioners stress the challenges of finding alternative uses for

[120] *Lawrence* (n 111) [36].
[121] Orme (n 16) 108.
[122] *Re St James, Kirk* [2022] Ecc Bla 3.
[123] Department of Culture, Media and Sport (n 3).
[124] ibid 16.
[125] Church Commissioners for England, *Review of the Mission and Pastoral Measure 2011, Draft Proposals, General Synod 2023*, GS 2315, 41.
[126] Church Commissioners for England, Mission, Pastoral and Church Property Group, *The Re-use of Closed Churches: An Analysis of Use Types and Sustainability from 1969–2019*, 3.
[127] ibid 5.

closed churches, given their 'unique building type'. Their report identifies 'access to buildings' as an issue.[128] Residential use has proved to be the most durable alternative use. A current review is seeking to simplify the legal process for closing churches, to add flexibility and to facilitate re-use.[129]

If land previously set aside for public worship is to be re-used, the associated proprietary rights need to be addressed. In *Collingwood King*, there was concern about the practical future of the site, given the outcome. The descendants of the original donor were held to own the vault (with an easement to access it), but the church itself was closed, with the intention of being re-purposed. Section 84 of the Law of Property Act 1925 provides the possibility of applying to modify or discharge covenants. This legislation has been used to facilitate new religious uses of buildings in the past.[130] Some types of religious buildings may need a covenant restricting them to religious use to be removed by agreement or under section 84. It is more likely that a closure will result in new covenants. Under the current Mission and Pastoral Measure 2011, where Church of England churches are closed and sold on for secular purposes, there is provision for the imposition of covenants to 'secure the suitable use of the building or land'.[131] It is fascinating, and again indicative of the privileges afforded to ecclesiastical land, that the Church Commissioners/Diocesan Board of Finance then retains the benefit to these covenants as if the Commissioners/Diocesan Board of Finance held neighbouring land, all the covenants are treated as negative (even if positive covenants), and covenants are given 'unusual effectiveness' by specific provision that they cannot be 'varied or released on an application to the Lands Tribunal'.[132] The same Measure also makes provision for conferring easements or taking over previously enjoyed easements.[133] There does not appear to be any way of getting rid of unwanted easements to facilitate new uses of the land. Section 84 of the Law of Property Act has no application to easements, and it is notoriously difficult to argue that an easement has been lost.[134] In 2011 the Law Commission recommended that section 84 be extended to newly created easements.[135] This would have limited impact for ecclesiastical rights, given how old they are. However, the recommendation that an easement not used for a continuous period of 20 years should raise a rebuttable presumption that it has been abandoned would be very relevant.[136] Elsewhere, Nield has

[128] ibid 4.

[129] See n 125 above.

[130] See n 10 above.

[131] Mission and Pastoral Measure 2011 (as amended), s 75(1); Code of Recommended Practice, vol 2 22.2.

[132] Mission and Pastoral Measure 2011 (as amended), s75(3); Code of Recommended Practice, vol 2 22.4.

[133] Mission and Pastoral Measure 2011 (as amended), s 72(1) and (2).

[134] Gaunt and Morgan (n 33) 564.

[135] Law Commission (n 4) 7.35.

[136] ibid 3.230.

discussed current accommodation of change on a 'micro' level within easements generally.[137]

The need to widen uses of land in the context of change in ecclesiastical settings is another reason to hope that the Law Commission's proposals will finally be progressed. This is an ever-growing list of reasons. In *Regency Villas*, Lord Briggs said the fact that the recreational rights were likely to be a burden 'long after the leisure complex … has outlived its natural life', given the current lack of a statutory basis for the modification and discharge of easements, was a reason against the recognition of them as easements in that case.[138] Section 84 is also one of the potential 'brake' factors on the breadth of the *Regency Villas* decision that Bevan identifies. Bevan suggests that the extension of section 84 to easements 'would be a powerful weapon in the armoury' to 'supervise over-burdensome easements' and achieve 'balance' between the rights of landowners.[139]

B. Ecclesiastical Easements as a Category of Rights

This chapter has shown that ecclesiastical easements are a complex and context-driven category of rights. Property lawyers have never needed or expected to see easements facilitating religious use, such as to pews or vaults, transposed to other types of land. The rights accommodate church use and belong in a church setting. Some other ecclesiastical easements, especially rights of way, have been restricted because of the character of the consecrated land. The legal history of this area of law has allowed the development of easements to accommodate specific settings.

As the possible categories of easements expand, property lawyers are allowed to be cautious about pressures to apply new types of easements across all settings generically. In 2009, Gray and Gray argued that '[t]he judicial animus against recreational easements has undoubtedly receded in recent times. It may be an index of a more hedonistic (or even more health-conscious) age that it no longer seems inappropriate to acknowledge the easement character of certain recreational facilities annexed to dominant land'.[140] *Regency Villas* has certainly taken us past that point. At the same time, the ecclesiastical easements defined in this chapter have been moving in the opposite direction. Writing in 2024, Hill describes the outworkings of the decision in *Aston Cantlow* as opening 'the way to secularism, side-lining religion into little more than a hobby or a

[137] S Nield, '(In)flexibility of Enduring Property Relations: The Easement Story' (2021) 3 *Conveyancer and Property Lawyer* 290, 291.

[138] *Regency Villas* (n 2) 79.

[139] Bevan (n 24) 69.

[140] K Gray and SF Gray, *Elements of Land Law*, 5th edn (Oxford, Oxford University Press, 2008) 612.

leisure pursuit'.[141] Whilst both sorts of land use are changing, they can still be served by easements appropriate to their own context. The detail of the variety of easements accommodating ecclesiastical purposes in this chapter show that character of the land is all important. If land law can recognise special types of easements for ecclesiastical land, then there are further grounds to suggest that recreational easements might be restricted to serve genuinely recreational settings like the 'country club' in *Regency Villas* alone. This could mirror the way in which ecclesiastical easements have served land set aside for religious purposes.

This chapter has also shown the variety of ecclesiastical easements. Later nineteenth-century and early twentieth-century editions of Gale continued to grapple with the detail of ecclesiastical easements. These rights do not always sit easily within the broader characteristics of easements subsequently set out by Cheshire in his *Modern Law of Real Property*, used in *Re Ellenborough* and followed in *Regency Villas*. The disjoint between the older ecclesiastical cases and the subsequently developed characteristics supports arguments to re-consider the voices of both Cheshire and Lord Evershed in *Re Ellenborough*. Anderson has explained the need for the first edition of Cheshire's work to set out the new 1925 legislation and guide practitioners with 'uncluttered accounts of changes from the past'.[142] The respect that Cheshire's efforts received from the judiciary as well as practitioners was very evident.[143] However, more recently, the impact of Cheshire's work on the subject has attracted debate.[144] The analysis of ecclesiastical easements in this chapter adds additional evidence to the view, from Bottomley and Lim amongst others, that with Cheshire, there was some 'mapping [of] an assertion of coherence onto much more complex phenomena'.[145]

V. CONCLUSIONS

This chapter has defined a distinct category of ecclesiastical easements facilitating the use of land for religious purposes. These rights provide an example of the value of including ecclesiastical property law in wider discussions of the

[141] Hill (n 8) 18.

[142] S Anderson, *Lawyers and the Making of English Land Law 1832–1940* (Oxford, Clarendon Press, 1992) 312.

[143] See especially FH Lawson, 'Geoffrey Chevalier Cheshire 1886–1978' (1980) 65 *Proceedings of the British Academy* 610, 630.

[144] See, eg, M Doupe and M Salter, 'Approaching Nature and History of Property Law: The Limits of the "Cheshire Worldview"' (2000) 11 *King's College Journal* 49; and W Swain, 'Professor Geoffrey Cheshire (1886–1978) and Professor Cecil Fifoot (1899–1975)' in J Goudkamp and D Nolan, *Scholars of Contract Law* (Oxford, Hart Publishing, 2022) 229–52.

[145] H Lim and A Bottomley, 'Feminist Perambulations, Taking the Law for a Walk in Land' in H Lim and A Bottomley (eds), *Feminist Perspectives on Land Law* (Abingdon, Routledge, 2007) 1, 12.

development of property rights. As a category of rights limited to the type of land that they serve, ecclesiastical easements demonstrate how easements can exist to accommodate particular land uses. The chapter uses ecclesiastical easements to suggest that the recognition of easements for recreational purposes after *Regency Villas* should be confined to distinctly recreational settings. Ecclesiastical easements also contribute to understandings of rights around creation of noise in connection to land use and add weight to calls for reform to address out-of-date easements as land use changes. Finally, the chapter suggests that the detail of the ecclesiastical easements of pews, vaults, ways and possibly bells is a timely reminder of the layers, breadth of rights and complexity that has always existed behind Cheshire's four defining characteristics of an easements that were established in *Re Ellenborough*.

5

Dicta and Dissent; Doubt and Indecision

Estate Disputes and An(other) Opportunity Missed by the Supreme Court?

HEATHER CONWAY AND SHEENA GRATTAN*

> [T]he Supreme Court does not exist to do justice in particular cases, but to sort out the law.[1]

I. INTRODUCTION

THE TENDENCY FOR split decisions of the UK Supreme Court[2] with substantial *obiter dicta* and/or long dissenting judgments is a phenomenon noted by Neil Duxbury in *The Intricacies of Dicta and Dissent*.[3] For various reasons, private law – and property law in particular – has appeared somewhat neglected since the Court came into existence in 2009, compared

* Thanks to the anonymous reviewers, and to our colleagues in the School of Law at Queen's University for their comments on an earlier draft – in particular, Dr Conor McCormick.

[1] Lord Sumption, 'Introduction' in S Worthington and W Day (eds), *Challenging Private Law: Lord Sumption on the Supreme Court* (Oxford, Hart Publishing, 2020). Lord Sumption is a former Justice of the Supreme Court.

[2] Most notably in recent years (other than the subject matter of this chapter), see *Fearn and Others v Board of Trustees of the Tate Gallery* [2023] UKSC 4.

[3] N Duxbury, *The Intricacies of Dicta and Dissent* (Cambridge, Cambridge University Press, 2021). See also NH Andrews, 'The Supreme Court of the United Kingdom and English Court Judgements', 3 February 2014, University of Cambridge Faculty of Law Research Paper No 23/2014, available at SSRN: https://ssrn.com/abstract=2399103 or http://dx.doi.org/10.2139/ssrn.2399103.

with developments in the public law arena.[4] However, those property law disputes and legal contests with property law themes that have made their way to the Supreme Court since its inception[5] have not escaped the trend noted by Duxbury. The thorny question of whether dicta and, more importantly, dissent actually 'sort out the law' in cases of this nature is the subject of this chapter.

Our focus is on succession law[6] as a classic area in which the certainty of property law collides with the discretion of family law.[7] Decisions of the highest appellate court have been rare in succession law,[8] but two recent occasions have given the Supreme Court the opportunity to provide clarity. Much scholarly ink has been spilled in analysing the decision in *Ilott v The Blue Cross*,[9] with the consensus being that it generates more questions than answers for family provision claims by adult children and the modern function of the jurisdiction more generally[10] – something that was brought into sharp focus by Lady Hale's dicta-dominated supplementary judgment in the case (with which Lords Kerr and Wilson agreed). Similar scholarly analyses are emerging following the ruling in *Guest v Guest*,[11] when the Supreme Court was presented with an opportunity to review the appropriate measure of relief in successful proprietary estoppel claims in the context of the large sway of modern cases involving family farms and how these should pass between generations.[12] The end result, some

[4] This is not to suggest that private law has stagnated since the inception of the Supreme Court – see, eg, the collection of essays in Worthington and Day (n 1). However, more decisions of the Supreme Court – both numerically and more prominently – have been dealing with public law issues, though there are signs that the proverbial tide is turning (at least in the number of private law cases).

[5] Another chapter explores how the Supreme Court has shaped the concept of property in these cases: see Evans and de Contreras, ch 6 in this volume.

[6] We use the term 'succession law' as encompassing the entire intergenerational transfer of wealth, and not restricted to the traditional view of transmission on death via the twin pillars of the testate and intestate succession – see, eg, G Miller, *The Machinery of Succession*, 2nd edn (London, Dartmouth Publishing, 1996).

[7] Another classic illustration is the constructive trust of the family home. For an interesting comparison of proprietary estoppel in the family context and constructive trusts, see M Dixon, 'Informality and Claims to Property: Untangling Lives, Untangling the Law' [2021] *Conveyancer and Property Lawyer* 1.

[8] In addition to the two UK Supreme Court decisions discussed here there is *Marley v Rawlings* [2014] UKSC 2 and, if a broad view is taken to the definition of 'succession law', the decision in *Unger and Another v Ul-Hasan (Deceased)* [2023] UKSC 22.

[9] *Ilott v The Blue Cross* [2017] UKSC 17, [2017] 2 WLR 979.

[10] See, eg, B Sloan, '*Ilott v The Blue Cross* (2017): Testing the Limits of Testamentary Freedom' in B Sloan (ed), *Landmark Cases in Succession Law* (Oxford, Hart Publishing, 2019) 30; H Conway and S Grattan, 'Children in Need and the Great Intergenerational Wealth Transfer: Squaring the Impossible Circle of Testamentary Freedom, Family Obligation and the Role of the State' in S Lennon and D Monk (eds), *Inheritance Matters: Kinship, Property, Law* (Oxford, Hart Publishing, 2023) 233.

[11] *Guest v Guest* [2022] UKSC 27, [2022] 3 WLR 911.

[12] See, eg, A Purewall, 'Addressing the "Lively" Controversy around Proprietary Estoppel' (2023) 29 *Trusts & Trustees* 79; A Waghorn, 'Promises at Equity and at Law: Proprietary Estoppel after *Guest v Guest*' (2023) 86 *MLR* 1504. As noted, succession law should be viewed in a broader context to include all disputes about intergenerational wealth transfer. The parties were still very much alive in *Guest*, as they have been in several other estoppel cases, including another seminal decision in *Gillet v Holt* [2000] 2 All ER 289.

10 months after the hearing, was a somewhat dense 108-page judgment, in which the dissenting judgment is longer than the lead judgment (53 pages compared to 41).

Both these judgments – like so many other Supreme Court decisions – speak to the concept of legal doctrine. Described by Tiller and Cross as the 'currency of the law', it is composed of the rules and standards contained in judicial opinions and 'sets the terms for future resolution of cases in an area'.[13] Adopting said functional approach, this chapter argues that the potential for resolving future cases is in danger of being compromised by split decisions of the Supreme Court in disputes such as *Ilott* and *Guest* that are highly fact-specific and (more importantly) where the relevant decision-making matrix is both fluid and flexible. Our starting point is that both dicta and dissent are important, not just as part of the rich tapestry of a common law legal tradition, but also as part of the judicial decision-making process broadly construed, and we explore this more fully in section II. The emphasis then shifts to dissenting judgments where there has been the barest of majorities in the Supreme Court, and the specific problems that this creates. Taking *Guest* as a paradigmatic illustration, section III provides a brief overview of the decision before considering the implications of dissenting judgments on smaller jurisdictions that take their lead from a larger legal system and its appellate court.[14] It is axiomatic that, for any jurisdiction – irrespective of size – 'legal doctrine exists within a decision-making hierarchy'.[15] However, our central argument is that dissenting judgments have the potential to be more problematic in small jurisdictions with their very distinct legal cultures. In doing so, we use our own jurisdiction of Northern Ireland as an exemplar, and identify its specific traits (and idiosyncrasies) in section IV. We then argue in section V that the climate of legal uncertainty triggered by bare majority judgments with lengthy dissents does not provide the necessary clarity for lower courts. This is problematic for two reasons. First, it fuels unhelpful human behaviours such as the taking of nuisance claims. The second, and not unrelated, reason is the impact that it has on testamentary freedom.[16] To date, the potential link between these concepts has not been interrogated in the literature.

[13] EH Tiller and FB Cross, 'What is Legal Doctrine?' (2006) 100 *Northwestern University Law Review* 517, 517. The authors acknowledge that they are adopting a 'conventional legal approach to the law … [as being] all about doctrine', with judicial decision-making (notwithstanding the views of critical legal studies scholars) being premised on the application of specific rules to the facts presented (at 518). For present purposes, our focus is also and unapologetically on this conventional approach.

[14] We define what constitutes a 'small' jurisdiction in section IV below.

[15] Tiller and Cross (n 13) 531.

[16] Whether this is a clear expression of testamentary intent in the will of the now-deceased property owner, or an intended estate distribution where the owner is still alive, but has informed the claimant that they will inherit nothing or significantly less than anticipated.

In essence, this chapter goes to the heart of 'how law works' and acts as a counterpoint to the received wisdom that Supreme Court judgments are definitive statements of legal doctrine. Moreover, the influence of these judgments extends beyond the narrow confines of the lower courts, to the resolution of those private law legal disputes (in fact, the vast majority) that resolve without court intervention. While our focus is on Northern Ireland, the observations have a wider resonance.

II. A BRIEF FORAY INTO DICTA AND DISSENT

The very nature of appellate courts means that judges 'typically decide the appeals before them as a group',[17] and separate analyses by Paterson and Cahill-O'Callaghan reveal concerted efforts to encourage a culture of collaborative working and collective decision-making within the UK Supreme Court.[18] The upshot may be a movement away from individualised judgments.[19] However, we can still point to rich seams of dicta and – more importantly – dissent that are an inevitable consequence of a multi-person panel replete with different personalities and different viewpoints on the law, facts and legal principles before it.[20] Both *Ilott* and *Guest* are obvious examples, but what purpose do dicta and dissent actually serve in judgments that go beyond that standard 'rule formulations applied to specific facts'?[21]

Though intrinsically different legal creatures, Duxbury sees both dicta and dissent as forms of legal reasoning that explain how decisions were reached and have great potential to shape the law.[22] They are deliberative acts that are designed to communicate particular points, and especially at the Supreme Court level, where judgments are reserved and then written after a period of reflection. Dicta are much more than mere evidence of a 'judicial predilection for reflection';[23] through varied means and indicative phrasing, these judicial observations articulate important incidental issues. What sets apart Lady Hale's comments in *Ilott*, however, is the use of a forceful supplementary judgment devoted exclusively to dicta – something that is very unusual in a unanimous

[17] RC Jubelirer, 'Communicating Disagreement Behind the Bench: The Importance of Rules and Norms of an Appellate Court' (2019) 82 *Law & Contemporary Problems* 103, 103.

[18] AA Paterson, *Final Judgment* (Hart Publishing, 2013) and R Cahill-O'Callaghan, 'When You Cannot Ask the Judge: Using Cases to Explore Judicial Culture in the UK Supreme Court' (2023) 13(S1) *Oñati Socio-Legal Series* S121–S144.

[19] According to Cahill-O'Callaghan (n 18), the decline in lone dissents in the Supreme Court is more noticeable; any decline in minority dissents is less pronounced.

[20] See generally C Hanretty, *A Court of Specialists: Judicial Behavior on the UK Supreme Court* (Oxford, Oxford University Press, 2020).

[21] Duxbury (n 3) 4.

[22] ibid.

[23] ibid.

decision.[24] Having observed that *Ilott* raised 'some profound questions'[25] about the nature of family obligations, the role of the state and concepts of testamentary freedom, Lady Hale concluded that the case itself could have resulted in 'three very different solutions',[26] all of which could have been deemed acceptable on the facts. The latter observations – while no doubt true – promulgate the sense of uncertainty that we are highlighting in this chapter.

The meaning and significance of dissent, meanwhile, may be shaped by a particular 'jurisdiction's adjudicative culture',[27] but disagreement with the majority view tends to be seen as an important part of the common law's evolutionary process when appellate judges are free to issue dissenting opinions.[28] These same opinions might be important in shaping the future development of the law.[29] From a more short-termist perspective, dissents are essential ways of promoting individual judicial responsibility and overall transparency in demonstrating how a particular decision was reached.[30] They might also 'provide some solace to the losing litigants and a sense that their case was indeed properly considered and dealt with',[31] though the point has also been made that 'depending on the mindset of the losing party, the knowledge that the court was divided might make matters worse'.[32] In the already febrile arena of contested estates, with all their familial tensions and emotional stressors,[33] the latter point is a pertinent one.

Running alongside these themes is the concept of audience and the fact that Supreme Court decisions have to speak to a diverse range of groups with 'very different attitudes and expectations'.[34] Of course, there are the parties

[24] The term 'supplementary judgment' appears in the UK Supreme Court's own press summary of the judgment and is doctrinally distinct from a concurring judgment by adding specific observations to the primary decision rather than, eg, reaching the same conclusion by way of different reasoning. Supplementary judgments are uncommon; any non-binding guidance is typically found within the main judgment(s). For the sake of completeness, it should be noted that the practice of issuing separate concurring judgments has been the subject of debate – see, eg, J Lee, 'A Defence of Concurring Speeches' [2009] *Public Law* 305.

[25] *Ilott*,(n 9) [65].

[26] ibid.

[27] Duxbury (n 3) 128.

[28] As well as Duxbury (n 3), see PW Hogg and R Armarnath, 'Why Judges Should Dissent' (2017) 67 *University of Toronto Law Journal* 126.

[29] Dissents 'underline the area of the law that is uncertain or ripe for development and invite dialogue about the law's development in those areas': FM Steel, 'The Role of Dissents in Appellate Judging' (2017) 67 *University of Toronto Law Journal* 142, 145.

[30] See Hogg and Armarnath (n 28), as well as J Alder, 'Dissents in Courts of Last Resort: Tragic Choices?' (2000) 20 *Oxford Journal of Legal Studies* 221.

[31] Steel (n 29) 145.

[32] Alder (n 30) 242.

[33] See generally M Izuhara and S Köppe, 'Inheritance and Family Conflicts: Exploring Asset Transfers Shaping Intergenerational Relations' (2019) 8 *Families, Relationships and Societies* 53. The same familial and emotional dynamics also make mediated settlements more challenging; we return to this briefly in section V below.

[34] See FP Shecaira and N Struchiner, 'Legal Audiences' (2018) 32 *Argumentation* 273, 275–76, where the authors discuss the nature of the audiences that are targeted and should be targeted by judges in the legal process to address the issue of what the authors describe as 'audience diversity'. See also A Mikva, 'For Whom Judges Write' (1987) 61 *Southern California Law Review* 1357.

themselves, who wish to know the outcome of their (expensive) legal travails, but we can add judges and lower courts, the legal profession, legal academics and researchers, and the general public to the list. However, for both lower courts and legal practitioners advising clients on the strength of a particular claim, dissent can be particularly problematic where the result is a bare majority decision that generates even more potential for doubt and indecision. This is especially true in the already uncertain and exclusively judge-made legal terrain of proprietary estoppel.

In *Guest*, the dissenting judgment of Lord Legatt (with whom Lord Stephens agreed) did not reject the appeal; like the majority decision, it allowed it. Instead, the dissent was premised on allowing the appeal on different grounds and substituting a different remedy in an extremely active area of law that is increasingly characterised by uncertainty where family farms and broken promises around inheritance trigger bitter litigation. As such, the decision has been criticised for not bringing much-needed clarity to the law and its 'lack of unanimity … [that] implies potential deviations in reasoning in future cases'.[35] However, the consequences for proprietary estoppel claims in Northern Ireland, as a small jurisdiction taking its lead from the Supreme Court, are more pronounced, as we shall see. Before that, the following section briefly rehearses the facts and rulings in *Guest*.

III. THE DECISION IN *GUEST*: AN OVERVIEW

'One day, my son, all this will be yours.'[36]

Time will tell, but these opening words of the judgment of Lord Briggs in *Guest* may become as well known as some of Lord Denning's most famous openings.[37] Moreover, in contrast to Lord Denning's colourful references to such matters as bluebells,[38] scripture rallies[39] and the four surnames of one Janet 'Eves',[40] Lord Briggs' opening points immediately to what he considers to be the major element of a proprietary estoppel claim: expectation. The facts of the case are well known and need only be reproduced briefly.

[35] CM Smyth and R Dunbar, 'Clear as Mud: Proprietary Estoppel after *Guest v Guest*' (2024) 30 *Trusts & Trustees* 229, 229.

[36] Guest, (n 11) [1]. The transmission of family farms on death is still dominated by gendered practices that favour sons, and the eldest male in particular – see, eg, JL Glover, 'Gender, Power and Succession in Family Farm Business' (2014) 6 *International Journal of Gender and Entrepreneurship* 276. However, daughters can also be potential inheritors (usually where there are no sons) and trigger the types of estoppel dispute that infuse this chapter – see, eg, *Davies v Davies* [2016] EWCA 463.

[37] Several of which are recorded in Sir Henry Brooke's 'Judgments: The Best Opening Lines and a Few More', https://sirhenrybrooke.me/2017/04/29/judgments-the-best-opening-lines-and-a-few-more.

[38] *Hinz v Berry* [1970] 2 QB 40.

[39] *Burgess v Rawnsley* [1975] Ch 429.

[40] *Eves v Eves* [1975] 1 WLR 1338.

The Guest family had farmed Tump Farm (hereinafter 'the Farm') since 1938. Mr and Mrs David and Josephine Guest held the Farm and dairy business in joint names, and in 1981 they had made wills leaving both assets to their two sons, Andrew (the claimant) and his brother, in equal shares. Andrew had left school aged 16 and worked full-time on the Farm until the relationship with his parents broke down in 2015. Andrew duly moved out of a tied cottage and his parents made new wills, removing Andrew entirely. They did, however, offer Andrew terms for continuing to work on the Farm under a farming business tenancy, a proposal which Andrew rejected on the ground of affordability. Andrew brought a claim for a beneficial interest in the Farm based on proprietary estoppel. The trial judge ordered Mr and Mrs Guest to pay Andrew a lump sum representing 50 per cent of the market value of the farming business and 40 per cent of the market value of the Farm. As a consequence, the property would have to be sold in order that Mr and Mrs Guest could realise the amount of the award. Not wanting to sell the Farm, Mr and Mrs Guest appealed to the Court of Appeal on the question of the appropriate remedy. The primary finding from the first instance decision – that Andrew had succeeded in establishing an equity based in proprietary estoppel on the ground that assurances had been made to him over many years (and on which he had relied) that he would inherit a substantial share of the Farm – remained constant in the subsequent appeals. Both appeals concerned the appropriate remedy to which Andrew was entitled as a result of the finding at first instance that a proprietary estoppel had arisen in his favour.

The Court of Appeal, relying heavily on the decision in *Davies v Davies*,[41] refused to interfere with the first instance decision, leaving the parents with no alternative but to appeal to the Supreme Court to achieve their objective of avoiding the sale of the Farm. As anticipated, the hearing before the Supreme Court distilled into a debate as to whether the starting point for considering the appropriate remedy in proprietary estoppel cases was the expectation which had arisen as a result of the representation ('expectation-loss') or, alternatively, the quest for a remedy which addressed the detriment that the promisee had suffered ('detriment-loss'). This so-called 'lively controversy' had been described by Lewison LJ in the following terms in *Davies* v *Davies*:

> One line of authority takes the view that the essential aim of the discretion is to give effect to the claimant's expectation unless it would be disproportionate to do so. The other takes the view that the essential aim of the discretion is to ensure that the claimant's reliance interest is protected, so that she is compensated for such detriment as she has suffered. The two approaches, in their starkest form, are fundamentally different.[42]

Lord Briggs for the majority (Lady Arden and Lady Rose concurring) rejected the proposition that remedies for proprietary estoppel had ever been

[41] *Davies* (n 36).
[42] *Davies* (n 36) [39].

(or should be) based on providing compensation for the detriment suffered by the promisee. While acknowledging that the remedy should not, without good reason, be out of all proportion to the promisee's detriment, Lord Briggs declared that this was no more than a useful cross-check for potential injustice. Rather, the appropriate remedy was, and always has been, the prevention or undoing of unconscionable conduct, and once the equity has been established, fulfilment of the promise will likely be the starting point. The correct approach would be to allow Mr and Mrs Guest to elect between putting the Farm in trust for their children, including Andrew, subject to a life estate in their own favour or making an immediate lump sum payment of compensation to Andrew (as per the trial judge), but sufficiently discounted to take account of the accelerated receipt (with a direction to remit to the Chancery Division for determination if a sum could not be reached by agreement).

Lord Leggart wrote the dissenting judgment, with which Lord Stephens agreed. They would have allowed the appeal in its entirety, substituting £610,000 payable to Andrew by his parents as equitable compensation, with a 40-paragraph appendix setting out the basis upon which this 'detriment-loss' sum had been calculated.

The practical outcome for Mr and Mrs Guest was that they were not forced to sell the Farm (which they would have been required to do on the first instance decision). Their appeal had therefore achieved what it had set out to do and their legal team had succeeded in acting in the best interests of their clients. Before we move on to consider the implications that this decision is likely to have for lawyers in Northern Ireland advising prospective proprietary estoppel claimants (and defendants) as to what is in their best interests, it might be appropriate to provide some background as to the Northern Ireland legal jurisdiction and the context and culture in which it operates.

IV. NORTHERN IRELAND: SMALL JURISDICTION TRAITS AND 'SMALL JURISDICTION SYNDROME'

In 'Navigating Law-Making and Law Reform in Small Jurisdictions',[43] Caroline Morris lists population size and geographical territory as two 'prominent indicators' of a small jurisdiction. In this respect, it seems self-evident that Northern Ireland, with its population of less than two million people[44] and a physical area just short of 5,500 square miles, meets the definition of 'small'.[45] Not only is Northern

[43] C Morris, 'Navigating Law-Making and Law Reform in Small Jurisdictions' in C Morris (ed), *Making and Changing Law in Small Jurisdictions* (Dordrecht, Springer International, 2024) 1.

[44] The latest Census for Northern Ireland, conducted in 2021, lists a population of 1,903,173 at the census date: see www.nisra.gov.uk/statistics/census/census-2021.

[45] Another 'objective measure' noted by Morris (n 43) is the size of the jurisdiction's economy (something that is also highlighted in World Bank definitions cited in P Giliker, 'Reforming Tort Law in Smaller Jurisdictions: Vicarious Liability as a Case Study' (2023) 29 *Tort Law Review* 101

Ireland a small jurisdiction on any objective standard, but it is also the smallest of the three separate legal jurisdictions that make up the United Kingdom.[46]

It is equally self-evident that any common law jurisdiction with such a modest population will have difficulty in generating a meaningful volume of jurisprudence on most substantive areas of law[47] and will instinctively look to its traditional 'legal metropolis' for guidance.[48] This presents obvious challenges to developing the common law in small legal jurisdictions, something that has attracted comparatively little attention in legal scholarship, with one notable exception being the recent research of Paula Giliker[49] on developing vicarious liability in Hong Kong, Singapore and the Republic of Ireland. In many respects, Northern Ireland is no different from other small jurisdictions dealing with issues around legal transplantability and the suitability – or otherwise – of laws imported from elsewhere.[50] However, as the following sections illustrate, the distinct nature of our focal jurisdiction presents its own complex and unique issues that simultaneously stunt the potential for developing the law while impacting on how legal disputes are actually resolved, especially in those areas that are entirely judge-made, such as proprietary estoppel.

A. The Northern Ireland Legal Landscape: A Thumbnail Sketch

As has been noted, Northern Ireland is a separate legal jurisdiction within the UK. Following partition in 1920, its Parliament was given authority to enact

and her associated reference to World Bank definitions of small jurisdictions). Moving beyond these so-called 'objective measures', Morris also cites a jurisdiction's 'perceptual size', and how it perceives itself (and is perceived) as an influential actor on the world stage as a relevant factor: Morris (n 43) 2. Since this could be an entire thesis in itself, the authors will not attempt any such categorisation of Northern Ireland!

[46] Taking population size – which directly correlates with other factors such as economic activity – Northern Ireland is smallest by a considerable margin, with a population of just over 1.9 million and significantly lower than that of England and Wales (60.8 million of which Wales is 3.16 million) and Scotland (approaching 5.5 million). At the time of writing, these are the latest figures, available from the Office of National Statistics: www.ons.gov.uk/peoplepopulationandcommunity/populationandmigration/populationestimates.

[47] This aligns with the theory presented by Davis (in the context of developing economies but also more generally) that small jurisdictions can also be characterised by low volumes of activity in different spheres, including their laws and legal systems: see KE Davis, 'Law-Making in Small Jurisdictions' (2006) 56 *University of Toronto Law Journal* 151. Of course, aberrations do exist, depending on the socio-political context of the jurisdiction and its particular historical and contemporary narratives. Northern Ireland, for instance, is known for a large volume of legal activity in the fields of criminal justice and human rights – see below.

[48] The 'legal metropolis' term was used by one of the current authors to denote the dominant 'law producer' that individual nations or states sitting within a particular country (in other words, the archetypal small jurisdiction) would instinctively look to when contemplating legal reforms or new policy initiatives. See H Conway, 'The Death of the Legal Metropolis? Law Reform and the Family Home in Northern Ireland' (2003) 38 *Irish Jurist (NS)* 124.

[49] Giliker (n 45).

[50] For a flavour, see Davis (n 47).

legislation for the 'peace, order and good government' of the new jurisdiction, immediately raising the question as to whether the Northern Ireland legislature should, as a matter of policy and political expediency, follow developments in English law on a step-by-step basis or choose to 'plough its own furrow'.[51] By way of illustration – and relevant to the theme of this chapter – the overwhelming desire for parity with the larger jurisdiction clearly influenced the work of the Committee on Family Provision in the 1950s. In its Final Report, the Committee readily acknowledges that:

> [O]wing to the size of the community in Northern Ireland there are never likely to be any Northern Ireland textbooks on the subject and very few reported cases ... so [we] recommend that if legislation is introduced ... it should follow the Inheritance (Family Provision) Act 1938.[52]

Equally, however, there are many illustrations from this era of the still-embryonic Northern Ireland legislature expressly choosing not to adopt precisely identical statutory provisions,[53] in what might be described as bouts of 'Small Jurisdiction Syndrome'. More fundamentally, the Northern Ireland Parliament expressly rejected restrictions on testamentary freedom in the late 1930s (when England and Wales had enacted the Family Maintenance Act 1938) and there would be a 22-year wait before the broadly equivalent Inheritance (Family Provision) Act (NI) 1960 was enacted in the midst of significant opposition. Today the law of succession in Northern Ireland is broadly similar to that in England and Wales, but with several significant differences.[54] Pertinent to the *Ilott* decision, the key provisions of the

[51] On the extent to which laws should be made and developed to suit local needs in the different context of social welfare law, see L Lundy, 'Parity, Parrotry or Plagiarism? Legislating for the Unemployed Poor in Northern Ireland 1838–1995' in N Dawson, D Greer and P Ingram (eds), *One Hundred and Fifty Years of Irish Law* (Belfast, SLS Legal Publications (NI), 1996) 1.

[52] Cmd (NI) 330 (1953), [37].

[53] See, eg, Administration of Estates Act (NI) 1955 (as amended), which is similar to the Administration of Estates Act 1925, but with significant differences regarding intestate entitlement, such as no restriction on statutory next of kin, no postponement of half-blood, and minors taking an absolute interest rather than on the statutory trusts. The Charities Act (NI) 1964 incorporated a blue-pencil provision as in some Commonwealth jurisdictions and section 56 of the Trustee Act (NI) 1958 is wider than the equivalent section 57 of the Trustee Act 1925 (section 56 is in identical terms to the legislation in Bermuda, which has been invoked to allow the alteration of beneficial entitlement of trusts).

[54] See, eg, Wills and Administration Proceedings (NI) Order 1994 (similar to the Wills Act 1837 as amended by the Administration of Justice Act 1982 and the Administration of Justice Act 1985), and the Succession (NI) Order 1996 (similar to Law Reform (Succession) Act 1995, but with minor differences). The general pattern has been that Northern Ireland eventually follows where England has led, with a time lag ranging from a year to 30 years. Unfortunately, the non-functioning of the Northern Ireland Assembly (ie, the devolved legislature for Northern Ireland) for sporadic periods since its inception in 1999 has resulted in there being several recent English statutes which do not yet have an equivalent here: see, eg, the Perpetuity and Accumulation Act 2009; the Estates of Deceased Persons (Forfeiture and Law of Succession) Act 2011; the Trusts (Income and Capital) Act 2013; and the Inheritance and Trustees' Powers Act 2014. Of more recent interest, Northern Ireland did not enact any concessions to allow the virtual witnessing of wills during the recent COVID-19 pandemic.

Inheritance (Provision for Family and Dependants) (NI) Order 1979 are identical to those in the Inheritance (Provision for Family and Dependants) Act 1975.[55]

The basic structure of the court system in Northern Ireland (in order of hierarchy) is the High Court, the Northern Ireland Court of Appeal and the UK Supreme Court. It should be noted that because Northern Ireland is a separate legal jurisdiction, its courts are not strictly bound by decisions of the English courts. In theory, the Northern Ireland High Court and the Northern Ireland Court of Appeal are only bound by a decision of the Supreme Court on a case which originated in Northern Ireland. In practice, however, any decision of the Supreme Court is of the very highest persuasive authority and such decisions are to be treated as effectively binding. Even decisions of the lower English courts are treated as of high persuasive authority.[56]

The reality of legal life in such a small common law jurisdiction is that there is often no relevant Northern Ireland precedent, whether in the interpretation of statutes or entirely judge-made law. Both lawyers and judges therefore constantly rely on decisions of the English courts, only declining to follow them if there is a very strong justification for doing so. Northern Ireland practitioners and judges also rely heavily on English textbooks and commentaries. Most typically, no distinction is made in a Northern Ireland court when Counsel is citing English authority or a Northern Ireland authority and there is no requirement, or even expectation, that Northern Ireland authorities should be listed separately to English cases in the list of authorities presented to the court.

B. Specific Challenges for Property Practitioners

Private law generally has had a much lower profile than public law in England and Wales over the last few decades – something that is evidenced by the comparatively lower volume of cases reaching the highest appellate court. In Northern Ireland, private law generally, but property law and – more specifically – what might be called 'private client' law, have all provoked little interest, with an attendant lack of legislation, a relatively modest body of jurisprudence from the courts in Northern Ireland and only one private law decision having been

[55] The two pieces of legislation are not precisely identical and Northern Ireland has not adopted any of the amendments introduced by the Inheritance and Trustees' Powers Act 2014. However, the basis of a claim, including one by an adult child, is identical.

[56] See generally B Dickson, *The Legal System of Northern Ireland*, 5th edn (Belfast, SLS Legal Publications (NI), 2025), where the author describes courts in Northern Ireland as being 'deferential' to earlier decisions of the English courts. Similarly, courts in Northern Ireland will treat decisions of the Court of Appeal in England and Wales as being strongly persuasive and will follow them unless there is good reason not to do so – see, eg, *Beaufort Developments v Gilbert Ash* [1997] NI 42. For a recent illustration of the dangers faced by lawyers in Northern Ireland advising on similar but not identical, statutory schemes, see *RM's Application for Judicial Review* [2024] UKSC 7.

heard by the Supreme Court.[57] In contrast, the cup of those lawyers, researchers and activists who are interested in public law and criminal justice in Northern Ireland floweth over with riches. The reality is that the socio-political context that dominates our cultural narrative has also dominated our legal narrative, as is confirmed by an analysis of Supreme Court decisions which have emanated from Northern Ireland.[58]

The challenges of 'keeping private law alive and thriving in UK universities' and the attendant consequences of developing and retaining private law academics was articulated by Lord Burrows almost a decade ago.[59] However, the problems are particularly acute in Northern Ireland, with a diminishing pool of academic expertise and a dearth of specialist private law legal texts.[60] Finally, it is also worth pointing out that, due to budgetary pressures, the Northern Ireland Law Commission has effectively been non-operational since April 2015, when it was wound down due to financial pressures facing the Department of Justice in Northern Ireland.[61] What Morris describes as a '[l]imited or non-existent infrastructure for systemic development and reform of the law'[62] is a significant barrier to substantive and reflective legal change in Northern Ireland. From a property law perspective, it means that ongoing projects around land law reform have simply 'withered on the vine',[63] and there seems little prospect of

[57] *Peninsula Securities Ltd v Dunnes Stores (Bangor) Ltd* [2020] 3 WLR 521. In its decision, the UK Supreme Court invoked the 1966 Practice Direction of the House of Lords ([1966] 1 WLR 1234) to overrule the 1967 decision of the House of Lords in *Esso Petroleum Co Ltd v Harper's Garage (Stourport) Ltd* [1968] AC 269. It has been suggested that the so-called 'gay cake' case (*Lee v Ashers Baking Co Ltd* [2020] AC 413) might also be classified as a 'private law' decision – see D Capper, 'Restrictive Covenants, Use of Land, and the Restraint of Trade Doctrine' (2021) 71 *Northern Ireland Legal Quarterly* 132.

[58] B Dickson and C McCormick, 'Northern Ireland Dimensions to the First Decade of the United Kingdom Supreme Court' (2020) 83 *MLR* 1133. While Dickson and McCormick conclude that the Supreme Court has established itself as an 'indispensable component' of the legal system in Northern Ireland, we suggest that this is not the case for private law in the jurisdiction, and for property law disputes in particular, where any potential to be involved here has not (yet) been realised.

[59] A Burrows, 'Challenges for Private Law in the 21st Century' (2016) Oxford Legal Studies Research Paper No 3/2016, available at SSRN: https://ssrn.com/abstract=2710270 or http://dx.doi.org/10.2139/ssrn.2710270.

[60] For instance, the seminal text on land law in Northern Ireland (and long since out of print) dates back to 1997: JCW Wylie, *Irish Land Law*, 3rd edn (London, Butterworths, 1997).

[61] In an appearance before the Committee for Justice in the Northern Ireland Assembly in March 2024, the Lady Chief Justice of Northern Ireland, the Rt Hon Dame Siobhan Keegan, emphasised that Northern Ireland 'loses out' by not having a structured law reform agenda and called for the Commission to be reinstated – see https://aims.niassembly.gov.uk/officialreport/minutesofevidencereport.aspx?AgendaId=32349&eveID=16578. However, it would be remiss not to record the achievements of the very cost-effective Law Reform Advisory Committee for Northern Ireland (LRAC), which operated between 1989 and 2007. The LRAC was a specialist independent body tasked with identifying and advising on specific areas of law reform in Northern Ireland, and the current authors both served as members. It was chaired by, inter alia, two very esteemed Chancery lawyers, the late Lord Carswell and Sir Paul Girvan, and was responsible for initiating several pieces of legislation, including that on business tenancies, deeds and escrows and marriage.

[62] Morris (n 43) 4. The author was articulating an issue facing small jurisdictions more generally.

[63] See, eg, Northern Ireland Law Commission, *Report on Land Law Reform – NILC 8* (2010), which proposed major reforms to modernise and simplify land law in Northern Ireland.

smaller-scale yet meaningful reforms enacted or proposed by the Commission[64] being taken forward today.[65]

V. *GUEST* IN THE NORTHERN IRELAND CONTEXT

The small population of Northern Ireland and the obvious challenges that this brings to a common law legal system have already been noted. In addition to its size, Northern Ireland has other specific characteristics that are relevant here.

A. Still a 'Country of Small [and Parsimonious and Taciturn] Farmers'

The debates of the Northern Ireland Parliament in the 1930s–1960s that preceded various statutory reforms in the property and succession law spheres were replete with frequent references that 'we are a country of small farmers'.[66] As we approach the second quarter of the twenty-first century, farms in Northern Ireland are still generally family-owned and of much more modest acreage than those in England and Wales.[67] Recent research from the University of Exeter confirms that farmers in Northern Ireland are less likely to make wills than their other UK counterparts.[68] Any practitioner from Northern Ireland will attest to the fact that even fewer of them have written partnership agreements, and the limited number that are in existence rarely reflect the 'position on the ground' or are compatible with the terms of a will.

Aligned with this, Northern Ireland is the most economically deprived area of the UK.[69] For many farming families, it will be necessary to supplement the farm income by one or other members being employed elsewhere while assisting on the farm in the evenings, weekends and during holidays – something that can

[64] Or by the Law Reform Advisory Committee for Northern Ireland as its predecessor.

[65] In some instances, these reforms resulted in Northern Ireland adopting a different legal approach from England and Wales – see, eg, art 34 of the Property (NI) Order 1997, which significantly alters the rules concerning the passing of the benefit and burden of freehold covenants in Northern Ireland where such covenants were entered into after January 2000. Of course, not all property law developments in Northern Ireland display this more radical approach, and the overall picture has generally been more mixed; see H Conway and S Grattan, 'Northern Ireland: A Forgotten Jurisdiction. Falling Behind or Forging Ahead?' in E Cooke (ed), *Modern Studies in Property Law*, Vol 2 (Oxford, Hart Publishing, 2003) 203.

[66] Usually as a means of special pleading to reject a particular reform.

[67] This in itself presents challenges as to how the UK tax system, including agricultural property relief for inheritance tax for a farmhouse on a small farmholding, operates equitably as between Northern Ireland and England and Wales.

[68] R Wheeler, M Lobley and R Soffe, *Farm Succession and Inheritance in England, Scotland and Northern Ireland*, July 2020, Centre for Rural Policy Research, University of Exeter, https://socialsciences.exeter.ac.uk/media/universityofexeter/research/microsites/centreforruralpolicyresearch/pdfs/Inheritance_and_succession_Final_report_for_NFUM_FINAL_version_30.07.20.pdf.

[69] See, eg, Statistics NI, *Northern Ireland Poverty and Income Inequality Report* (2024).

also be the genesis of a proprietary estoppel claim. There is also a reluctance to spend money on professional services, particularly those that do not yield an immediate return, such as estate planning.[70] No doubt, no Lincoln's Inn client 'of testamentary capacity would expect a professional to work for nothing',[71] but there will be few involved in private client work in Northern Ireland who have not met clients who, although as capable of making a will as their lawyer, nonetheless expect not to be charged. The daily lot of the average private client practitioner is also very different from, in particular, their counterparts based in the more affluent south-east of England. For example, few clients with descendants are troubled by inheritance tax because the nil-rate bands, ordinary and residence, generally exhaust the chargeable estate – at least for those with spouses or registered civil partners. The small volume of work means that it is less viable for solicitors to specialise,[72] and a large number of sole-practitioner and two or three partner firms still exist.[73]

There is also the Northern Ireland 'psyche'. While 'taciturn and undemonstrative men'[74] are obviously not unique to the farming context here, there is undoubtedly a preponderance of 'strong, silent types'. The culture is not to show emotion and not to discuss private matters such as intergenerational transfers even within the family. Anyone who has practised in the area (as one of the authors has done) will be familiar with the retort, in response to a lawyer's enquiries as to promises and representations, that the deceased 'was a man of his word and said it only once' – and never with an independent witness present.

B. The Peculiarities of Practice: Procedural Rules and Costs in Northern Ireland

There is a tendency for academic commentators to ignore the role played in estate litigation, in the 'real world', by the rules of procedure and the burden of costs. It is important to note that what might loosely be termed as 'practice' is fundamentally different in Northern Ireland on the one hand and England and Wales on the

[70] Note the exhortation by Deeny J, the then Chancery Judge, encouraging lay people who own property to make wills and with a solicitor: *Kinney v McKittrick* [2011] NI Ch 24, [26].

[71] As noted by James Kessler KC in his *Drafting Trusts and Will Trusts* series.

[72] However, the Northern Ireland branch of the Society of Trusts and Estate Practitioners (STEP) has done sterling work since its inception in 2006 to promote specialisation in wills and estates matters.

[73] In 2022, 27 per cent of NI law firms comprised a sole practitioner, a further 25 per cent had a sole principal and a total of 93 per cent of firms had less than four partners: see the Solicitor Profession in Northern Ireland, www.lawsoc-ni.org/study-into-solicitor-profession-in-northern-ireland-published. Conversely, Belfast also has the largest number of large international law firms in any UK city other than London, which is one of the most pressing issues for the legal profession in Northern Ireland (and by extension for those of us who teach undergraduate law students).

[74] Of that central to the proprietary estoppel claim in *Thorner v Major* [2009] 3 All ER 945.

other hand. Northern Ireland has not (or at least not yet) adopted a counterpart to the civil procedure rules post-Woolf.[75] This gulf in practice is especially evident in the Northern Ireland Chancery Division. English-based clients who encounter a Northern Ireland dimension to an estate dispute (most typically large English charities that are beneficiaries under a Northern Ireland will that is being challenged on the basis of proprietary estoppel or an inheritance claim) are often frustrated by what they consider to be lack of speed, and the fact that procedural time limits (like Italian traffic lights) appear to be 'advisory' only.

There is also the entrenched 'seize' culture to settle cases very late when high costs have already been incurred (most typically on the morning of the first day of trial and sometimes on the second or subsequent mornings). As in England and Wales, costs are always at the discretion of the judge, with the default position being that 'costs follow the event'. The reality (again, based on one of the current author's extensive practical experience) in Northern Ireland is that a high preponderance of estate disputes will settle at some stage before the claim runs to full hearing and adjudication, but the estate beneficiaries will invariably end up bearing the costs in order to get a settlement 'over the line'.

C. Proprietary Estoppel Cases in Northern Ireland Post-*Guest*

One of the aims of this chapter was to explore the impact that the Supreme Court decision in *Guest* might have on the application of the doctrine of proprietary estoppel in Northern Ireland, both in the judicial decisions of the Northern Ireland Chancery Division (and the Court of Appeal) and in the increasing number of compromise settlements (whether following arbitration, mediation or otherwise). Most of the spate of first-instance English decisions that culminated in the Supreme Court judgments in *Guest* have involved farming disputes.[76] Likewise, in Northern Ireland, the majority of proprietary estoppel disputes (often linked with partnership issues) involve farms, albeit invariably of a much lower value.[77] The reported decisions are only the tip of a litigation

[75] The Woolf reforms (named after the Lord Woolf) were a series of reforms designed to make the civil justice system more accessible, fair and consistent, and resulted in the Civil Procedure Rules 1998 in England and Wales. Northern Ireland's reticence to adopt similar measures is discussed in D Capper, 'Keeping Woolf from the Door: The Reform of Civil Procedure in Northern Ireland' (1999) 50 *Northern Ireland Legal Quarterly* 434.

[76] These cases include *Suggitt v Suggitt* [2012] EWCA Civ 114, *Thompson v Thompson* [2018] EWHC 1338, *Gee v Gee* [2018] EWHC 1393, *Davies v Davies* [2016] EWCA 463, *Moore v Moore* [2018] EWCA 2669 and *Habberfield v Habberfield* [2019] EWCA 890. Land values (and the number of farming estoppel cases) can be expected to increase yet further if the current UK government honours the promise made in the October 2024 Budget to build 1.5 million homes over the course of this Parliament – see J Butler, 'Value Judgment' (2024) 6 *STEP Journal*, https://journal.step.org/step-journal-issue-6-2024/value-judgement.

[77] See, eg, *Re Little* [2007] NI Ch 7, *Re Johnston* [2008] NI Ch 11, *Kinney v McKittrick* [2011] NI Ch 24, *Graham v Graham* [2021] NICA 25 and, most recently post-*Guest*, *Irvine v Drain* [2024] NI Ch 1.

iceberg, for – as has been noted – the vast majority of proprietary estoppel disputes will settle before or even during trial.

It is the authors' view that the Supreme Court decision in *Guest* will encourage more nuisance claims in Northern Ireland. Prior to the ruling(s), much of the debate during pre-trial negotiations in the standard estoppel case concentrated on whether a 'detriment-loss' or an 'expectation-loss' analysis was appropriate, with the reality being that in many cases where one or other of the components was weak (whether representation or reliance), parties were readily persuaded to settle on a 'detriment-loss' basis. In other words, 'your [or their] case is not the strongest but you [or they] will be awarded something'. Now that the starting point appears to be expectation, it is foreseeable that fewer claimants will be prepared to compromise on a detriment-loss basis, shifting the focus more to the nature of the promise itself as a means of sifting out weaker cases. As has been noted, it is not uncommon for the alleged promise to have been made only once, with only the representee present,[78] so the representee and his or her advisers may be emboldened to risk that the representee's oral evidence will persuade the judge, now that the ultimate 'prize' is most likely to be the representee's full expectation being satisfied.

The jury is still out on the practical outcome of *Guest* in the Northern Ireland courts as there has only been one reported decision, namely *Irvine v Drain*.[79] Rather against the trend, the plaintiffs did not succeed. The judge, Huddleston J, the Chancery Judge in Northern Ireland and who, unusually for a Northern Ireland judge, was previously a private client solicitor, makes only one reference to *Guest* in his 12-page judgment and then only to refer to Lord Briggs' endorsement of the succinct summary of the legal principles of proprietary estoppel in the decision of the English Court of Appeal in *Uglow v Uglow*.[80] Speaking extra-judicially at a joint academic-practitioner event at Queen's University Law School in June 2024, the same month as the judgment in *Irvine v Drain* was handed down, Huddleston J side-stepped any discussion of *Guest*, but again endorsed the *Uglow* principles as encapsulating the doctrine of proprietary estoppel as he understood it. Whether *Guest* has a more pervasive influence in future cases in Northern Ireland therefore remains to be seen.

D. The Nuisance Claim and Potential Threat to Testamentary Freedom in Northern Ireland

If one accepts, as the current authors and others do, that testamentary freedom should be the starting point in intergenerational wealth transfer,[81] it is important that it is protected. Academics have long argued that complete testamentary

[78] Notwithstanding the fact that *Guest* involved a living plaintiff, it is still the case that the vast majority of representors are deceased – or have lost mental capacity and are unable to give evidence.
[79] *Irvine v Drain* (n 77).
[80] *Uglow v Uglow* [2004] EWCA Civ 987.
[81] A key theme in the Supreme Court's judgment in *Ilott* (n 9).

freedom is a myth,[82] not just because of express restraints such as discretionary family protection mechanisms, but also in light of more subtle restraints whereby the courts have sought to protect certain 'expected' and morally acceptable testation patterns in, inter alia, the interpretation of the will itself, of the statutory formalities and of the testamentary capacity principles. However, the current authors consider that there is a much more pernicious threat to testamentary freedom whereby parties are effectively forced to settle cases.

Concerns have been expressed for some time that 'those advising clients can all too readily see estoppel as a panacea for all ills'.[83] Aligned with this is the prevalence of the nuisance claim (which pervades all categories of estate dispute) and is perhaps the single biggest threat to testamentary freedom in Northern Ireland.[84] The estate will be diminished by both the amount paid to the nuisance claimant (however modest) and legal costs (which in a nuisance claim will invariably exceed the award).[85] When confronted with a palpably weak claim, making a nuisance payment may be more cost-effective than risking court and, in particular, disproportionately excessive legal costs. When one adds long, convoluted judgments with no clear principles into this mix, one potentially ends up with a much higher preponderance of nuisance claims.

Of course, not everything can be laid at the door of the Supreme Court. Other factors, in addition to those listed above, in many ways create the perfect storm: judges with lengthy lists and limited time to hear cases; the attendant judicial 'encouragement' to settle cases; the trend to send people to mediation and again the encouragement to settle there – with some mediators referring to their 'success rate'.[86] Against this backdrop, appellate judgments from the Supreme Court as the final arbiter that point in different directions are certainly unhelpful. As Davis has noted about small jurisdictions more generally, '[l]egal uncertainty that leads to divergent beliefs about the outcome of trial may impede informal settlement of disputes'.[87] Like so many legal conflicts, proprietary estoppel claims are 'precipitated by incompatible aspirations involving access to

[82] MB Leslie, 'The Myth of Testamentary Freedom' (1996) 38 *Arizona Law Review* 235.

[83] M Dixon, 'Proprietary Estoppel: The Law of Farms and Families' [2019] *Conveyancer and Property Lawyer* 89, 89 (repeating similar concerns aired a decade earlier; see M Dixon, 'Estoppel: A Panacea for All Wills' [1999] *Conveyancer and Property Lawyer* 46).

[84] Of course, in the paradigm case of *Guest*, the parties were still alive; however, the resultant litigation and its outcome had the effect of subverting the parents' testamentary freedom at significant financial cost.

[85] Sadly there are now several reported estate dispute decisions in which the amount of the award is far exceeded by the legal costs of that party. One illustration is the mutual wills case of *Shovelar and Others v Lane* [2011] EWCA Civ 802. Ward LJ, expressing horror that the claimant's costs alone were £320,000 when the entire estate was worth £134,000, added that the 'great British public must think that something has gone wrong somewhere': [2011] EWCA Civ 802, [61].

[86] See generally B Speers, 'When is Mediation Not Mediation?' *The Writ (Journal of the Law Society of NI)*, Winter 2024.

[87] Davis (n 47) 160. The author makes the point that the resultant formal resolution of disputes in areas of law characterised by uncertainty increases aggregate costs, and has implications from a law and economics perspective; see, eg, RA Posner, 'An Economic Approach to Legal Procedure and Judicial Administration' (1973) 2 *Journal of Legal Studies* 399.

finite resources';[88] the fact that most of these claims 'hide a larger story about fractured relationships'[89] and trigger intense emotions for everyone involved presents additional challenges for reaching a mediated settlement.[90]

Perhaps what Northern Ireland urgently needs is: less judicial enthusiasm for foisting mediation on the parties when the estate defendant has expressed the view, in good faith, that the case as pleaded has no merit; renewed judicial enthusiasm for weeding out palpably weak cases; and listing these for hearing expeditiously, in accordance with procedural time limits. If claimants fail to succeed in court, they should be condemned in indemnity costs, and the costs decision published so that advisers are properly equipped to advise future nuisance claimants. Whether the judiciary has the appetite or resources for this particular course of action remains to be seen. In the meantime, those advising on the potential merits of such claims still lack the sense of legal clarity that might have been expected (no pun intended) from *Guest*, with its two very persuasive judgments. Of course, there is some helpful guidance in the decision. However, like *Ilott*, the Supreme Court's ruling in *Guest* will generate more uncertainty, and while the focus has been on Northern Ireland, some of the problems that we have highlighted (for example, the nuisance claim) will also present themselves elsewhere. In this sense, *Guest* may turn out to be another important opportunity missed.

VI. CONCLUSION

> [Appellate] courts perform a public service by delivering binding decisions which develop and clarify the law. But it is a public disservice for this major source of law to be contained in judgments which might take half a day to read and require close re-reading in order to discern subtleties, especially differences of emphasis and formulation between different members of the same appeal panel.[91]

A decade ago, Neil Andrews concluded the paper from which the above quotation is taken by observing that a major challenge facing the UK Supreme Court is writing shorter judgments that are easier to understand and apply.[92] The virtues of being more concise and of a more judicious use of judicial editing have been highlighted more recently by Lord Burrows in a 2021 conference paper, though his Lordship also acknowledged that judgment writing 'is a particularly difficult form of legal writing' and that the 'potential audience … is very wide and varied'.[93]

[88] J Macfarlane, 'Why Do People Settle?' (2000) 46 *McGill Law Journal* 663, 691.
[89] Dixon, 'Proprietary Estoppel' (n 83) 89.
[90] See generally Macfarlane (n 88); HL Munsinger and DR Philbin, 'Why Can't They Settle: The Psychology of Relational Disputes' (2016–17) 18 *Cardozo Journal of Conflict Resolution* 311.
[91] Andrews (n 3) 3, who suggests that one solution would be to impose a word limit on judgments.
[92] ibid 18.
[93] Lord Burrows JSC, 'Judgment Writing: A Personal Perspective', Annual Conference of Judges of the Superior Court in Ireland, May 2021, https://supremecourt.uk/uploads/judgment_writing_a_personal_perspective_lord_burrows_aa1b4f5676.pdf.

Perhaps the danger is not simply one of length and trawling through pages of arguments from counsel, extracts from previous judgments and expansive judicial reasoning; rather, it is length and the absence of a definitive statement of legal principle. To paraphrase a different judicial comment, such judgments can give more 'grist to academics' mills'.[94] However, they also give more grist to (potential) litigants' mills and are problematic for those in the legal profession who are at the quotidian sharp end of 'how law works'.

To underline a central theme in this chapter, dicta and dissent have important roles to play in a common law legal system, and the latter is a good thing when collective decision-making is simply not possible. However, just as the well-known quotation implores 'all things in moderation', we would argue that lengthy dissents in bare majority decisions have significant potential for generating doubt and indecision.[95] When the Supreme Court gets a rare opportunity to pronounce on a property law topic where discretion is concerned, it is better to have some clarity. Of course, bright-line rules may not be possible with a topic as necessarily fluid and malleable as proprietary estoppel that operates on the basis of core principles as opposed to set legal rules. Regardless, a decision of the highest appellate court should, ideally, still be about probing the juristic concepts while distilling legal principles that will guide both judges deciding future cases and those advising the parties. Otherwise, the result – paradoxically – is to generate more litigation and, in doing so, potentially to subvert testamentary freedom. As Andrews has argued, 'the "duty" to give reasons' has become a tyrannical procedural precept'[96] – and, in the Northern Ireland context in particular, we would argue that it is a precept that is far from helpful.

The final word is reserved for Martin Dixon, who draws the analogy with the spate of litigation in the 1970s and 1980s concerning the family home and beneficial interests acquired under a constructive trust,[97] which culminated (initially) in the then House of Lords ruling in *Lloyds Bank v Rosset*.[98] Lamentably, *Guest* has not brought the same clarity to an area of law that is also beset with uncertainties surrounding real property and who is entitled to what. As a result, understanding, explaining and predicting the proper reach of proprietary estoppel in any given case is – to borrow Dixon's own descriptor – still akin to an exercise in 'trying to herd cats'.[99]

[94] To paraphrase the comments of Baroness Hale of Richmond in *OBG Ltd v Allan* [2007] UKHL 21, [303], albeit that they were made in advocating for single majority judgments in the then House of Lords.

[95] By way of an interesting comparison with the 104-page *Guest* decision, virtually the entire body of reported jurisprudence on the Settled Land Acts 1882 to 1890, which still apply in Northern Ireland, amounts to 270 pages (comprising 37 cases).

[96] Andrews (n 3) 8.

[97] Dixon, 'Proprietary Estoppel' (n 83); Dixon (n 7).

[98] *Lloyds Bank v Rosset* [1991] 1 AC 107. The constructive trust 'can of worms' was, of course, re-opened by the Supreme Court in *Stack v Dowden* [2007] 2 AC 432 and *Jones v Kernott* [2012] 1 AC 276, albeit in relation to constructive trusts where title to the family home was in joint names (as opposed to one person's name as in *Rosset* and other cases).

[99] Dixon, 'Proprietary Estoppel' (n 83) 89.

6

The Supreme Court: 15 Years of Shaping 'Property'

Defining Property and Socio-legal Themes*

VICTORIA EVANS AND CATHERINE DE CONTRERAS**

I. INTRODUCTION

THE SUPREME COURT of the United Kingdom[1] turned 15 in 2024. This milestone provides the ideal opportunity to consider how the Supreme Court has shaped the concept of 'property' through its judgments. As the Court's own materials tell us: 'The impact of Supreme Court decisions extend far beyond the parties involved in any given case, shaping our society, and directly affecting our everyday lives.'[2] This chapter aims to elucidate some of the 'themes' that arise from a consideration of Supreme Court decisions relating to 'property'. This work is important as while many of the cases we discuss have been studied and debated in great detail, others

* The second part of this project focuses on the remaining eight themes: Catherine de Contreras and Victoria Evans, 'The Supreme Court: 15 Years of Shaping "Property": Part Two: The Power and Role of the Court and Policy (and Other) Reasoning Themes' (2025) 89 *Conveyancer and Property Lawyer* 30.

** Emails: vicki.evans@kcl.ac.uk and catherine.de_contreras@kcl.ac.uk. The authors are very grateful to their colleagues at KCL who gave feedback on early iterations of this project at the Staff Seminar Series and the King's Private Law Forum. We would also like to thank the organisers and attendees at Modern Studies in Property Law at Cambridge and the Association of Law Property and Society Conference at Pepperdine University for the opportunity to present this chapter and for their helpful comments on earlier drafts. We would like to thank our research assistant, Lee Curran, who was a vital part of this research: thanks also to the King's Undergraduate Research Fund (KURF) scheme and the Dickson Poon School of Law for the funding to hire Lee. Without this (and him), the research would not have been possible. Finally, a big thank you to Dr Jenny Russell for her generous help with editing this chapter.

[1] Hereinafter referred to as 'the Supreme Court' or 'the Court'.

[2] 'Significance of the Supreme Court', www.supremecourt.uk/about-the-court#significance-to-the-uk.

have not, and this provides an opportunity for two key contributions. First, we give the decisions a fresh review within thematic groupings. Second, we contrast how specific themes are dealt with across decisions and analyse their internal consistency. This chapter is the first instalment in a series of papers for this project and it intends to give a doctrinal and descriptive overview of both the 'property' decisions handed down by the Supreme Court, and the first seven themes that arise from consideration of them, as a foundation for future exploration.

Section II explains this chapter's methodological approach and section III explores the seven themes that are the focus of this paper. In section III, we also consider how each theme arises and has been developed in the case law.

II. METHODOLOGY

To explore how the Supreme Court has shaped the concept of 'property', we surveyed all decisions handed down by the Supreme Court since its establishment in 2009 until 2024 to identify any that had a 'property' dimension. 'Property' was initially given a generous and broad interpretation, the aim being to be over-inclusive at the outset. As the research developed, some areas were sidelined[3] to allow for a focus on cases more strictly relevant to 'core' property rights and law.[4]

The research, which was supported by a research assistant,[5] used thematic analysis as a method to identify, analyse and report patterns (themes) within the data (which were the judgments of the Supreme Court).[6] This involved identifying and reading all the cases which had a 'property element' and adopting an inductive/bottom-up coding approach.[7] Here, the authors summarised the decisions and pulled out quotations from the cases, and at the same time jotted down any

[3] This included those that focused purely on intellectual property rights, those that related primarily to criminal law (mainly those relating to proceeds of crime and related legislation), cases that could be considered part of family law, tax decisions solely planning decisions etc.

[4] We kept cases related to land law (eg, proprietary estoppel, leases, covenants, easements and co-ownership), other property law cases (eg, those relating to chattels and anything relating to the property torts, such as trespass (to land and goods) and private nuisance), and equity and trusts cases (eg, those relating to wills, trusts and insolvency). This is what we consider the 'core' of 'property'. Judgement calls were made in this process, and if an author was unsure, they asked for a second opinion. We soon realised that difficult cuts needed to be made, and lines drawn, as it was possible to 'see' property in many cases.

[5] Thank you to our research assistant Lee Curran who worked very hard on the project.

[6] V Braun and V Clarke, 'Using Thematic Analysis in Psychology' (2006) 3 *Qualitative Research in Psychology* 77, 79. Inspiration of how this can work as a method within property law was gained through consideration of E Walsh, 'Security of Tenure in the Private Rented Sector in England: Balancing the Competing Property Rights of Landlords and Tenants' in B McFarlane and S Agnew (eds), *Modern Studies in Property Law*, vol 10 (Oxford, Hart Publishing, 2019).

[7] Braun and Clarke (n 6) 83.

keywords/terms/themes. At the end of this process, all the keywords were collated to identify broader themes, which were then refined.[8] These themes were also grouped into larger categories for ease of discussion. As this was a relatively small data set, manual coding was employed.[9]

The themes and categories raised are presented in Table 6.1 below. The initial papers arising from this research project seek to explore the core and re-occurring themes that emerged through this process: the 'keyness' of a theme is not necessarily dependent on quantifiable measures, as discussed by Braun and Clarke, 'but rather on whether it captures something important in relation to the overall research question'.[10] Within each theme, we focus on analysing and comparing the cases that emerged as the strongest illustrations of their particular theme. For most themes, this was an exhaustive list; however, for space reasons, where there was overlap with other parts of the two papers, cases were omitted. This chapter, as the first instalment of our broader project,[11] focuses on the first seven themes that fall within the 'Defining Property' and 'Socio-legal' category, which are bolded in Table 6.1.

Table 6.1 Themes and categories identified through thematic analysis

Category	Individual themes
'Defining Property' themes	**1. Understanding the Essential Characteristics of Property Rights** **2. The Boundaries of Property** **3. Defining Key Terms in Relation to Land and Property**
'Socio-legal' themes	**1. Balancing the Rights of Property Holders Against Those Who are Less Propertied or Relatively Less Possessed** **2. Rights of the Property Holder as Balanced against the Community at Large** **3. Homelessness and the Concept of Home** **4. Gender**
'The Power and Role of the Court' themes	1. The Relationship between the Legislature and the Court 2. The Power of the Courts over the Property of Others 3. The Influence of Previous Decisions 4. The Relevance of the Intentions of the Parties (and Interpreting Them)

(continued)

[8] See ibid 79 for the process adopted. This was also the process used by Walsh (n 6).

[9] As opposed to using a qualitative data analysis software package such as NVivo.

[10] Braun and Clarke (n 6) 82.

[11] The second part of this project focuses on the remaining eight themes: Catherine de Contreras and Victoria Evans, 'The Supreme Court: 15 Years of Shaping "Property": Part Two: The Power and Role of the Court and Policy (and Other) Reasoning Themes' (2025) 89 *Conveyancer and Property Lawyer* 30.

Table 6.1 *(Continued)*

Category	Individual themes
The Influence of Policy (or Other Reasoning) themes	1. Public Policy Influence 2. The Balance Struck in Cases Where One Party was a Bank/ Commercial Lender 3. Human Rights and Civil Liberties Influence 4. Modernising the Law

III. THEMES

A. 'Defining Property' Themes

i. Understanding the Essential Characteristics of Property Rights

'[T]here is certainly no consensus on the definition of what property is.'[12]

Any search for an authoritative definition of property ends with a (seemingly endless) list of important elements or characteristics of property rights. The usual starting point is *National Provincial Bank v Ainsworth*,[13] where Lord Wilberforce said that 'before a right or an interest could be admitted into the category of property, it must be definable, identifiable by third parties, capable in its nature of assumption by third parties, and have some degree of permanence or stability'.[14] Usual additions to this list are the characteristics of 'certainty, exclusivity, control and assignability',[15] or the incidents of 'alienability, excludability and exigibility',[16] depending on the context in which a definition is sought. This theme explores how decisions of the Supreme Court help us to understand these different features and their importance, and to draw inferences about property more generally. This theme explores the characteristics of (i) permanence and stability and (ii) excludability and exclusion. We do not suggest that the Court adopts a specific theory, but instead highlight the two characteristics of property that came through strongly in a variety of scenarios in which the Court's interaction with them calls for analysis.

a. Degree of Permanence and Stability

An important element of property rights is their permanence and stability; the idea that property rights continue and remain effective, constant and enforceable.

[12] J-P Robe, *Property, Power and Politics* (Bristol, Bristol University Press, 2000) 44.
[13] *National Provincial Bank v Ainsworth* [1965] AC 1175.
[14] ibid 1247–48.
[15] See UK Jurisdictional Task Force, *Legal Statement on Cryptoassets and Smart Contracts*, https://technation.io/wp-content/uploads/2019/11/6.6056_JO_Cryptocurrencies_Statement_FINAL_WEB_111119-1.pdf, [39].
[16] M Bridge et al, *The Law of Personal Property*, 3rd edn (London, Sweet & Maxwell, 2021) [1.008].

Some of the literature surrounding this idea focuses on how permanence means that rights can be enforced in bankruptcy or insolvency proceedings,[17] and there are Supreme Court cases which illustrate this characteristic of property.[18] More broadly, the idea of permanence is that a person's proprietary entitlement is protected, enduring and consistent in application and extent. However, many Supreme Court decisions seem to undermine this idea to varying degrees, questioning the continuing relevance of this 'distinguishing feature' of property rights.

For example, the mere existence of compulsory acquisition diminishes the enduring nature of proprietary rights. And even though the Court recognised in *R (Sainsbury's Supermarkets Ltd) v Wolverhampton City Council*[19] that compulsory acquisition was a 'serious invasion of proprietary rights'[20] which required a strict approach to the application of planning law principles, the fact that proprietary rights can be interfered with or removed on the basis of ordinary planning principles allows us to question the centrality of permanence and stability to the definition of a property right. The same could be argued with respect to *Jones v Kernott*,[21] where the Court held that the extent of a beneficial interest in land through a common intention constructive trust could change over time – in effect, changing the property rights of the two cohabitating parties on the basis of 'logical inferences' made by the judge about the parties' proprietary holdings in view of the context pertaining to their relationship and break-up.

More recently, questions about permanence arose in relation to restrictive covenants over land (both freehold and leasehold) in two different contexts (and jurisdictions): *Alexander Devine Children's Cancer Trust v Housing Solutions Ltd*[22] and *Peninsula Securities Ltd v Dunnes Stores (Bangor) Ltd (Northern Ireland)*.[23] Both decisions recognised that there was scope to challenge and remove covenants, the former on the basis of section 84 of the Law of Property Act (LPA) 1925 and the latter on the basis that the covenant was an unreasonable restraint on trade. While ultimately finding that the covenant in *Peninsula* was valid as it was the type of covenant that 'passed into the accepted and normal currency of commercial or contractual or conveyancing relations',[24] the case shows the ability of other right holders to question and seek removal of other parties' proprietary entitlements. In *Devine*, the Supreme Court was given the opportunity to clarify the remit of discretion in the modification or discharge of

[17] Bridge described this as the touchstone for establishing the proprietary nature of rights. See M Bridge, *Personal Property Law*, 4th edn (Oxford, Oxford University Press, 2015) 42.

[18] See, for example, *FHR European Ventures LLP v Cedar Capital Partners LLC* [2014] UKSC 45, which recognised a proprietary right, enabling the claimant to trace even in bankruptcy/insolvency to the detriment of creditors. But see also *Akers v Samba Financial Group* [2017] UKSC 6, which held, in contrast, that a 'limited' property right of the kind concerned there could be overridden.

[19] *R (Sainsbury's Supermarkets Ltd) v Wolverhampton City Council* [2010] UKSC 20.

[20] ibid [71].

[21] *Jones v Kernott* [2011] UKSC 53.

[22] *Alexander Devine Children's Cancer Trust v Housing Solutions Ltd* [2020] UKSC 45.

[23] *Peninsula Securities Ltd v Dunnes Stores (Bangor) Ltd (Northern Ireland)* [2020] UKSC 36.

[24] ibid [46].

covenants under section 84 LPA for the first time. The decision itself held that the cynical breach by the developer by building in breach of covenant could be considered at the discretion stage of the section 84 test. But, in doing so, the Court confirmed that there is a potentially significant role for judicial discretion within this section and generously interpreted the provision. This stream of cases allows us to question whether permanence and stability really do continue to play a significant role in property rights.

b. Excludability and Exclusion

While the importance of permanence appears to be diminishing, the importance of exclusion and excludability does not seem to be suffering from quite the same fate. The right to exclude is often said to be at the heart of property rights; depending on one's theoretical persuasion, it might constitute an important stick within the bundle of rights or be the irreducible core and basis of property.[25] The importance of a property owner's right to exclude is emphasised in a number of Supreme Court judgments.

For example, while the Court in *Secretary of State for Environment, Food and Rural Affairs v Meier*[26] decided that it could not justify possession orders over land not yet occupied by travellers,[27] it was clear that owners have strong rights to remove people from land, enforcing their right to exclude. More recently, a similar issue relating to how local authorities can protect their land from possession by the travelling community came up in *Wolverhampton City Council v London Gypsies and Travellers*,[28] where the Court held that there is a power to grant injunctions against persons who are unknown and unidentified at the date of the grant of the injunction, and who have not yet performed, or even threatened to perform, the acts which the injunction prohibits; these are known as 'newcomer injunctions'. This remedy bolsters landowners' exclusionary rights and shows that courts are willing to take significant steps to protect these rights.

However, in *Fearn v Board of Trustees of the Tate Gallery*,[29] the Court arguably questioned the importance of the right to exclude. Here, it was held that visual intrusion caused by people looking or peering into flats and taking photos

[25] We recognise that these are not the only two conceptions of property, but they are the dominant conceptions. For further discussion on these two conceptions, see the works of Hohfeld for the former, which is said to lay the intellectual foundations for the theory: WN Hohfeld, 'Some Fundamental Legal Conceptions as Applied to Judicial Reasoning' (1913–14) 23 *Yale LJ* 16, 21–22; WN Hohfeld, 'Fundamental Legal Conceptions as Applied in Judicial Reasoning' (1916–17) 26 *Yale LJ* 710, 720. For the latter, see S Douglas and B McFarlane, 'Defining Property Rights' in J Penner and H Smith (eds), *Philosophical Foundations of Property Law* (Oxford, Oxford University Press, 2013).

[26] *Secretary of State for Environment, Food and Rural Affairs v Meier* [2009] UKSC 11.

[27] ibid [64].

[28] *Wolverhampton City Council v London Gypsies and Travellers* [2023] UKSC 47.

[29] *Fearn v Board of Trustees of the Tate Gallery* [2023] UKSC 4.

from the Blavatnik's viewing gallery was capable of being a private nuisance. In coming to that conclusion, the Court confirmed that emanations do *not* underlie, or are not the basis of, a nuisance action, and so nuisance does not protect the right to exclude. The implication of this is that the right to exclude cannot be seen as the core of property, or at least not the only element of property that needs protecting. Property rights encompass more than merely the right to exclude, as remedies are on offer without any physical interference.

These Supreme Court decisions, through elucidating and applying the characteristics of permanence and excludability, tell us something more broadly about property. They show a view of property where exclusion is (generally) key – almost reinforcing the traditional Blackstonian view of absolute control to the exclusion of others, where a man's home is his castle – but, equally, where stability and permanence are sidelined. Thus, these 'strong exclusionary' rights are relatively impermanent, or at least are amenable to change and removal.

ii. The Boundaries of Property

This theme concerns situations where the Supreme Court is attempting to draw (or push) the boundaries between proprietary rights and personal, or no, rights. Although a relatively clear boundary between proprietary rights and non-proprietary rights is often thought to exist, the cases in this theme suggest that this boundary is blurred and easily moved. We see that, when the boundary is moved, it gives rise to those incidents of property seen in the previous section, with exclusion being particularly prioritised.

This idea is represented in *Manchester Ship Canal Company Ltd v Vauxhall Motors Ltd*,[30] where the Court held that a licensee could claim relief from forfeiture, thereby implying that a licence can, at least in limited circumstances, be upgraded so that it has proprietary status.[31] However, this was said to be a 'very unusual' licence,[32] which granted virtually exclusive possession in giving the Ship Canal Company the ability to exclude others from access to pipelines. The choice here was between recognising a property right (albeit a relatively weak possessory right) and limiting the claimant's entitlements to its contractual rights, which would not have given access to the remedy of relief from forfeiture. Thus, one implication of this case is that the Court is willing to stretch the idea of possession to grant access to proprietary remedies. Another is

[30] *Manchester Ship Canal Company Ltd v Vauxhall Motors Ltd* [2019] UKSC 46.

[31] Not all would agree with this interpretation of the case. Note that Martin Dixon has recently argued that there is a distinction in how possession is used within the case law. Possession can be used in a definitional sense, but also in a remedial sense. He argues that when possession is used in a remedial sense, it should not be tied to the existence of a proprietary claim – this is how he interprets *Manchester Ship Canal*. See M Dixon, 'Real Property, Licences and the Slippery Idea of Possession' (2023) 139 *LQR* 552, 569.

[32] *Manchester Ship Canal Company Ltd v Vauxhall Motors Ltd* (n 30) [46].

that the features of control and exclusive use are very important factors in determining the scope of property, potentially expanding and pushing its boundaries. In fact, even a right which is (or was) not considered proprietary can be made so (or at least made to have quasi-proprietary status or proprietary implications) if these features are found. This trend of stretching what could be considered property is also seen in *Fearn*, where the Court held that being free from visual intrusion, or at least some degree of privacy, is part of property that can be protected via nuisance. This stretches the concept of freehold or leasehold title to encompass some right of the holder to be free from visual intrusion. In a sense, it also stretches the boundary of 'land' itself, since the visual field interrupted by the decision includes the airspace around the viewing gallery. We see something similar occurring in *Regency Villas v Diamond Resorts*,[33] where the Court expanded the category of easements, including not only rights of recreation (which to some extent had already been accepted in some limited sense),[34] but also rights dependent upon step-in access by the dominant owners to secure maintenance. When we examine what is significant about the 'property-ness' of this right, we can see that it is permanence: the ability to demand access to the recreational facilities, use them and maintain them would *endure* for successors and be enforceable against successors. In his dissent, Lord Carnwath argued that this decision was elevating *permanent* membership of a country club into a proprietary right.[35]

A contrasting decision is *Akers v Samba*.[36] Here, an individual declared himself trustee of shares he owned for a corporate beneficiary, which subsequently became insolvent. He later transferred the shares to Samba, a bank in Saudi Arabia. The key issue before the Court was whether the beneficiary's equitable interest under the trust was 'bitten' by section 127 of the Insolvency Act 1986, which provides that a 'disposition' of a company's 'property' made after the commencement of winding-up proceedings is void, subject to a court discretion to re-validate it. Having assumed either that Samba was a bona fide purchaser or that principles of private international law would make Samba the outright owner, the Court needed to consider the meanings of 'disposition' and 'property'. It noted that the definition of 'property' under section 426 of the Insolvency Act 1986 was extremely broad – extending even to personal obligations. As such, the question of whether the beneficiary's interest was proprietary did not need to be resolved.[37] The Court nevertheless showed a strong inclination

33 *Regency Villas v Diamond Resorts* [2018] UKSC 57.

34 See, for example, *Re Ellenborough Park* [1955] EWCA Civ 4, [1955] 3 WLR 892; and *Mulvaney v Gough* [2003] 4 All ER 83, which concern the use of a park/communal garden and a garden respectively. So while some recreational use had been recognised, it was expected that easements should not be for 'pure recreation'.

35 *Regency Villas v Diamond Resorts* (n 33) [96].

36 *Akers v Samba* [2017] UKSC 6.

37 ibid [44] and [51] (Lord Mance), [81] (Lord Sumption).

to say in dicta that it was proprietary,[38] but that it is an inherently limited right that is vulnerable to being overridden by a transfer to a third party. The Court assumed that such overriding had occurred, and interpreted this as the *destruction* of the beneficiary's interest. In turn, it was not possible to then extend the meaning of 'disposition' under section 127 to embrace destruction; therefore, the provision could not bite on the transaction. This might suggest a sliding boundary between proprietary and non-proprietary rights, with some *weaker* proprietary rights sitting in between the two concepts given their inherent susceptibility to becoming defeasible against a third party. It seems possible to think of proprietary status as a spectrum as opposed to two distinct positions.[39] Here, the Court deployed an orthodox view that very firmly situated equitable interests under a trust somewhere in the middle of the spectrum, being unwilling to stretch even the meaning of the insolvency provision (which would normally have voided alienations of the insolvent's property) to give the right in question more permanence. Thus, despite strong dicta favouring the proprietary side of a long-running debate about the nature of a beneficiary's interest, this proprietary status still could not save the right from destruction upon transfer by the trustee.[40]

Akers notwithstanding, in considering property's boundaries, the Court has occasionally shown a willingness to stretch the concept and accord stronger rights (for example, excludability) to the claimant than they would otherwise have enjoyed.

iii. Defining Key Terms in Relation to Land and Property

Supreme Court decisions have sometimes fleshed out key terms in relation to land and property. The cases have clustered around two categories: the first includes land and the buildings on it, and the second is the concept of possession. While the Court's definitions in the former category depart from lay conceptions and can even create paradoxes, its definitions in the latter category have created a conception of possession that is unbounded and flexible.

a. Land and the Built Environment

Sometimes the Court offers counter-intuitive definitions of concepts relating to land and the built environment. Its definitions of the terms 'land', 'home', 'house', and 'dwelling' bolster strong property rights.

[38] ibid [16] (Lord Mance), [82] (Lord Sumption).

[39] See S Agnew and B McFarlane, 'The Nature of Trusts and the Conflict of Laws' (2021) 137 *LQR* 405, who argue why the decision is consistent with the 'right against rights' or 'relational' theory of the beneficiary's interest under a trust, which views it as a modified personal right.

[40] See C de Contreras, '*Samba*-Dancing around the Nature of a Beneficiary's Interest' in J Russell and L Graham (eds), Private Law and the UK Supreme Court: Key Cases and Decisions (Abingdon, Routledge, 2026).

For a term so central to property law, 'land' is not well defined by statute. Many will agree that the definition in section 205 of the Law of Property Act 1925 is incomplete and self-referential. Consequently, case law is needed to help elucidate this concept. A key case here is *Star Energy v Bocardo SA*,[41] where the Court held that the ancient brocard 'cuius est solum eius est usque ad coelum et ad inferos'[42] still applied below the surface, meaning that land, for the purposes of trespass to land, extends below the surface until it reaches the point of absurdity.[43] This granted the owner strong property rights over terrain they had no prospect of using, enabling them to charge the appellant a licence fee.

Land and the buildings on it provide the structures that support homes, commercial development and vital infrastructure. In defining everyday concepts, paradoxes have arisen. A 'home is where a family lives together' and local authorities may be required to provide homes in that sense,[44] but temporary accommodation is not a 'dwelling',[45] and a grand terrace in London is not a 'house' if it has been used as short-term tourist accommodation, or some, but not all, of its floors have been converted to offices.[46] The Court is of course constrained by wider legislative and policy schemes in construing terms within each statutory scheme. In *ZH and CN*, a bare majority adopted the position that temporary accommodation provided by local authorities was not offered as a 'dwelling'. Consequently, the applicants were unable to rely on section 3 of the Protection from Eviction Act (PEA) 1977 and the local authority could re-take possession without a court order. The majority's interpretation aims to ensure a coherent statutory scheme for the provision of temporary accommodation, but it has the paradoxical result that the closest thing the applicants had to a home was not a 'dwelling'.[47]

The Court's role has often been to supplement statutory definitions; in doing so, we have seen that it has offered meanings that might surprise a non-lawyer. At the same time, in a number of notable cases that surprised *lawyers* too, it has taken the opportunity to re-fashion core property concepts.

b. Possession

While Supreme Court case law has supplied definitions of land and the built environment that are quite detailed (albeit unusual), its treatment of possession has been less precise. Questions concerning possession are often at the forefront of decisions relating to the protection of property rights through torts,

[41] *Star Energy v Bocardo SA* [2010] UKSC 35.

[42] Translated as: 'The person who owns the land owns everything reaching up to the very heavens and down to the depths of the earth.'

[43] *Star Energy* (n 41) [26].

[44] *Sharif (FC) v London Borough of Camden* [2013] UKSC 10, Lord Kerr (dissenting) [59].

[45] In the view of the majority in *R (ZH and CN) v London Borough of Newham and London Borough of Lewisham* [2014] UKSC 62.

[46] *Day v Hosebay Ltd* [2012] UKSC 41.

[47] *ZH* (n 45) Lord Hodge [33]. See also Lady Hale, dissenting [140].

but also arise in cases concerning Article 1, Protocol 1 (A1P1) of the European Convention on Human Rights (ECHR), and cases about leases and easements that rely heavily on the concept of possession to define and delineate these rights. The concept of possession is important as any definition has far-reaching consequences, but the Court has not advanced one core concept of possession across the range of cases. Instead, it has interpreted possession differently in these varying contexts and has been flexible and vague in applying the concept. This risks cross-fertilisation between the Court's own different meanings of possession, thereby blurring the meaning of this central property concept. This can be seen in cases involving possession of land, as Dixon has recently argued, on the basis that possession does not always entail the assertion of a property right, and instead possession, at least in the context of land, can sometimes be 'definitional' and other times 'remedial'.[48] We tentatively suggest that the Court should be clearer in how, and why, it uses the concept of possession in relation to land and other 'things'.

Often the Court has equated possession and ownership, working in both directions so that possession means ownership and ownership means possession. These terms are obviously interrelated, and the Supreme Court's continued link between them reminds us of the importance of relativity of title in property disputes. For example, the Court held in *Star Energy* that the paper owner will be presumed to be in factual possession of the 'land'.[49] Meanwhile, in *Hurstwood Properties v Rossendale Borough Council*,[50] it was held that the definition of 'owner' was 'the person entitled to possession'.[51]

Within A1P1 discussions, the approach to 'possessions' has been broader: often, the decisions side-step defining or limiting the concept of a possession for the purposes of the article. One example is *R (SG) v Secretary of State for Work and Pensions*,[52] where Lady Hale took the time to elucidate the term, suggesting that possessions, for this purpose, include entitlement to welfare benefits.[53] A similar point was made in obiter dicta in *Re an Application by Denise Brewster for JR*,[54] where it was said that '[i]t is not in dispute that the denial of a [cohabiting] survivor's pension falls within the ambit of A1P1'.[55] Both cases show that a possession for A1P1 purposes is an almost unbounded concept. Nevertheless, it is unclear whether the concept of a possession in A1P1 is the same as that of possession in the English property law sense. It might be that the Court is simply using the term 'possessions' as a synonym for 'a thing we can enjoy property

[48] See Dixon (n 31).
[49] *Star Energy* (n 41) [31].
[50] *Hurstwood Properties v Rossendale Borough Council* [2021] UKSC 16.
[51] ibid [1].
[52] *R (SG) v Secretary of State for Work and Pensions* [2014] UKSC 16.
[53] ibid [178].
[54] *Re an Application by Denise Brewster for JR* [2017] UKSC 8.
[55] ibid [44].

over', and so any explanation of possession in this context does not feed into broader debates or questions of possession in other contexts.

Questions relating to possession also arise in the context of leases and easements, where the concept delineates the right in question: possession forms an essential element of the test for leases,[56] and helps to differentiate leases and easements (the former being about possession and the latter use).[57] We argue that, in this context, possession is often equated with control, and the cases show a tendency to 'find' possession any time factual control is found, even if this would not normally be possession in the legal sense (the sense where it is an important proprietary concept). Thus, the presence of control is equated with possession, which in turn has proprietary consequences. For example, in *Manchester Ship Canal Company Ltd v Vauxhall Motors Ltd*, relief from forfeiture was allowed for a licence because the licence granted such extensive control that it amounted to possession. This allowed the Court to side-step the fact that it was not possible to view the right granted as a lease.[58] *Regency Villas* also interacts with possession in its implicit adoption of the 'possession and control' test for whether a putative servient owner has been 'ousted' and a prospective easement has been invalidated. Again, the Court is eliding concepts: while the test looks for 'possession and control', the Court is really asking whether the dominant owners had *control* of the servient land on the facts rather than whether they had *possession* of it. The assumption that 'possession and control' is the correct test, in turn, makes it easier not to infringe the ouster principle and therefore find an easement, again allowing for proprietary consequences as in *Manchester Ship Canal*.

Here, we build on Dixon's 'reflexive scholarship'[59] approach to delineating possession, tracking how the concept has been elucidated (or not) in a series of Supreme Court decisions. Overall, we can see that the Court has not given 'possession' a single meaning; it has different meanings or connotations in different contexts. Interestingly, this has allowed the courts to adopt generous interpretations which can benefit the relatively weaker party in a dispute (those lacking a freehold or leasehold, or dependent on benefits or pensions). This seems broadly consistent with the Court's emerging willingness (when it is not constrained by housing statutes) to help a specific type of applicant: one holding a weaker or non-property right. We will delve into this next.

[56] *Street v Mountford* [1985] AC 809.

[57] This is primarily done through the ouster principle – this is discussed in cases like *London & Blenheim Estates v Ladbroke* [1993] 4 All ER 157 and *Moncrieff v Jamieson* [2007] UKHL 42.

[58] See, for example, *Bruton v London & Quadrant Housing Trust* [1999] UKHL 26. Here, and in *Manchester Ship Canal*, Dixon has argued that the 'remedial' version of possession is engaged, and that this differs from and should not alter the 'definitional' idea of possession; however, the case law implies that the concept of possession *has* been changed. See Dixon (n 31).

[59] See Dixon (n 31) 553–54.

B. 'Socio-legal' Themes

i. Balancing the Rights of Property Holders against those who are Less Propertied or Relatively Less Possessed

How do the courts seek to balance the rights of property holders against those who are less propertied (or relatively less possessed)?[60] Traditional methodologies of property law scholarship have arguably been applied to prioritise the claims of 'more propertied' parties and marginalise those 'less propertied' parties.[61] Consequently, the property outsider (the less propertied person) has been rendered invisible within legal analyses, arguments and decision-making.[62] This theme explores whether the Supreme Court has continued this trend or whether it purports to re-address the balance.

Overall, the Supreme Court's decisions are a bit of a 'rag-bag', with three distinct case law strands emerging: (i) cases where the Court clearly *sees* the less propertied person and uses a range of techniques to ensure they are 'protected'; (ii) cases at the opposite end of the spectrum, where there is a strong push to support the more propertied person with the less propertied person being perceived as 'trying it on'; and (iii) cases in the middle, where attempts are made to think about the less propertied party – but in a limited way, with the more propertied party ultimately being preferred. Although examples of all three positions can be found in the Court's jurisprudence, there is a significant number of cases which fall into the first category, showing that the Court has found space to innovate when helping a specific type of more vulnerable claimant. Further, these examples span different eras of the Court, suggesting that this is not the work of isolated judges.

a. 'Seeing' the Less Propertied/More Vulnerable Party

There are cases where the Court has clearly attempted to think about the less propertied person and centre them within the analysis, often using creative techniques. This can be seen in *Austin v London Borough of Southwark*,[63] which considered whether a brother could inherit a secured tenancy. The local authority had already obtained a possession order against the deceased, but never sought to enforce it. In trying to find a solution, the Court held that the brother

[60] We understand these terms as including those with seemingly weaker or more vulnerable property rights. We left out cases in this theme which dealt with how a local authority dealt with homelessness and tenancy issues in order to avoid repetition in the following theme. We recognise that some of the same arguments arise.

[61] L Fox O'Mahony, 'Property Outsiders and the Hidden Politics of Doctrinalism' (2014) 67(1) *Current Legal Problems* 409.

[62] ibid.

[63] *Austin v London Borough of Southwark* [2010] UKSC 28.

could act as personal representative and apply to set aside the possession order (as the arrears had been paid) and receive a secure tenancy. *Berrisford v Mexfield Housing Co-operative Limited* also shows the Court employing creativity to protect a less propertied party.[64] Rather than finding that Mrs Berrisford lacked a tenancy due to an uncertain term, the court side-stepped traditional property principles and held that section 149(6) LPA turned this uncertain term into a lease for 90 years. Accordingly, the landlord could not seek possession unless the tenant breached the terms of the agreement. Finally, this phenomenon can also be seen in *Guest v Guest*,[65] where the Supreme Court again showed a willingness to help the (relatively) dispossessed, in asking, as Lord Briggs did: 'What if anything can the law do for Andrew [Guest]?'[66]

Moreover, a series of less extreme examples, which nonetheless champion the position of the more vulnerable through a strict interpretation of legislation, also exist. One example is *Royal Bank of Scotland plc v John Patrick McCormack Wilson (Scotland)*,[67] where the Court upheld a strict interpretation of the Scottish statutory process for lender repossession of family homes under section 5 of the Heritable Securities (Scotland) Act 1984. This interpretation was to the disadvantage of the bank and the advantage of the borrowers, who were able to stay in their homes (at least temporarily). This interpretation was reached notwithstanding concerns that the borrowers and their spouses were 'trying it on'; after all, the defendants were said to know 'perfectly well what they have been asked to pay and they have had ample opportunity to put forward their defence',[68] Another case is *S Frances Ltd v The Cavendish Hotel (London) Ltd*,[69] which concerned qualified security of tenure for business tenancies. Here, the landlord fell into one of the grounds exempting him from granting a new tenancy, but admitted that the only reason for 'reconstructing' (the relevant exemption ground) was to *allow* him not to grant a new tenancy. In considering the case, the Court questioned whether the landlord really did 'intend' to carry out the works, defining intention in a tenant-friendly way so that work only being done to avoid security would not qualify as 'intended'. As such, it was held that a new tenancy should be granted.[70] Here again, the Court used interpretation to benefit the more vulnerable party. The same is true in *Croydon London Borough Council v Kalonga*,[71] where the Court interpreted the relevant legislative provisions with the starting point that Parliament 'could not be taken as intending to expose a tenant to a loss of contractual security of tenure earlier than the landlord could have

[64] *Berrisford v Mexfield Housing Co-operative Limited* [2011] UKSC 52.
[65] *Guest v Guest* [2022] UKSC 27.
[66] ibid [3].
[67] *Royal Bank of Scotland plc v John Patrick McCormack Wilson (Scotland)* [2010] UKSC 50.
[68] ibid [33].
[69] *S Frances Ltd v The Cavendish Hotel (London) Ltd* [2018] UKSC 62.
[70] ibid [16].
[71] *Croydon London Borough Council v Kalonga* [2022] UKSC 7.

obtained possession under the terms of the tenancy',[72] showing a tenant-focused approach.

b. Prioritising the More Propertied Party

At the other end of the spectrum, there are cases where the more propertied person is prioritised. In doing so, rather than emphasising the less propertied person's vulnerability, there is an accompanying discourse that they are 'chancing it' and 'trying their luck'. This pattern can be seen in *Southern Pacific Securities 05-2 plc v Walker*,[73] a mortgage case which concerned the interpretation of 'credit' within a mortgage agreement, where, after finding against the borrower, the Court noted that it expected the claimant to raise an issue regardless of how the 'credit' was defined in the agreement. *Daejan Investments Limited v Benson*[74] provides another example: Lord Neuberger questioned why a dispensation of the consultation requirements for maintenance work on the building would not be granted where the extent, quality and cost of the works were unaffected by the landlord's failure to comply with them. The undertone is that the less propertied party was seeking to take advantage of a small error by the landlord, and so the Court sought to re-balance the two parties' interests in light of the protection already afforded to the tenants.

c. Middle Ground: Recognising Vulnerability, but Protecting the More Propertied

Finally, there are cases which fall in the middle ground, such as *Secretary of State for Environment, Food and Rural Affairs v Meier*. Despite recognising that injunctions could operate disproportionately in this scenario – with the threat of prison, which would not be appropriate[75] – against the less propertied and more marginalised party, the Court still emphasised the need for better landowner protections. Another case that falls into this category is *Nottingham City Council v Parr*,[76] which concerned whether regulations governing the size of rooms in Houses in Multiple Occupation (HMOs) should apply to student housing. While recognising the reasons behind the regulations of 'providing acceptable living standards' and 'protecting vulnerable or potentially vulnerable groups that tend to occupy HMOs' were (as the trial judge put it) 'commendable',[77] the Court decided that the proposed mode of occupation

[72] ibid [40].
[73] *Southern Pacific Securities 05-2 plc v Walker* [2010] UKSC 32.
[74] *Daejan Investments Limited v Benson* [2013] UKSC 14 and [2013] UKSC 54.
[75] *Meier* (n 26) [14].
[76] *Nottingham City Council v Parr* [2018] UKSC 51.
[77] ibid [25].

should be considered.[78] As such, the size limit under the regulations did not apply to student houses if the HMO licence was limited to students.[79]

This theme shows that the Court is sometimes, though not always, willing to be creative and interpret provisions in ways that prioritise the vulnerable party. While this theme explored how rights are balanced between two different (often individual) parties, one being a property right holder and the other being a more marginalised individual, the next section questions how the Court strikes the balance when questions are raised relating to the needs of the wider community.

ii. Rights of the Property Holder Balanced against the Community at Large

Some cases cite the needs of the wider community as part of the justification for depriving individuals of rights to or relating to property. The Supreme Court has referred to the need for 'give and take' between neighbouring users or owners of land,[80] to the power to subordinate the defence of property rights via injunctions to the general good of the community (for compensation),[81] and to local authorities' duties to consider their housing stock and to protect social tenants' safety.[82] Notions of the greater good as a self-justifying reason to cut away property rights, or dispossess individuals, are implicit in some of the Court's reasoning. Using this lens, this category explores the Court's approach to the tension that arises between robust private property rights on the one hand, and the needs and wishes of the community at large on the other.

Determining a dispute between private property owners necessarily has implications for the community, whether this community is defined as tourist families looking at modern art or children in need of palliative care. A series of cases explore the question, as Lord Sumption put it, 'how is one to reconcile public and private law in the domain of land use where they occupy much the same space?'[83] In *Fearn v Tate Gallery*, the Court showed a robust concern with vindicating private property rights. This came at the cost of upsetting the amenity value of the Tate Modern: 'It is not a justification for carrying on an activity which substantially interferes with the ordinary use of your land that the community as a whole will benefit from the interference.'[84] Yet, Lord Leggatt noted that while the benefit to the community was not a reason to deny a remedy at all, it may be considered in deciding whether damages might be more appropriate than an injunction. Thus, the way in which the Court reconciles the

[78] ibid [26].
[79] ibid [35].
[80] *Fearn* (n 29) [229] (Lord Sales).
[81] *Coventry v Lawrence* [2014] UKSC 13 [161].
[82] *Manchester City Council v Pinnock* [2011] UKSC 6 and 45 [52].
[83] *Coventry* (n 81) [155].
[84] *Fearn* (n 29) [121]. However, he continued by recognising at [122] that: 'There are circumstances in which [property rights] … may be subordinated to the general good of the community.'

recognition of a private property right with the needs of the community is to consider the latter, not in determining the existence of property rights themselves, but rather at the remedial stage in exploring the appropriate consequence for an individual's interference with those rights.

This analysis is consistent with views expressed nine years earlier in *Coventry v Lawrence*,[85] in which the claimants had bought a house near a stadium with a motocross track, where various racing activities took place. They brought a nuisance claim and sought an injunction to stop the noise-causing activities. The use had planning permission (a decision in which the public interest is necessarily considered) and no limits had been placed on the noise made. The Court did not think that planning permission could make the noise an established part of a neighbourhood so as to bar a nuisance claim. As with *Fearn*, it pushed consideration of the public interest issue to the remedial stage. Indeed, Lord Sumption viewed the Court's remedial discretion as '[w]hat saves, or could save the law from anomaly and incoherence',[86] resulting from the clash between public interest-focused planning decisions and private law claims defeating that public interest. And, at this remedial stage, we see strong support for the community. Lord Sumption expressed this most strongly, stating (obiter) that injunctions to stop activities 'should not normally be granted in a case where it is likely that conflicting interests are engaged other than the parties' interests'.[87]

By contrast, *Alexander Devine Children's Cancer Trust v Housing Solutions Ltd* involves the public interest at an earlier stage. The developer manipulated the situation so that it would no longer be in the public interest to maintain the covenant in its present form (given that affordable housing was already being built and much of it had been completed), thus engaging the public interest jurisdictional ground for discharge or modification under section 84(1) LPA. Recognising this, Lord Burrows held that the developer's cynical breach was relevant to the Court's *discretion* to discharge or modify, meaning that an application could potentially be refused on that basis. Unlike *Coventry* and *Fearn*, in *Devine* consideration of the public interest was mandated by statute in determining the claim's existence (ie, whether jurisdiction lies under section 84(1)). Interestingly, though, if a section 84(1) application is rejected so that the covenant remains and there is then a breach, the courts can still presumably avail themselves of the *Coventry* remedial approach and consider the community when deciding whether damages or an injunction would be more appropriate.

Thus, in *Fearn* and *Coventry*, the needs of the community are a potential factor in courts' wide discretion to grant an injunction or to consider granting damages in lieu, while in *Devine*, the public interest (though not fully defined) is one of the sufficient factors for a claim to arise. Yet, in each of these scenarios,

[85] *Coventry v Lawrence* [2014] UKSC 13.
[86] ibid [157].
[87] ibid [161].

the needs of the community had *already* been considered at the planning stage. The re-inclusion of the community in determining private property claims (regardless of how this is done) in itself suggests a greater role for the community, and a smaller role for property rights, than one might have imagined.

Nevertheless, impairing neighbours' lives and economic positions is sometimes the inevitable result of applying a statute. In *Barratt Homes v Dwr Cymru Cyfyngedig (Welsh Water)*,[88] the Court held that owners' 'absolute right'[89] under section 106 of the Water Industry Act 1991 to connect to a public sewer was not constrained even where the resulting overload led to foul water escapes.[90] Thus, here, enforcing a strong property right is the natural result of applying the relevant statute, in spite of its likely adverse effects on the wider community as well as the opponent. We can imagine that community needs might weigh less heavily when the individual claimant risks losing their home and this is perhaps especially true in the private contractual sphere. In *Telchadder v Wickland Holdings Ltd*,[91] a landowner terminated a licence agreement with an occupier of a mobile home after a second instance of anti-social behaviour against a neighbour. The issue was whether the occupier had failed to redress the original breach within a reasonable time, meaning that the agreement could be terminated forthwith under the Mobile Homes Act 1983.[92] The Court, however, held that a fresh notice was required: Lord Wilson noted that, otherwise, the first breach in this case would give the occupier no second chances if a reasonable time was too broadly defined.[93] The Court thus upheld security for the claimant, but at the expense of other licensees in his community concerned about the prospect of continued anti-social behaviour.

The balance radically shifts when a case engages the social tenancy regime under the Housing Act (HA) 1996: here, the Court is constrained by the wide-reaching policy enacted by that statute. We could therefore expect cases to be at the community-favouring extreme. Nevertheless, the Court attempts to give a sensitive approach, in line with European Court of Human Rights jurisprudence. *Manchester City Council v Pinnock*[94] concerned a possession order made in respect of a demoted tenancy following repeated anti-social behaviour from household members. The Court held that compatibility with Article 8 ECHR required courts to be able to assess the proportionality of orders for possession, but that, in any event, it would have been proportionate in this case to make

[88] *Barratt Homes v Dwr Cymru Cyfyngedig (Welsh Water)* [2009] UKSC 13.

[89] ibid [23].

[90] While Welsh Water submitted that this exposed them to criminal liability, the Court remarked that it was their duty to deal with the consequences of discharge: ibid [27].

[91] *Telchadder v Wickland Holdings Ltd* [2014] UKSC 57.

[92] In sched 1, pt I, ch 2, para 4 (provided that an application to court is made, and that the court is also satisfied that the termination is reasonable).

[93] *Telchadder v Wickland Holdings Ltd* (n 91) [34]. Lord Carnwath agreed that the lapse of time 'was too great' (at [96]), but preferred to ask whether there was effectively a continuing failure to comply (at [91], [92]).

[94] *Manchester City Council v Pinnock* [2011] UKSC 6 and 45.

the order. Lord Neuberger had regard to the needs to be balanced in this kind of case: not only did the authority have ownership rights to be vindicated, but it also owed duties to others which would reinforce the proportionality of a possession order. These included:

> [T]he fair allocation of its housing, the redevelopment of the site, the refurbishing of sub-standard accommodation, the need to move people who are in accommodation that now exceeds their needs, and the need to move vulnerable people into sheltered or warden assisted housing … [as well as] the need to remove a source of nuisance to neighbours.[95]

This high hurdle placed in front of occupiers is maintained by *Powell*,[96] in which Lord Hope remarked that counsel was right to say that 'in only a small proportion of cases' would there be an arguable case on proportionality.[97] Echoing Lord Neuberger, he said that: 'Local authorities hold their housing stock, as do other social landlords, for the benefit of the whole community. It is in the interests of the community as a whole that decisions are taken as to how best it should be administered.'[98]

Nevertheless, Lord Carnwath had less time for appeals to local authority struggles in *Sharif v London Borough of Camden*.[99] Here, the local authority offered two separate flats on the same floor to a family, offering one flat to the applicant and her sister, and the other to their father, for whom the applicant cared. Reviewing the decision, Lord Carnwath noted that '[a]lthough the problems of housing authorities, particularly in urban areas, are well known, there is no specific evidence to support a submission that this particular requirement would pose unacceptable problems'.[100] It was ultimately held (by a majority) that the offer that had been made was sufficient to discharge the duty, as the flats would be close enough for the family to live together, but Lord Carnwath warned that this decision did 'not give authorities a free hand'.[101]

Meanwhile, in *Hotak v London Borough of Southwark*,[102] Lord Neuberger considered the extent to which strained resources can be considered in assessing whether an applicant was in priority need, in this case for reasons of vulnerability under section 189(1)(c) HA 1996. He remarked that, following a determination of the applicant's status, 'their duty to that applicant is as

[95] ibid [52].
[96] *London Borough of Hounslow v Powell, Leeds City Council v Hall, Birmingham City Council v Frisby* [2011] UKSC 8.
[97] ibid [35].
[98] ibid.
[99] *Sharif v London Borough of Camden* [2013] UKSC 10. However, see *Poshteh v Royal Borough of Kensington and Chelsea* [2017] UKSC 36, where Lord Carnwath noted that a local authority is entitled to have regard to the 'allocation of scarce resources'.
[100] *Sharif v London Borough of Camden* (n 99) [23].
[101] ibid.
[102] *Hotak v London Borough of Southwark* [2015] UKSC 30.

defined in the Act: the fact that the authority may be very short of money and/or available accommodation cannot in any way affect whether an applicant is in priority need'.[103] Similarly, Lady Hale's dissent in *ZH and CN* emphasises that strain does not remove duty:

> We can, I think, take it for granted that it would indeed make life more difficult for hard-pressed housing authorities who are having to cope with increasing numbers of homeless persons and diminishing resources with which to do so. However, as Lord Hodge himself [for the majority] acknowledges,[104] this would not by itself be determinative.[105]

The duty-resource tension was particularly highlighted in *Nzolameso v Westminster City Council*.[106] The applicant, who had chronic health problems, had been renting a privately owned property in the City of Westminster with the help of housing benefit, but could no longer afford the rent after a cap was introduced. She was offered accommodation in Bletchley,[107] owing to the 'severe shortage of accommodation in Westminster',[108] although this would have required a change of schools for her children and a long commute for her. The Court considered that the local authority had not discharged its duty under section 193(2) HA 1996 to provide accommodation. For instance, no questions about the practicability of moving out of the area were asked.[109] Nevertheless, the Court recognised the strains on resources that rest on the shoulders of local authorities and over which they have no control.[110]

While there is emerging consideration of public interest concerns in disputes between neighbouring right holders (especially *Fearn*, *Coventry* and *Devine*), the needs of the community have received the most detailed attention in local authority cases. Here the strain on resources, and therefore the needs of the community, is a key variant in decisions. There is a relatively light-touch property analysis when it comes to defining the authorities' needs *qua* owners, but authorities are at the same time a stand-in for the community, owing the community a vast range of duties; thus, their rights as owners are subordinated to what they hold those rights *for*.

iii. Homelessness and the Concept of 'Home'

We saw earlier that legal definitions of common terms such as 'home' may not reflect a lay understanding. In conceptualising the 'home' and related words, the

[103] ibid [39].
[104] *ZH* (n 45) [36].
[105] ibid [166].
[106] *Nzolameso v Westminster City Council* [2015] UKSC 22.
[107] A housing authority 'shall' secure that accommodation is available for the applicant's occupation 'in their district', but only '[s]o far as reasonably practicable' (HA 1996, s 208).
[108] *Nzolameso* (n 106) 4.
[109] ibid [36].
[110] ibid [38].

Supreme Court is in many cases constrained by its duty to give meaning to terms in legislative schemes that have different aims.

We see two polar-opposite interpretations of an everyday property term in the conjoined appeal in *R (ZH and CN) v Newham London Borough Council and Lewisham London Borough Council*, with radically different consequences. Both applicants' mothers were given temporary accommodation under section 188(1) HA 1996. The local authorities had determined that they owed the mothers limited duties under section 190, inter alia, to 'secure that temporary accommodation would be available to them', where they could have a reasonable opportunity to find other accommodation. The local authorities then terminated the temporary accommodation on the basis that they had discharged these duties. The applicants argued that a safeguard in the PEA 1977 was engaged: where sections 3(1) and 3(2B) apply,[111] an owner must give 28 days' notice[112] and bring court proceedings in order lawfully to recover possession, provided that the premises have been let or occupied 'as a dwelling'. The issue therefore turned on whether the temporary accommodation was provided as a 'dwelling', and a 4:3 majority held that it was not. Lord Hodge held that 'as a matter of nuance, "dwelling" as a general rule suggests more settled occupation than "residence" and can be equated with one's home'.[113] He viewed the authorities' limited duties in section 190, which, for example, meant that an applicant might be asked to move accommodation, as inconsistent with such settlement.[114] The majority acknowledged that while a hotel, for example, is unlikely to be a 'dwelling',[115] precarity *in itself* is not the determining factor:[116] the problem here was that the section 190 set-up, with the possibility of day-to-day licences, in their view ruled out the level of permanence needed for a dwelling.[117] Lady Hale, dissenting, noted that '"residing" and "dwelling" and "living" somewhere generally mean the same thing',[118] and that '[r]eserving the right to change the accommodation provided at little or no notice does not prevent the accommodation being provided as a home if that is what it is'.[119] Meanwhile, Lord Neuberger's dissent emphasised that these protective sections merited a wide meaning: 'They do not represent a substantial incursion into the property rights of the owners of premises, and they reflect a policy that people who have been

[111] It applies to 'any premises [that] have been let as a dwelling under a tenancy which is neither a statutorily protected tenancy nor an excluded tenancy' (s 3(1)), as well as 'to any premises occupied as a dwelling under a licence, other than an excluded licence' (s 3(2B)).
[112] As required under s 5(1A) PEA 1977.
[113] *ZH* (n 45) [45].
[114] ibid [33]–[36].
[115] ibid [27].
[116] ibid [56].
[117] ibid [45] (summarising the decision).
[118] ibid [159].
[119] ibid [164].

lawfully living in premises should not be summarily evicted or locked out.'[120] We thus see entirely opposed views on whether the premises could, in effect, be considered to be 'homes'.

The Court has also considered how sharing a space affects the 'home'-ness of a place. In *Sharif* (see above), Lord Kerr's dissent emphasised that a 'home' is 'where a family lives together',[121] while Lord Carnwath's majority decision did not differ on that point, but held that the offer of two flats on the same floor did enable the family to live together. This can, however, be criticised on the basis that this was in fulfilment of the authorities' full duty to secure long-term accommodation under section 193(2), and being divided into two physical spaces with their own kitchens and front doors does seem to be a barrier to forming a 'home'. In *Hotak* (see above), Lord Neuberger noted that there was a potential paradox (as put forward by counsel's 'very powerful point') – that is, an applicant receiving care from a family member might not qualify as having priority need and thus both would be refused accommodation, whereas an applicant whose family member refuses to care for them would be in a better position, as they might then be in priority need.[122] However, 'at least on its own, the fact that a statutory provision is capable of producing a distasteful result in some circumstances cannot justify some sort of judicially created legislative exception',[123] an exception which would in turn have further implications in the sense that it might 'place an excessive burden on housing authorities and work unfairly on other applicants, if it was disregarded when assessing the applicant's vulnerability'.[124] The problem of housing authority resources again rears its head. Finally, in *Yemshaw v London Borough of Hounslow*,[125] the Court considered the local authority's interpretation of domestic violence in assessing whether the applicant was homeless. One condition for homelessness is that it is not reasonable to continue to occupy current accommodation: under the previous version of section 177(1) HA 1996, one ground for this is that it is 'probable that [staying in their current occupation] will lead to domestic violence or other violence'. The Court criticised the authority's narrow view of 'probable … domestic violence', which excluded controlling behaviour on the part of the applicant's husband and seeming to require physical harm or the threat of it. In a sense, the Court recognised that an applicant in this situation can be both homed and not homed, as she was lacking the tranquillity needed for it to be reasonable to stay where she was.[126] An amendment to section 177(1) in 2021 replaced the

[120] ibid [135].
[121] ibid (n 41).
[122] *Hotak* (n 102) [66].
[123] ibid [67].
[124] ibid [68].
[125] *Yemshaw v London Borough of Hounslow* [2011] UKSC 3.
[126] For discussion of this idea, see L Fox O'Mahony, *Conceptualising Home: Theories, Laws and Policies* (London, Bloomsbury, 2006).

terms 'domestic violence or other violence' with 'violence or domestic abuse'. This finally made the statute reflect the Court's more realistic assessment of the 'home'-ness of a place.

While statutory duties (and the strains on resources referred to in the previous section) can mean that there is no duty to give someone a place to live for a given period, it is an entirely separate question whether that person has a *home*. The answer to that question ought to (and does) impact the protection given, but the Court has unfortunately not been consistent in how it defines the 'home'. Nevertheless, it is encouraging to see occasional warnings from the bench when local authorities do not go far enough to respect the boundaries of where people live – including a powerful dissent in *ZH* from Lady Hale. The following text discusses the impact her Ladyship has had on a broader issue: whether property law puts women at a disadvantage.

iv. Gender

A final theme that arose in this category was how gender was discussed in relation to property; there were a series of cases where the justices, and particularly Lady Hale, took the time to make an explicit statement regarding gender in the decisions.

Lady Hale's dissent in *Radmacher v Granatino*[127] (on whether a husband was bound by a pre-nuptial agreement) argued that the enforceability of pre-nuptial agreements is usually an issue that will disproportionately affect female spouses,[128] and because of this 'gender dimension', some might think that it an issue 'ill-suited to a decision by a court consisting of eight men and one woman'.[129] Similarly, in *Yemshaw*, a case discussed above relating to homelessness and domestic violence, Lady Hale once again took the opportunity to remind everyone that this is disproportionately an issue affecting women.[130] The Court's wider view of 'violence' shows a concern with protecting more women in the future. Lady Hale similarly emphasised the gender dimension of abuse in *R (Carmichael and Rourke) v Secretary of State for Work and Pensions*,[131] which concerned the bedroom tax, and appeals based on non-discrimination and other property-related human rights claims. In her dissent, she suggested that the removal of the claimant's housing benefits on the basis that she was housed in a three-bedroom house (which was then 'fortified' to keep her and her son safe after fleeing violence), when she only required two bedrooms, was an interference with their right to respect for 'home'.[132] She continued to spearhead this issue in *R (SG) v Secretary of State*

[127] *Radmacher v Granatino* [2010] UKSC 42.
[128] ibid [137].
[129] ibid.
[130] *Yemshaw* (n 125) [1].
[131] *R (Carmichael and Rourke) v Secretary of State for Work and Pension* [2016] UKSC 58.
[132] ibid [76].

for Work and Pensions, a case concerning the benefit cap and the interaction with human rights (including A1P1) where she recognised the prejudicial effect of the cap and said that: 'This prejudicial effect has a disproportionate impact upon lone parents, the great majority of whom are women, and is also said to have such an impact upon victims of domestic violence, most of whom are also women.'[133]

The Court, and Lady Hale in particular, has also done much work on developing a legal regime for cohabiting couples recognising the unfairness that the application of resulting trusts or even constructive trusts, as governed by decisions like *Lloyds Bank v Rosset*,[134] creates for, predominantly, female cohabitees.[135] This was recognised by Lord Wilson in *Jones v Kernott*, who 'warmly applaud[ed] the development of the law of equity, spear-headed by Lady Hale and Lord Walker in their speeches in *Stack v Dowden*[136] and reiterated in their judgment in the present appeal'.[137] The Supreme Court, however, has been clear that Parliament should step in to create a legislative regime, and the Court sought to emphasise this in *Gow (AP) v Grant (Scotland)*[138] concerning Scottish cohabitation legislation. Here, the majority (including Lady Hale) took the time to say that: 'The Act has undoubtedly achieved a lot for Scottish cohabitants and their children. English and Welsh cohabitants and their children deserve no less.'[139]

It is interesting to see this theme of gender come through, and it seems to be a recognition by Lady Hale and the Supreme Court that decisions in property, while appearing to be value-neutral and apolitical (focusing on things like certainty, autonomy and efficiency), are concealing and propagating an area of law that reflects society's inequalities and inherently favours 'insiders' over 'outsiders'.[140] Historically, women were not able to be property holders and thus not property insiders. It was only in the 1980s that we have recognition in the decision in *Boland*[141] that a wife's occupation can be occupation *in her own right*, as opposed to being seen as a 'mere shadow of the husband's', allowing her to potentially have a right which could override the bank's charge in a mortgage priority dispute. In fact, it was this decision which spurred banks into wanting both husbands and wives to be a party to a mortgage – but, as can be seen in *Wilson* (see above), at least some banks still fail to respect the wives who

[133] *R (SG)* (n 52) [180].
[134] *Lloyds Bank v Rosset* [1991] 1 AC 107.
[135] Other issues relating to cohabitation have been raised in the Court and by Lady Hale in cases like *Re an Application by Denise Brewster for JR* [2017] UKSC 8 and *Re an Application by Siobhan McLaughlin for JR* [2018] UKSC 48.
[136] *Stack v Dowden* [2007] 2 AC 432.
[137] *Jones* (n 21) [78].
[138] *Gow (AP) v Grant (Scotland)* [2012] UKSC 29.
[139] ibid [56].
[140] Fox O'Mahony (n 61).
[141] *Williams & Glyn's Bank v Boland* [1981] AC 487.

are party to these agreements. In this case, despite the wives being personally liable, the bank never alerted the wives of the situation or demanded payment of them before seeking to gain possession. Lady Hale pointed out the unfairness of the bank's actions, remarking that it was sexist to presume the wives did not have sums to pay.[142]

Lady Hale taking the time to note how women are disproportionately disadvantaged by aspects of property law was a notable feature of the early years of the Court, and we can question what has been lost since Lady Hale's retirement and whether the Supreme Court should have a more active role in solving the inequality that property law creates.

IV. CONCLUSION

This chapter has explored how the Supreme Court has shaped property through its decisions, in exploring the first seven themes which arose from our thematic analysis. The identification of the themes is, in itself, one of the core contributions of this chapter. A further key contribution is that, by grouping and theming the decisions in this way, the research has allowed for new reflections on cases to emerge, showing some cases in a new light and allowing for comparisons between cases not previously linked.

The research has identified that while there are some key themes that arise throughout the data set, how the themes are dealt with, or how they arise in the different cases, is not necessarily consistent. Rather, within the themes discussed, there seem to be varying interpretations and applications of ideas, sometimes at opposite ends of the spectrum. Interestingly, the Court sometimes gives greater weight to protecting the vulnerable, and it often bolsters the exclusionary aspect of property. Our research shows that both protection and exclusion are emerging as key features in how the Court has shaped property.

One issue that cuts across the different themes identified is the impact that individual judges have on how themes are raised or applied. To some extent, the themes show that the different iterations of the court are not determinative – for example, different judges still push to protect the vulnerable parties or emphasise the importance of exclusion. But in other areas, single judges can be seen as spearheading different ideas and themes. This is especially true of Lady Hale and gender.

It is our hope that this chapter sparks new debates and provokes thought along new lines.

[142] *Wilson* (n 67) [81].

7

The Doctrine of Abandonment

Lost Cause or Chimera?

SUSAN PASCOE*

I. INTRODUCTION

THE SUPREME COURT decision in *Hillside Parks Ltd v Snowdonia National Park Authority*[1] that there is no principle of abandonment or extinguishing by abandonment of planning permission raises issues of wider importance in land law in relation to the doctrine of abandonment. This chapter will examine four main areas. First, whether planning permission is a property right will be analysed, as well as whether the property rights analogy is helpful in relation to modern planning permissions. It is notable that common law abandonment remains a key concept in relation to other aspects of planning law where questions of whether a use has been abandoned arise. Second, an analogy is drawn with the doctrine of abandonment in relation to other rights in land, such as easements. By reference to Hickey's exploration of the doctrinal structures operating in the context of abandonment of easements by physical relinquishing/non-use and a corroborating manifest divesting of intention, it will be examined whether Hickey's reasoning that disputes could be managed through informal express release rather than implied release by abandonment could be applied in the framework of *Hillside*. If abandonment of easements can justified only where there are no alternative means of achieving the same objective, the alternatives accepted by Supreme Court in *Hillside* may be too blunt a tool that does not enable nuanced analysis.

Third, in the area of adverse possession, it will be evaluated whether abandoned property is treated differently from a legal perspective, and if there are unifying and underlying themes. The discussion includes, inter alia, the differentiation highlighted by Rostill between the destructive abandonment of an

* I am very grateful to Professor Alison Clarke for initial discussions on this topic and also for very helpful suggestions from participants in the MSPL conference. The usual disclaimers apply.

[1] *Hillside Parks Ltd v Snowdonia National Park Authority* [2022] UKSC 30, [2022] 1 WLR 5077.

interest in land/extinctive abandonment and the abandonment of possession of land, compares it with Penner's extinction/creation 'directional abandonment' model and considers their congruity in this context. Lastly, despite the fact that abandoning interests in land requires justifications different from those applicable to abandonment of ownership of land, the chapter investigates whether any insights can be discerned from the more general discourse of abandonment of ownership of land in the writings of American academics, such as von Schütz, Peñalver and Strahilevitz.

Planning permission had been granted in *Hillside* in 1967 for 401 houses to be built. Between 1996 and 2011, the local planning authority granted six planning permissions relating to specific areas of the site which were implemented. In total, only 41 houses were built, none of them in accordance with the 1967 plan. In 2017 the authority told the developer to cease all works, because implementation of the 1967 permission had become impossible by the developments carried out under the later permissions – for example, houses had been built where some of the roads were meant to be under the 1967 plan, and a road had been laid where a row of houses was supposed to stand. The developer brought proceedings for a declaration that the 1967 permission remained valid and could be carried on to completion. The Supreme Court ruled in favour of the planning authority on three main grounds: the test of physical impossibility applied to the whole site covered by the 1967 permission and not just part of it; permission for a multi-unit development in 1967 was not severable; and later planning permissions were not variations of the 1967 permission and meant that the 1967 permission could not be implemented according to its terms, which had made it physically impossible to implement the 1967 permission.

The primary reasoning in relation to abandonment of the Supreme Court in *Hillside*, in the judgment delivered jointly by Lord Sales and Lord Leggatt (with whom the other judges agreed), was based on the following main points. The first is that there is no principle in planning law whereby a planning permission can be abandoned.[2] The Supreme Court did not accept that the decision in *Pilkington v Secretary of State for the Environment*[3] can be explained on the basis of a principle of abandonment. *Hillside* approved the House of Lords decision in *Pioneer Aggregates (UK) Ltd v Secretary of State for the Environment*,[4] where the House of Lords unanimously held that there is no principle, and no room for any principle, in planning law whereby a planning permission may be extinguished by abandonment.

The second justification in *Hillside* is that planning permission is governed exclusively by legislation. In agreeing with Lord Scarman in *Pioneer Aggregates*, the Supreme Court in *Hillside* explained that:

> Parliament has provided a comprehensive code of planning control and the courts should not introduce into planning law principles or rules derived from private law

[2] ibid [35].
[3] *Pilkington v Secretary of State for the Environment* [1973] 1 WLR 1527.
[4] *Pioneer Aggregates (UK) Ltd v Secretary of State for the Environment* [1985] AC 132.

> unless expressly authorised by Parliament or necessary to give effect to the purpose of the legislation.[5]

The Supreme Court quoted approvingly from Lord Scarman's judgment that 'only the statute or the terms of the planning permission itself can stop the permission enuring for the benefit of the land and of all persons for the time being interested therein'.[6] The rationale, explained by the Supreme Court, is that:

> Introducing a doctrine of abandonment into planning law would be inconsistent with this, as it would allow the land to lose the benefit of a planning permission by a means not provided for either by the legislation or by the terms of the planning permission itself.[7]

The third justification given in *Hillside* was that the planning register needs to be conclusive. Planning permission is binding on everyone with an interest in the land, but its abandonment would not be in the register. As the Supreme Court stated, again referring to Lord Scarman in *Pioneer Aggregates*:[8]

> Lord Scarman emphasised that the existence or otherwise of a valid planning permission should be capable of ascertainment by inspection of the planning register and of the land in question. That follows from the nature of planning permission as running with the land and as affecting third parties. Introducing a doctrine of abandonment, not provided for in the planning legislation, would be inconsistent with this requirement of public accessibility.[9]

The Supreme Court applied the test of physical impossibility that it would be unlawful to carry out the development proposed in the unimplemented planning permission, since it had become physically impossible to do so, having regard to what had been done under the implemented permissions. Where the test of physical impossibility was met, the reason why further development carried out in reliance on the permission was unlawful was simply that the development was not authorised by the terms of the permission. The Supreme Court provided further guidance on application of the *Pilkington* principle.[10] Where there are two planning permissions for the same site, what matters is whether it is physically possible to carry out the unimplemented planning permission. A mere inconsistency between the two planning permissions does not prevent the other planning permission from being carried out.[11]

Referring specifically to multi-unit developments, the Supreme Court agreed with the view expressed by the Court of Appeal in that case that where

[5] *Hillside* (n 1) [35], citing *Pioneer Aggregates* (n 4) 140–41.
[6] *Hillside* (n 1) [35], citing *Pioneer Aggregates* (n 4) 141.
[7] *Hillside* (n 1) [37].
[8] *Pioneer Aggregates* (n 4) 139.
[9] *Hillside* (n 1) [38].
[10] ibid [41], [43], referring to *Pilkington* (n 3).
[11] See also M Greig, 'Physical Impossibility of Implementing Planning Approval' [2022] *Scottish Planning and Environmental Law* 138.

planning permission is granted for the development of a site, such as a housing estate, comprising multiple units, it is unlikely to be severable: 'The scheme for development … which was the subject of the 1967 permission seems to us to be a paradigm instance of such an integrated scheme which cannot be severed into component parts.'[12] The Supreme Court did not, however, rule out the possibility that planning permission of a multi-unit development could be severable where construction of the permissions authorised this. Section 110 of the Levelling-up and Regeneration Act 2023, which is not yet in force, will introduce a new section 73B into the Town and Country Planning Act 1990, which would enable local planning authorities to grant new permissions for developments that are substantially the same in effect as an existing permission, whilst only considering the ways in which the new permission would differ from its predecessor.[13] The provision was not drafted with *Hillside* in mind, but was intended to supplement and simplify the process of amending permissions.[14]

II. THE NATURE OF PLANNING PERMISSION AS A PROPERTY RIGHT

The Supreme Court was faced with difficult questions about the nature of rights arising when planning permission is granted. Following the first Town and Country Planning Act in 1947, planning permission was treated as a quasi-property right, because it is binding on anyone with an interest in the land and is contained within special planning registers held by local authorities. However, it is not a right within the traditional sense, because it is not within the land registration system and so cannot be an interest which overrides. The Supreme Court treated it as a self-enclosed statutory principle, applied their own ideas of what is a property interest and decided that the physical impossibility test is the true basis for the so-called abandonment principle, which the Supreme Court held had no place in planning law.

Since any grant of planning permission to develop land (except insofar as the permission otherwise provides) is for the benefit of the land and of all persons with an interest in it,[15] planning permission does, therefore, transfer to the buyer upon sale, since planning permission attaches to the land. Planning permission stays with the property and not the owner, because it is statutory and not due to being proprietary. When planning permission is granted with or without conditions, it is entered into the local authority planning register, at which point it becomes a property right. Despite what the Supreme Court stated in *Hillside* about abandonment of planning permissions, common law abandonment

[12] *Hillside* (n 1) [72].

[13] See further N Gooch, 'A View from *Hillside*: How the Supreme Court Decision is Shaping Planning in Practice' (2023) 13 *Journal of Planning and Environment Law* OP67, OP88.

[14] ibid.

[15] Town and Country Planning Act 1971, s 33(1).

remains a key concept in relation to other aspects of planning law where questions of whether a use has been abandoned arise.

There was a very helpful summary of the case law that had considered abandonment of planning permission in *R (on the Application of Ocado Retail Ltd) v Islington London Borough Council*.[15] Holgate J considered that abandonment was a doctrine that could be considered and applied in relevant cases. In that case, a lawful planning right which had accrued upon the expiry of a time limit was not lost merely because subsequently that right was not exercised for a period of time. The requirement was that the right remained in existence at the date when the lawfulness of what it authorised was in issue and had not been lost by a supervening event, such as abandonment.

The Supreme Court in *Hillside* did not refer to the *Ocado* case in its judgment or to the other cases considered by Holgate J. For example, in *Hartley v Minister of Housing and Local Government*,[17] the Court of Appeal held that the use of a site, such as an established use, could be abandoned, and its resumption would require planning consent. The test applied was:

> Has the cessation of use (followed by non-use) been merely temporary, or did it amount to an abandonment? If it was merely temporary, the previous use can be resumed without planning permission being obtained. If it amounted to abandonment, it cannot be resumed unless planning permission is obtained.[18]

Holgate J contrasted this with the decision in *Pioneer Aggregates*[19] that a planning permission which remains capable of being implemented cannot as a matter of law be abandoned. Planning permissions may, however, terminate by time limits for the commencement of development.[20]

In another case referred to in *Ocado*, *Hughes v Secretary of State for the Environment, Transport and the Regions*,[21] the Court of Appeal accepted that abandonment can be assessed by the planning authority by reference to four criteria: '(i) the physical condition of the building; (ii) the length of time for which the property had not been used for residential purposes; (iii) whether it had been used for any other purposes; and (iv) the owner's intentions'.[22] Despite this, the Court of Appeal in *Hughes* held that the test is an objective one and the subjective intentions of the actual owner are not determinative. The objective

[16] *R (on the Application of Ocado Retail Ltd) v Islington London Borough Council* [2021] EWHC 1509 [74]–[80].

[17] *Hartley v Minister of Housing and Local Government* [1970] 1 QB 413, considered in *Ocado* (n 16) [74].

[18] *Hartley* (n 17) 420 (L Denning MR).

[19] *Pioneer Aggregates* (n 4). Holgate J also refers to *Camden London Borough Council v McDonald's Restaurants* (1993) 65 P & CR 423.

[20] Town and Country Planning Act 1990, ss 91–93.

[21] *Hughes v Secretary of State for the Environment, Transport and the Regions* (2000) 80 P & CR 397.

[22] ibid 398, applied in *Trustees of the Castell-y-Mynach Estate v Secretary of State for Wales* [1985] JPL 40.

test is based on the view that would be taken by a reasonable person with knowledge of all the relevant circumstances.[23] The inspector was entitled to conclude that residential user had been abandoned due to its physical condition and the period since it was last used as a residence, even though the intention of the appellant was to live at the property. As stated by Thorpe LJ: 'It would not be right to elevate the intentions of its owners to a paramount status, or conversely to subordinate other relevant considerations to intention.'[24] Unfortunately, this case was not considered in *Hillside*.

In *Swale Borough Council v First Secretary of State*,[25] also considered in the *Ocado* case, Keene LJ, relying on *Hartley v Minister of Housing and Local Government*,[26] stated that: 'The concept of abandoning the use is, in my judgment, best confined to the topic of established use rights where it is a well-recognised concept.'[27] However, as explained in *Ocado*, Keene LJ 'was using the expressions "established use rights" and "lawful use rights" interchangeably',[28] because the issue was whether abandonment was relevant to an accrued use right being lost, but not to whether it had accrued in the first place.[29] *Swale* was cited in *Staffordshire County Council v Challinor*,[30] where the leading judgment was also given by Keene LJ. Neither of these cases were discussed in *Hillside*, which meant that a significant body of case law on abandonment was not analysed in that specific context, with the consequence that abandonment is still relevant in relation to use of a planning permission.

Gray and Gray refer to planning controls as an example of the 'property absolutism of a bygone era being replaced by a property relativism which holds that the estate owner's "bundle of rights" contains no entitlement ruthlessly to exploit land resources regardless of the communal good'.[31] This is, however, a statement of political and economic philosophy rather than of legal truth. The grant of planning permission makes the concession to the homeowner of an increased degree of socially permitted control over that land, and the homeowner's bundle of rights is augmented by the conferment of an extra component of property. When the state curtails its possible use or development, the state is effectively withdrawing from the homeowner certain important kinds of 'property' in respect of that land.[32] This demonstrates that the state retains an eminent domain or overriding 'property' in all land, which Gray and Gray identify as perhaps the most significant present-day manifestation of the Crown's

[23] *Hughes* (n 21) 402 (Kennedy LJ); see also the discussion in *Ocado* (n 16) [76].
[24] *Hughes* (n 21) 402–03.
[25] *Swale Borough Council v First Secretary of State* [2005] EWCA Civ 1568.
[26] *Hartley* (n 17).
[27] *Swale Borough Council* (n 25) [30] (Keene LJ).
[28] *Ocado* (n 16) [79], referring to *Swale Borough Council* (n 25) [7], [9], [15].
[29] *Ocado* (n 16).
[30] *Staffordshire County Council v Challinor* [2007] EWCA Civ 864, [2008] 1 P & CR 161 [31].
[31] K Gray and SF Gray, *Elements of Land Law*, 5th edn (Oxford, Oxford University Press, 2009) 1.5.54.
[32] ibid 1.5.55.

radical title, with the state holding the dominating stake in the determination of land use priorities.[33] Such an approach is arguably evident in *Hillside*, with the Supreme Court rejecting the doctrine of abandonment and ensuring property relativism with the test of physical impossibility.

The hybrid, quasi-property right nature of planning permission is demonstrated by the analysis of Lees of an increasingly sophisticated series of responses, particularly from the courts, in assessing how private law rules interact with the rapidly changing legal landscape in respect of, inter alia, planning law controls.[34] As Lees has examined in the context of *Coventry v Lawrence*,[35] planning permissions are effectively a public assessment of relative need and benefit within a local area, but they are not determinative of the scope of private property rights, acquired as part of title to land.[36] It is not a defence to an action in nuisance that the defendant had planning permission. The Supreme Court in *Coventry* confirmed that planning permissions of any sort will never alter the balance of factors applied by the courts in determining the existence of a nuisance, but may, however, influence the remedy which courts will grant with damages, rather than injunctions, becoming the normal remedy.[37] As demonstrated by Lees, the case left the door open for future problems in the interaction between private and regulatory law with a gap in the planning system that no compensation is awarded.[38] Where there are competing proprietary entitlements to use land in a way which oversteps the normal balance between neighbouring owners, *Coventry* demonstrates where the balance lies in finding a mutual accommodation between the principles of the private law in the tort of nuisance, and the public interest and public benefit encapsulated in planning law.[39] *Hillside* is an example of how the courts adapt and direct their case law to continually strive to articulate the extent to which land law rules should constrain and shape public law and vice versa.

The test of physical impossibility is not a test usually applied in land law. Gray and Gray consider the test of impossibility in the context of the court's historic jurisdiction to strike down conditions or limitations attached to a grant in fee simple where the constraints have been impossible or illegal or against public policy on moral, social or economic grounds.[40] They acknowledge that the judicial power to override the expressed wishes of grantors has always represented a significant diminution of the owner's right under English law to dispose of any assets.[41] It is likely that the test of impossibility will be confined

[33] ibid.

[34] E Lees, *Principles of Property Law* (Oxford, Oxford University Press, 2020) 15–16.

[35] *Coventry v Lawrence* [2015] UKSC 50, [2015] 1 WLR 3485.

[36] Lees (n 34) 598.

[37] ibid 598.

[38] ibid 599.

[39] ibid 603. See also M Dixon, 'The Sound of Silence' [2014] *Conveyancer and Property Lawyer* 79.

[40] Gray and Gray (n 31) 3.1.37, referring to W Blackstone, *Commentaries on the Laws of England*, vol 2 (1766) 156.

[41] Gray and Gray (n 31).

to planning permissions and not have a broader reach into other areas. *Hillside* was followed in *R (on the Application of Dennis) v Southwark London Borough Council*,[42] where, on its true construction, the planning permission was not severable. The provisions for the development to be carried out in phases were entirely consistent with the grant of a single, integrated planning permission, and did not amount to a contra-indication pointing to severability of the phases, and the test of physical impossibility was applied.[43] As a result of *Hillside*, planning permission as a property right needs to be analysed through this lens which makes the right relative as opposed to absolute.

III. ANALOGY WITH THE DOCTRINE OF ABANDONMENT IN RELATION TO OTHER RIGHTS IN LAND

A comparison with other rights in land, especially easements, provides insights into potential cognitive dissonance between the operation of abandonment in private law and planning law. In relation to easements, mere non-user is not enough by itself,[44] even if accompanied by a mistaken belief that the right has been extinguished.[45] If the dominant owner shows an intention to release an easement or profit, it will be extinguished by implied release. An intention to abandon the right, which is a question of fact, must be shown,[46] although non-user for a long period may raise a presumption of abandonment.[47] Twenty years non-user will usually be sufficient,[48] but even then the presumption may be rebutted if there is another explanation.[49] The non-user may be explained by the fact that the dominant owner had no need to use the easement, in which case it will not be enough to establish abandonment.[50] A presumption of abandonment will arise where there are circumstances adverse to the user and sufficient to explain the non-user, combined with a substantial length of time during which the dominant owner has acquiesced in that state of affairs or where the dominant owner does some act clearly indicating the firm intention that neither he nor any successor in title of his should thereafter make use of the easement.[51] Abandonment is not to be lightly inferred, since owners of property

[42] *R (on the Application of Dennis) v Southwark London Borough Council* [2024] EWHC 57.
[43] ibid [115].
[44] *Ward v Ward* (1852) 7 Exch 838, 839; *Gotobed v Pridmore* (1970) 115 SJ 78, as discussed in R Megarry and HWR Wade, *The Law of Real Property*, 5th edn (London, Stevens & Sons Ltd, 1984) 897.
[45] *Obadia v Morris* (1974) 232 EG 333, discussed in Megarry and Wade (n 44) 897.
[46] *Swan v Sinclair* [1924] 1 Ch 254, affirmed [1925] AC 227.
[47] *Crossley & Sons Ltd v Lightowler* (1867) 2 Ch App 478, 482; see Megarry and Wade (n 44) 897–98.
[48] *Moore v Rawson* (1824) 3 B & C 332, 339, as compared with *Lawrence v Obee* (1814) 3 Camp 514.
[49] *Ward v Ward* (n 44); *James v Stevenson* [1893] AC 162; *Treweeke v 36 Wolseley Road Pty Ltd* (1973) 128 CLR 274.
[50] J Gaunt and P Morgan, *Gale on Easements*, 21st edn (London, Sweet & Maxwell, 2020) [12-72].
[51] ibid.

do not normally wish to divest themselves of it unless it is to their advantage to do so, even though they may have no present use for it.[52] The law as to the abandonment of an easement can be contrasted with the rules for the abandonment of the benefit of a contract.[53] It is not possible to have a unilateral abandonment of the benefit of a contract, but it seems possible to have a unilateral abandonment of the benefit of an easement.

Although many of the cases of abandonment of easements can be considered in terms of estoppel by acquiescence, or other estoppels,[54] this analysis is not appropriate for all the decisions. *Gale on Easements* differentiates the law based on whether the easements are continuous or discontinuous. The law as to abandonment of continuous easements does not require a fixed amount of time during which this cessation must continue, and the key issue is whether there was an intention to abandon the right.[55] In relation to discontinuous easements, the rule would appear to be that mere non-user without more, however long, cannot amount to abandonment. Such non-user is evidence from which abandonment may be inferred, but must be regarded in the context of the circumstances as a whole.[56] Whether a person intends an abandonment is not a subjective question; it is always a question of fact to be ascertained from the surrounding circumstances as to whether the act amounts to an abandonment or was intended as such.[57]

It is notable that Strahilevitz argues that when the beneficiary of an easement releases it, there is no abandonment, because the transfer necessarily benefits the owner of the servient tenement.[58] His rationale is that abandonment of real property necessarily entails indifference as to the identity of the subsequent owner, so it is wrong to refer to the abandonment of an incorporeal hereditament because when such an interest is 'abandoned', the interest in question reverts to the owner of the previously burdened estate. Therefore, in Strahilevitz's view, real property, both corporeal and incorporeal, cannot be abandoned under the common law. His view is problematic in relation to incorporeal hereditaments, because the intention of the owner of the dominant tenement is to cease permanently using the easement rather than having a positive intention to transfer the benefit of the easement. This contrasts with the view of Peñalver that the benefit of easements and covenants can be 'abandoned' and will 'disappear' with the rights being restored to the owner of the burdened possessory estate, which Peñalver treats as a borderline case of abandonment.[59] Only the benefit of an easement can be abandoned, because the burden can only be terminated with the consent of the benefitted party.

[52] ibid.

[53] ibid [12-30].

[54] Ibid, referring to *Lester v Woodgate* [2010] EWCA Civ 199, [2010] 2 P & CR 21.

[55] See, eg, *Moore v Rawson* (n 48); *Ecclesiastical Commissioners for England v Kino* (1880) 14 Ch D 213; and the cases discussed in Gaunt and Morgan (n 50) at [12-32]–[12-71].

[56] Gaunt and Morgan (n 50) [12-72].

[57] Ibid, discussing *Odey v Barber* [2006] EWHC 3109, [2008] Ch 175 – see also other cases at [12-72]–[12-117].

[58] LJ Strahilevitz, 'The Right to Abandon' (2010) 158 *University of Pennsylvania Law Review* 355, 377.

[59] EM Peñalver, 'The Illusory Right to Abandon' (2010) 109 *Michigan Law Review* 191, 200, 212.

A. Limits on Unilateral Divestment

Hickey analyses whether it is possible in English law to unilaterally divest title or abandon property.[60] As he states, the law of abandonment contains many paradoxes, as demonstrated by the fact that there are few decided cases where abandonment has been allowed, and most of these are explicable on grounds other than a unilaterally accomplished divesting of title.[61] This has produced a lack of consensus on abandonment, to the point where commentary has both vigorously asserted and denied the very existence of the possibility.[62] Hickey argues that the law would better reflect the values of private property if it regarded owners as obligated to facilitate the transfer of the property to some other person, rather than free to dispose of it unilaterally. Such recognition would more fairly balance a regard for owner-autonomy with the broader distributive and community-focused aims of private property.

As argued by Hickey, doctrinally divesting abandonment is framed as an obverse of the common law's foundational maxim of possessory acquisition.[63] If factual possession and intention to possess serve to generate an original property right for the possessor, the cessation of possession with an intention to relinquish operates to divest such an interest. His argument is persuasive that this overstates the role of autonomy in justifying the creation or extinction of property rights.[64] The decision in *Hillside* is emblematic of the rejection of the autonomy of a property right holder, which Hickey describes as a principal animating value of our system of property law, and reminds us that property rights are responsive to the interests of others. This approach cautions against recognition that a property right holder may unilaterally divest title without restrictions.[65]

B. Implied Release?

Hickey argues that the judgment in *Annetts v Adeleye*[66] makes clear in relation to easements that what we currently think of as abandonment relates to whether, in the circumstances, it is equitable to treat the easement as having been impliedly released, since what is required is a more bilateral enquiry as to the effect of conduct between the dominant and servient owners.[67] This would

[60] R Hickey, 'The Problem of Divesting Abandonment' [2016] *Conveyancer and Property Lawyer* 28.

[61] ibid.

[62] ibid 28, citing A Hudson, 'Is Divesting Abandonment Possible at Common Law?' (1984) 100 *LQR* 110; Peñalver (n 59); J Griffiths-Baker, 'Divesting Abandonment: an Unnecessary Concept?' (2007) 36 *Common Law World Review* 16.

[63] Hickey (n 60) 36.

[64] ibid.

[65] ibid 38.

[66] *Annetts v Adeleye* [2018] EWCA Civ 555, [2018] 1 WLR 4539.

[67] R Hickey, 'Abandoning "Abandonment" for the Implied Release of Easements: *Annetts v Adeleye* [2018] EWCA Civ 555; [2018] 2 P & CR DG9' [2018] *Conveyancer and Property Lawyer* 289, 289–90.

link to cases on informal express release of easements, providing 'a more robust framework for decision-making, facilitating the autonomy and action of the parties, and jettisoning some of the well-ingrained common law antipathy to abandonment that lurks in the background of these cases'.[68]

The court in *Annetts*[69] held that a right of way over an access road had not been abandoned on a transfer of land which included it and that a covenant by the purchaser to fence the boundary of the access road did not demonstrate an intention to extinguish the right of way. As stated by Arden LJ, the court has to find:

> [T]he objective intention of the person alleged to have abandoned the right of way as reasonably perceived by the servient owner. It is irrelevant whether the servient owner actually knew about the transaction because the test is one of the reasonable perception of the servient owner and what he would conclude as to the dominant owner's intentions.[70]

What was key was that 'the hypothetical servient owner would not have concluded that the right of way had been abandoned'.[71] The principles in *Dwyer v Westminster City Council*[72] made it clear that abandonment was not to be lightly inferred.

Implied release is not suitable in the *Hillside* context, because the Supreme Court was rejecting in its approach a test of physical relinquishing/non-use and a corroborating manifest divesting intention. Hickey has praised this test due to the virtues of provenance and doctrinal elegance, whilst also recognising its limitations.[73] In relation to provenance, Hickey argues that they are taken to replicate to a large extent the Roman law on divesting abandonment, except for the well-known Roman school dispute about whether or not something had to be assumed by another in order for the divesting effect to occur, in which case, abandonment in Roman law is better understood as a form of indirect transfer.[74] Instead, the Supreme Court's test of physical impossibility is rigid and leads to the result that where actioning part of the unimplemented planning permission would be impossible, the court is thereby disallowing other parts of the original permission that could still be implemented. It is arguable that the decision in *Hillside* does not leave sufficient room for flexibility and is a one-size-fits-all approach unless the planning permission on its construction can be interpreted to allow severance. There may need to be more scope for the possibility of severance of parts of the unimplemented planning permission which are still feasible and achievable.

[68] ibid 290.
[69] *Annetts* (n 66).
[70] ibid [10].
[71] ibid [54] (Arden LJ).
[72] *Dwyer v Westminster City Council* [2014] EWCA Civ 153, [2014] 2 P & CR 7, referred to in *Annetts* (n 66) at [49].
[73] Hickey (n 67) 292.
[74] ibid.

The test of physical impossibility is necessarily an objective test and appears to leave no space for developers to argue that they will reverse parts of what have already been constructed to achieve their current goals. The objective nature of this test links with the approach in *Annetts*[75] of the reasonable perceptions of a hypothetical owner of the servient tenement. As Hickey has pointed out, generally where abandonment is understood as a unilateral divesting act, the law is agnostic as to who sees or hears the evidence of intention to abandon: it matters just that it was manifested.[76] His view in disputes relating to easements is that they might be more usefully managed through the law on informal express release on estoppel principles, where it would be inequitable for the dominant owner to assert that the easement still exists, rather than implied release through abandonment.[77] Abandonment should depend on the manifested intention of the dominant owner rather than the perceptions of the hypothetical servient owner. The Supreme Court decision in *Hillside* typifies the common law's misgivings and cynicism in relation to abandonment in refusing to apply it or even consider the implications and nuances of doing so in this context. The consequence is that developers need to take extreme care to ensure they do not invalidate retrospectively any planning permissions obtained due to this benchmark of physical impossibility and that the blunt instrument accepted by Supreme Court in *Hillside* is not equally effective as abandonment.

The Law Commission considered the problems which arise from the current law as to implied release or abandonment of easements.[78] They took into account two competing concerns relating to the extinguishment by abandonment:

> One is the need to preserve property rights and avoid any unlawful deprivation of property, while the other is the need to ensure that land is not burdened by rights that are obsolete. It benefits no-one to have titles encumbered by easements and profits that are never going to be used; but those who hold such interests should not be obliged to defend their rights by constant use.[79]

Although restrictive covenants can be discharged by the Lands Chamber pursuant to section 84 of the Law of Property Act 1925, there is no such jurisdiction for easements and profits, despite the recommendations of the Law Commission.[80] This is obviously not directly relevant in relation to planning applications, but the one-dimensional and inflexible approach adopted in *Hillside* highlights the potential need for one that is more malleable. This can be contrasted with the position in Scotland, where easements (servitudes) can be extinguished[81]

[75] *Annetts* (n 66).
[76] Hickey (n 67) 292.
[77] ibid 296.
[78] Law Commission, *Making Land Work: Easements, Covenants and Profits à Prendre* (Law Com No 327, 2011) [3-212]–[3-231].
[79] ibid [3.214].
[80] ibid [3.215] and see also [3.228].
[81] Title Conditions (Scotland) Act 2003, s 90.

because they are a 'title condition'.[82] Property rights are often lost by non-use for 20 years, whereby negative prescription extinguishes them.[83]

IV. COMPARISON WITH ABANDONMENT IN ADVERSE POSSESSION

Fee simple estates cannot be abandoned.[84] This derives from the feudal system of landholding after the Norman Conquest of England in 1066. Adverse possession does, however, enable abandoned land to be brought into productive socio-economic use. Adverse possession reflects the law giving precedence to the actual possession and use of the land, so that there is a possessor and subsequently an owner taking responsibility for it. Fox O'Mahony and Cobb argue that possession could be viewed, legitimately, as taking precedence over ownership, through an application of the concept of a duty of stewardship in relation to land. This also resonates with contemporary philosophical and policy analysis that seeks to foster productive use of land and the role of property law as potentially transformative in relation to social justice and citizenship.[85] The goal of ensuring effective stewardship of land is arguably a justifiable objective of the doctrine of adverse possession to deter poor management of land.[86] Research into the role of land tenure systems in promoting sustainability, economic development and social inclusion has highlighted the promotion of productive land use and stewardship as core values.[87]

Rostill draws a distinction between destructive abandonment of an interest in land (what he terms 'extinctive abandonment') and the abandonment of possession of land.[88] Rostill explains that extinctive abandonment occurs if an interest is extinguished by virtue of the interest holder's intention to divest of the interest, possibly together with some further element, such as physical separation.[89] The case of *Mount Carmel Investments Ltd v Thurlow*,[90] relating to an adverse possessor, was arguably not an example of extinctive abandonment, as Rostill explains, because the adverse possessor had a possessory title

[82] ibid s 122(1).

[83] Prescription and Limitation (Scotland) Act 1973, s 8, but note exceptions in sched 3, including ownership of land. See also *The Scottish Environment Protection Agency and Others v The Joint Liquidators of the Scottish Coal Company Ltd* [2013] CSIH 108; *Joint Liquidators of the Scottish Coal Co Ltd, Noters* [2013] CSOH 124.

[84] *Ironmonger v Bernard International*, CA (9 February 1996, unreported), discussed in L Rostill, *Possession, Relative Title, and Ownership in English Law* (Oxford, Oxford University Press, 2021) 92.

[85] L Fox O'Mahony and N Cobb, 'Taxonomies of Squatting: Unlawful Occupation in a New Legal Order' (2008) 71 *MLR* 878, 904.

[86] ibid. The duty of stewardship is derived from JP Karp, 'A Private Property Duty of Stewardship: Changing Our Land Ethic' (1993) 23 *Environmental Law* 735.

[87] Fox O'Mahony and Cobb (n 85) 905.

[88] Rostill (n 84) 91.

[89] ibid.

[90] *Mount Carmel Investments Ltd v Thurlow* [1988] 1 WLR 1078.

only, which was lost when he gave up possession. Rostill considers, in the alternative, that *Thurlow* could be a case of extinctive abandonment if it is argued that the adverse possessor's title was destroyed not because he lost possession, but because he manifested an intention to divest himself of his title.[91] It is, however, likely that the court in *Thurlow* merely assumed that it was possible for an adverse possessor to abandon their interest and the court did not examine this point, which means that *Thurlow* is not a strong authority that the interest acquired by a possessor may be abandoned.[92] The terminology of destructive and extinctive abandonment to describe where an interest is extinguished, because of the interest holder's intention to divest of the interest together with physical separation, may be seen to indicate some innate frustrations by Rostill in conceptualising the law of abandonment. Rostill's theory may, nevertheless, be useful as providing the basis for the threshold for a doctrine of abandonment of planning permission, whilst achieving the same overall result as in *Hillside*, without the necessity to resort to the doctrine of physical impossibility.

Penner's justification for abandonment is an individual's autonomy interest, since: 'It would indeed be a funny turn of events if … property in essence gave the things a person owned a power over him.'[93] An owner cannot by his act alone destroy his title, but can relinquish title, whereupon a subsequent owner's possession may give good title.[94] Penner favours symmetry between a system of laws that gives an individual the freedom to choose whether to acquire, and whether and when to be rid of property.[95] He acknowledges that avoidance of harm to others, which also incorporates the social interest, is an important counter-interest to ascribe responsibility to a person for the harms which their property may cause. As Penner states, the rules of title reflect both the owner's right of exclusive use and the general right not to be harmed.[96]

Penner examines Hohfeld's extinction/creation model of transfer, attributing to Hohfeld that his 'power to alienate' is also a 'power to abandon', and demonstrates why the directional abandonment model does not work.[97] The model relies on two normative powers: the power to abandon and the power to acquire title to unowned property by taking possession of it. Penner's discussion of the directional abandonment model, which is in effect a unilateral transfer of ownership or abandonment as transfer, focuses on whether a transfer can amount to successful abandonment and is a re-evaluation of abandonment as a specific way to transfer ownership. Directional abandonment followed by appropriation is a matter of empirical success, but fails as

[91] Rostill (n 84) 92.
[92] ibid 93.
[93] JE Penner, *The Idea of Property in Law* (Oxford, Oxford University Press, 1997) 79.
[94] ibid.
[95] Ibid; see also discussion in Strahilevitz (n 58) 371.
[96] Penner (n 93) 80.
[97] JE Penner, *Property Rights: A Re-examination* (Oxford, Oxford University Press, 2020) 132.

a normative substitute of mimicking the normative relationship of transferor and transferee.[98]

Penner's model has another very counter-intuitive implication, because it brings into play the nature and justification of acquiring rights by appropriating unowned things in every case of transfer and highlights the issue of whether deficiencies in the transferor's title pass to the transferee.[99] He is right in rejecting this model of transfer because, as he states, the model cannot distinguish between the case where a person acquires land as a successor in title from a previous owner by a conveyance, and the case where a person acquires a title to land by adverse possession, whereby the adverse possessor acquires an entirely new title in the land, which can be transferred to someone else.[100] The revocable licence to appropriate only achieves abandonment when someone else has appropriated the property. But more compelling reasons for rejecting this form of delayed or conditional transfer are that the abandonment would only be successful if someone else takes ownership, since unilateral relinquishment of title is not possible.[101] Penner's model is unsuitable and inappropriate in the context of planning permissions, and in repudiating the doctrine of abandonment in *Hillside*, the Supreme Court is demonstrating a legitimate concern about the coherence and unpredictability of abandonment as a congruous principle in planning law.

It is worth examining the views of a couple of American scholars on adverse possession in this context. Strahilevitz considers the relationship between adverse possession law and the law of abandonment.[102] Adverse possession may function as a substitute for abandonment, though it is an awkward one. The primary conceptual difference between abandonment and adverse possession stems from adverse possession's requirement of non-permissiveness. Strahilevitz argues that if the owner has intentionally relinquished title, then the trespasser's presence on the land becomes permissive, precluding the possibility of adverse possession.[103] In English law, however, the key issue is whether the possession is without consent and not whether the owner intentionally relinquished title, so adverse possession could be established in these circumstances. Since adverse possession takes so many years before the title transfers, this creates a great deal of uncertainty in the meantime and, in Strahilevitz's view, abandonment would be far more attractive than adverse possession to a landowner who wishes to divest themselves of their interest in land.[104]

[98] ibid 133.
[99] ibid 134.
[100] ibid 135.
[101] See also K von Schütz, 'Keeping it Private: The Impossibility of Abandoning Ownership and the *Horror Vacui* of the Common Law of Property' (2021) 66 *McGill Law Journal* 721, 735.
[102] Strahilevitz (n 58) 415–16.
[103] ibid 415.
[104] ibid 416.

Strahilevitz acknowledges that there may be good reasons to continue permitting the bad-faith adverse possession of real property, but it is almost impossible to construct a set of arguments under which bad-faith adverse possession of land should be permitted while the abandonment of positive-value real estate is prohibited.[105] He defines a bad-faith adverse possessor as someone who enters another's property knowing that it belongs to someone else or indifferent as to the state of title, and does not have an incentive to put the property in their possession to its highest-value use until the time limit expires. This compares with a good-faith adverse possessor, who Strahilevitz defines as someone who will not hesitate to put the land to its highest-value use, because they believe that the property in question is theirs.[106] He argues that if abandoned real property is not overwhelmingly characterised by negative value and the courts have the institutional capacity to sort between valuable and valueless property, abandonment should be permitted. That would, however, be excessively onerous in the English system of law. Incorporating and adapting notions of good-faith and bad-faith abandonment of planning permissions would inevitably introduce unnecessary and unwarranted layers of complexity.

Richardson has an interesting alternative solution for abandoned property, which is adverse possession with a reformed possession requirement.[107] She argues that the traditional application of the possessory requirement for adverse possession should be modified when the true owner has vacated the property, that actual possession should be unnecessary and, instead, a notice of intent to possess should be sufficient to acquire abandoned property through adverse possession. Technology might help in providing notice with, for example, a website maintained by the government that would allow individuals to register their notice of intent online.[108] Her view is that this would be an efficient solution for private parties to acquire ownership of abandoned properties, while still offering a temporal safety net to protect true owners. She argues that it would encourage adverse possessors and true owners to transfer ownership through voluntary bilateral transactions, which may result in a sale rather than adverse possession. Adverse possession could then become an unused relic of past property law.[109] Such a proposal is, however, fraught with difficulties and is an extremely unlikely solution in English law. From an evaluation of the theories examined above, Rostill's extinctive abandonment has the greatest potential to bring value added to the discussions on abandonment and could provide a springboard for further debate, although there was distinctly and unequivocally no support for such an approach in *Hillside*.

[105] ibid 418.
[106] ibid 417.
[107] SB Richardson, 'Abandonment and Adverse Possession' (2015) 52 *Houston Law Review* 1385.
[108] ibid 1416.
[109] ibid 1429.

V. ADDITIONAL LESSONS FROM THE WRITINGS OF AMERICAN ACADEMICS

The views of a few American academics have already been discussed in relation to specific areas examined to widen the scope of the debate. Further views are considered here in relation to abandonment in broader contexts.

A. Dualist Ownership Model Favouring Abandonment

Von Schütz makes a very helpful analysis of the fear that motivates the restrictions on abandonment, which is the *horror vacui* of common law ownership in its specific normative significance.[110] The way in which the common law conceives of ownership and distributes the roles between private owners and the state commits the common law to 'keep it private' in order to ensure that property remains in private ownership for as long as possible.[111] This is due to various factors: feudal heritage,[112] the need to prevent owners escaping liability for negative externalities,[113] and proprietary responsibility to determine the normative position of others to prevent creating a normative vacuum.[114] She contrasts civilian jurisdictions where ownership of land can be abandoned in a large number of those jurisdictions, with the state stepping in as the 'owner of last resort'.[115]

Von Schütz demonstrates how the dualist ownership model for public entities on the possibility of abandonment is operated by the property laws of France and Quebec, which are different from those in England. The 'public ownership of last resort' mechanism makes it legally possible to abandon with the abandonment never failing for lack of a designated successor, but it does not turn abandonment into transfer. Nevertheless, 'public ownership of last resort' restrictions and liability mechanisms directed at past owners take effect even if public entities assume ownership. A public ownership regime is reconcilable with the imposition of further obligations for ex post contributions or financial compensation when someone's dealing with an ownable resource generates

[110] Von Schütz (n 101).
[111] ibid 725–26.
[112] ibid 739–41; see also J Baker, *An Introduction to English Legal History*, 5th edn (Oxford, Oxford University Press, 2019) 245–47.
[113] Von Schütz (n 101) 741–42.
[114] ibid 743–45, discussing L Katz, 'Exclusion and Exclusivity in Property Law' (2008) 58 *University of Toronto Law Journal* 275, 306; L Katz, 'The Moral Paradox of Adverse Possession: Sovereignty and Revolution in Property Law' (2010) 55 *McGill Law Journal* 47, 71, 77–78; L Katz, 'Ownership and Offices: The Building Blocks of the Legal Order' (2020) 70 *University of Toronto Law Journal* 267, 269.
[115] Von Schütz (n 101) 745–50. See also the discussion by Strahilevitz (n 58) 394–95 on escheat, whereby abandoned property automatically becomes the property of the jurisdiction in which it is abandoned or in which the abandoning owner resides.

harm or undue burdens. In addition, the doctrine of domanial duty lets public entities assume ownership of an abandoned property under the private ownership modality.[116]

Recourse to a model of 'public ownership of the last resort' is barred in common law jurisdictions. Von Schütz enumerates three crucial features that characterise common law ownership and shape the legal rules on abandonment. First, common law ownership is monist, because the only modality that the common law knows is the private one, based on a fear of the absence of private ownership.[117] Abandonment is to be prevented unless a designated private successor comes forward. Second, it is grounded in a private ownership paradigm, which has the consequence that it is considered highly undesirable to vest ownership in public entities. Lastly, it assigns proprietary responsibility exclusively to private owners,[118] who have complete proprietary responsibility for property. Public entities, if they assume ownership, cannot flexibly switch between different modalities as happens in civil law jurisdictions. Instead, the common law's conception of ownership implements a strict separation between private owners and public entities. This strengthens the role of private ownership, even if such owners are prevented from abandoning, because it makes private ownership truly private.[119] There are very limited exceptions, such as the intestate death of an owner, but the common law does not extend this to a private owner's decision to abandon, as was demonstrated in *Hillside* in a different context.

B. Autonomy versus Obligation

Peñalver examines how the unilateral and relatively unqualified nature of the right to abandon is an example of the law's concern to safeguard the individual autonomy interests that lie at the heart of the concept of private ownership.[120] He analyses the law of abandonment as a useful case study of the law's recognition of the interplay between autonomy and obligation. He argues that viewed through the lens of land, the right to abandon virtually any form of tangible property, even chattels, is an illusion, because the legal prohibition of abandoning land dramatically qualifies the unilateral right to abandon chattels almost to the point of insignificance.[121] He states that what typically passes for 'abandonment', which is a purely unilateral act, of other types of property are actually bilateral acts, which are seamless conveyances of property from one person to

[116] Von Schütz (n 101) 749–50.
[117] ibid 750–51.
[118] ibid 753–55.
[119] ibid 755.
[120] Peñalver (n 59).
[121] ibid 194.

another that require the consent of both.[122] His view is that the appropriate question to ask is why the common law expresses such suspicion of abandonment as a whole, and answers that ownership is a social practice suffused with obligation and duty. Land ownership is revealed to be an obligation-laden institution through which the law can both enforce and disseminate norms of ownership.[123]

Peñalver argues that amongst conveyances, the doctrine that comes closest to abandonment is the law of gifts, but recognises that the legal act of giving a gift is a cooperative process that is quite distinct from the unilateral act of abandonment.[124] By way of contrast, forfeiture, which he discusses in the context of American law, and abandonment resemble each other in their unilateral operation and the absence of an intention by the owner to direct the property to a particular person. In forfeitures, however, the loss of ownership rights is the consequence of some other act, operating independently of the original owner's intentions and often against their wishes.[125]

Peñalver makes a valuable distinction between the law of abandonment as a post hoc means of resolving disputes over ownership and the right to abandon as an affirmative power or privilege from an ex ante perspective. It is this ex ante power of abandonment that matters most to exclusion theorists.[126] The rule relating to abandonment of land is one example of the common law's use of private ownership as a crucial tool for enforcing and disseminating property norms.[127] Peñalver is in favour of broadening the discussion beyond efficiency and autonomy to include the question of obligations to have a more nuanced defence of the common law's suspicion of abandonment.

C. The Permissive View of Abandonment

By way of contrast to Peñalver's view, Strahilevitz argues that the common law's complete prohibition on the abandonment of corporeal interests in real property is misguided and that legal rules prohibiting abandonment ought to be replaced with a more permissive regime in which both the value of the underlying resource and the steps that the abandoning owner takes to ensure that would-be claimants are alerted to the resource's availability are what matters.[128] Permissive abandonment would allow the owner to walk away from the resource and liability. He also advocates the law of abandonment being harmonised for real property and chattels,[129] and, as already discussed, criticises the law's

[122] ibid 195.
[123] ibid 196.
[124] ibid 198.
[125] ibid 199.
[126] ibid 208.
[127] ibid 209.
[128] Strahilevitz (n 58) 355.
[129] ibid 412–13.

preference for adverse possession over abandonment as a means of transferring title in cases in which these mechanisms might function as substitutes.

Strahilevitz analyses the common historical explanation for the distinction in the legal treatment of corporeal and incorporeal interests, which is that in the English feudal system, the Crown could not tolerate the non-ownership of land between the time of abandonment and reclamation, because no feudal incidents would be paid in the interim.[130] He argues that real property taxes are the modern-day equivalent of feudal incidents and that abandoned real property often has negative market value, in which case the state should not be levying taxes against it. He prefers the argument that the common law rule prohibiting abandonment is not based on a static rule of the requirement to pay taxes, but a dynamic one that encourages individuals to use the property in a more sustainable way. This would improve social welfare and maximise the long-term value of the property, and so would be a defence against economic conditions that encourage short-sighted uses of land.[131] But this argument is more applicable to corporeal than to incorporeal interests, and so does not justify real and incorporeal interests being treated the same in relation to abandonment.

Strahilevitz discusses the identification by Merrill and Smith of the core condition that leads to abandonment, which is an asset possessing negative value.[132] Such an asset comes bundled with a liability that exceeds its positive intrinsic value. Permissive abandonment would preserve the intrinsically valuable asset while imposing the same loss on the mortgagee.[133] With abandonment being prohibited, his opinion is that the better option is for the mortgagee to be required to take possession and sell the property. Nevertheless, he argues that an owner seeking to abandon property should be able to do so upon improving the property to give it positive market value.[134] This would, however, be difficult in mortgaged property where there is negative equity. He argues that an owner should not be forced to find a seller to take their property in light of the substantial transaction costs associated with land sales.[135] Yet, that argument does not deal adequately with the problems caused by abandoned land, does not encourage landowners to maintain effective scrutiny and stewardship over their unused property, and ignores the fact that the proceeds of sale would be used to pay the transaction costs.

With respect to positive market value property, Strahilevitz's view, in relation to American law, is that the law should permit abandonment of corporeal interests, requiring only that the owner record a notice of abandonment, so that

[130] ibid 399.
[131] ibid 400–01.
[132] ibid 362.
[133] ibid 388.
[134] ibid 418–19.
[135] ibid 419.

all parties interested in land will learn of its availability. The successful claimant then registers their interest in the land, so that third parties and government taxing authorities are informed of the title transfer.[136] However, he argues that there are numerous instances in which property with positive market value is abandoned. He identifies three main motivations for this. First, the owner may abandon property for profit-maximising purposes, seeking to acquire revenue streams for services that those claiming the abandoned property will need to purchase. Second, the owner may abandon property for reputation-enhancing purposes. Third, the owner may abandon property for more altruistic reasons.[137] The primary benefits of abandonment are reduced transaction costs and decision costs.[138]

There are, however, two principal problems associated with the abandonment of positive-value resources. First, abandonment may create confusion as to the state of ownership of the property. Second, abandonment may result in the deterioration of an asset's value while it remains unowned. In some cases involving worthless property, abandonment may also impose disposal costs onto society. In other cases involving valuable property, abandonment may spark violent disagreements among would-be claimants.[139] Strahilevitz recognises that the randomisation entailed by abandonment seems to undermine distributive justice.[140] He analyses how the law might be improved and should strive to permit abandonment as well as attempting to mitigate confusion costs, deterioration costs and error costs, while reducing disposal costs in the case of negative-value property and lawless race costs in the case of positive-value property.[141]

VI. CONCLUSION

The above analysis of a selection of American scholars has been useful in providing an overview of the dilemmas and complexities of the law of abandonment. The breadth of ideas examined demonstrates that abandonment invokes disparate and diverse discourse amongst academics favouring enhanced and augmented scrutinisation and application of abandonment, whereas the Supreme Court in *Hillside* displayed a resolute determination to bypass and circumvent abandonment. Nevertheless, it may be appreciated, and potentially welcomed, that the Supreme Court in *Hillside* decided to apply a straightforward test of physical impossibility rather than the intricacies of abandonment.

[136] ibid 418.
[137] ibid 370.
[138] ibid 372.
[139] ibid 372.
[140] ibid 378.
[141] ibid 405.

Hillside may represent a further step towards the demise of the doctrine of abandonment, although it remains to be seen to what extent planning law will influence private law. The impact of *Hillside* is likely to be minimal, because of the view taken by the Supreme Court that planning law is a self-contained statutory area. Cases of abandonment are relatively rare and the difficulty is that abandonment revolves so much on the facts. The policy justifications of the Supreme Court in refusing to apply the doctrine of abandonment in this area of planning law are to preclude developers and homeowners implementing parts of different planning permissions to prevent a pick-and-mix approach which may be outside the scope of the overall planning scheme. The decision gives more power to local planning authorities over developers, which will be welcome to local authorities.

The law has other tools to tackle potential problems of abandonment, such as Empty Dwelling Management Orders (EDMOs), created by the Housing Act 2004,[142] to bring empty private-sector property back into use as housing with two types of management order in relation to empty dwellings: interim EDMOs and final EDMOs.[143] EDMOs are used very rarely, but they were always envisaged as a last resort. Local authorities will normally engage with owners of empty properties and persuade them to bring property back into use.

Due to the shortage of housing, it is of concern that abandoned property removes important assets from the economy. Negative externalities associated with abandonment are considerable and the common law policy of not allowing abandonment of fee simple estates is a sound one to maximise individual, social, communal and housing welfare. The doctrine of abandonment highlights one of the dilemmas in English land law, which is the relationship between the 'community' or 'social' interest in land and the individualism of private ownership.[144] According to the social obligation norm, the support which landowners owe their communities may involve sacrificing personal preference-maximising uses of property.[145] It is hoped that the lively debates and range of views investigated in this chapter will bring renewed interest to the issue of abandonment in English land law.

[142] Chapter 2 of pt 4 of the Housing Act 2004.

[143] See further House of Commons Briefing Paper, *Empty Dwelling Management Orders (EDMOs)* No 04129 (2019), https://commonslibrary.parliament.uk/research-briefings/sn04129.

[144] GS Alexander, 'The Social-Obligation Norm in American Property Law' (2009) 94 *Cornell Law Review* 745, 757, discussed in Peñalver (n 59) 213. See also S Pascoe, 'Social Obligation Norm and the Erosion of Land Ownership?' [2012] *Conveyancer and Property Lawyer* 484.

[145] Alexander (n 144) 795.

8

Conservation Covenants

A New Opportunity?

MICHAEL W POULSOM

I. INTRODUCTION

CONSERVATION COVENANTS, COMPRISING obligations entered into by landowners with 'a responsible body', 'of a qualifying kind', having 'a conservation purpose' and being 'intended by the parties to be for the public good'[1] were proposed by the Law Commission in 2014.[2] Their introduction in England and Wales[3] in 2022 by Part 7 (sections 117–39) of the Environment Act 2021 ('EA 2021') leaves questions about their conceptual foundations, their implementation in practice and their integration into existing land law regimes wholly or partially unaddressed.

Conservation covenants have been described as 'private, voluntary arrangements between a landowner and a responsible body, such as a conservation charity or public body, allowing for positive or restrictive obligations to fulfil a conservation objective'.[4] They are capable of 'binding not only … the landowner, but also subsequent landowners' and of delivering 'lasting conservation benefits for the public good'.[5] Like conventional freehold and leasehold covenants, conservation covenants privately and voluntarily regulate the use of the covenantor's land. Like leasehold covenants, and freehold covenants, the burdens of which 'run' in equity, they will automatically bind both covenantors and their successors in title. They differ, however, from conventional freehold covenants in three ways. First, they bind successors in title not by applying equitable principles and entering a notice under section 32 of the Land Registration

[1] Environment Act 2021, s 117(1)(a).

[2] Law Commission, *Conservation Covenants* (Law Com No 349, 2014).

[3] EA 2021 s 117(2)(a)(i) states that Conservation Covenants apply to land 'In England'; EA 2021, s 146(7) states that pt 7 'extends to England and Wales'.

[4] Department for Environment, Food and Rural Affairs, *Consultation Outcome, Summary of Responses and Government Response*, www.gov.uk/government/consultations/conservation-covenants/outcome/summary-of-responses-and-government-response, 3.

[5] ibid.

Act 2002, but by express provision in section 122(2)(b) EA 2021. Second, they can bind successors whether they are negative or positive, as their definition as 'provision[s] … requiring [a] landowner … to do, or not to do, something on land'[6] makes clear. Third, by omitting any requirement that covenantees should own benefiting land, Part 7 allows conservation covenants to bind covenantors' successors irrespective of whether such land exists.

The examination in this chapter of aspects of Part 7 EA 2021 neither challenges the principle of conservation nor argues against statutory or other legal means of encouraging or compelling conservation activities. It argues first that existing land law mechanisms might be more creatively employed to achieve the conservation objectives which Part 7 envisages. It argues further that Part 7 defines conservation covenants in broad and potentially unclear terms. These broad terms contrast with the specific, established and well recognised (if not always well understood) limitations of the conventional covenants regime. It argues that conservation covenants may be misaligned with the problem they seek to address, and that this lack of alignment may discourage their use. It concludes that if their use becomes widespread, it may do so on a compulsory (and hence contrary to their characterisation as 'voluntary') basis, and that they may not meet the long-term conservation objectives for which they are intended.

II. THE SUITABILITY OF METHODS OTHER THAN CONSERVATION COVENANTS FOR PURSUING CONSERVATION OBJECTIVES

Conservation covenants are designed to address the absence of effective existing private law mechanisms to pursue conservation objectives. This arises in part from the inability of freehold covenants automatically to bind covenantors' successors if they are positive, or if the covenantee owns no land which those covenants benefit. Conservation covenants appear to solve both problems. Assessment of what their introduction might achieve, however, requires analysis of what precisely they can do which methods available before their introduction could not.

A landowner wishing to conserve land and to ensure that that conservation continues after disposal can employ existing mechanisms. A perhaps underappreciated method of conservation, at least until a change in ownership, involves no legal obligations: A landowner might voluntarily conserve the land without legally committing to do so. There is some evidence that this can be effective. In a study of 26 conservation covenantors in New Zealand, Saunders found that almost 60 per cent thought that the covenant had had 'no effect on the conservation interest in the land … because they would have protected the

[6] EA 2021, s 117(2)(a).

[land] in any case'.[7] Such covenants merely reinforce existing intentions, and possibly safeguard against those intentions changing. Even if they are viewed in more 'legalistic' terms, they are, as between original covenantors and covenantees, doing no more than could be achieved with a conventional covenant or a contractual promise.

On disposal of land, a former landowner's ability to ensure that conservation continues is likely to diminish, unless they can personally influence the successor's conduct. Various private voluntary arrangements, existing independently of conservation covenants, might be used to require successors to continue conservation activities.

A. Dispositions to Conservation Bodies or Creation of Charitable Trusts

A landowner might ensure that conservation activities continue after a disposition by choosing a disponee whose identity is characterised by commitment to conservation objectives. That disponee might be an existing conservation body, a limited company, the objects of which include social or environmental purposes, or a charitable trust, holding the land 'for the advancement of environmental protection or improvement',[8] 'for the advancement of the arts, culture, heritage or science'[9] or 'for the advancement of citizenship or community development'.[10] While evaluation of these methods of securing conservation is beyond the scope of this chapter, their conceptual simplicity perhaps suggests that effective conservation might depend less on the creation of novel obligations and more on the care with which established land law mechanisms, and the parties to those mechanisms, are considered and chosen.

B. Sales and Leases Back

A freehold disposal of the relevant land is likely to prevent the original landowner retaining possession. By transferring the freehold estate to a conservation body and taking a lease back, or by granting a lease and taking a sub-lease back, the landowner can retain possession and use the capacity of leasehold covenants, whether positive or negative, automatically to bind the current parties to

[7] C Saunders, 'Conservation Covenants in New Zealand' (1996) 13(4) *Land Use Policy* 325, 326. For a detailed UK study, pre-dating the EA 2021, of conservation activity by 500 farmers, see Wildlife and Countryside Link, 'Farmers and Conservationists on the Same Page about a Brighter Farming Future', June 2019, www.wcl.org.uk/farmers-and-conservationists-on-the-same-page-about-a-brighter-farming-future.asp.

[8] Charities Act 2011, s 3(1)(i).

[9] ibid s 3(1)(f).

[10] ibid s 3(1)(e).

the lease. The Law Commission noted that the Royal Society for the Protection of Birds (RSPB) and the Woodland Trust use leaseback arrangements.[11]

Some of the objections to using leaseback arrangements, and by implication the arguments in favour of conservation covenants, deserve attention: Pulman and Hopkins note that the Woodland Trust and others considered leaseback arrangements cumbersome to negotiate and implement, particularly in relation to the non-conservation aspects of the lease, including rent, term and forfeiture.[12] Where leaseback arrangements are created for conservation purposes, the lease or sub-lease is not primarily granting exclusive possession for a term at a rent, but is operating as a vehicle to enable the enforceability of positive covenants. It is unclear why such a lease requires a forfeiture clause or why the rent could not be purely nominal.

In relation to the lease term, and therefore the duration of the conservation obligations contained within it, the creation of conservation covenants might not necessarily ease the negotiation process significantly. Their duration and obligations would require negotiation in any event. More broadly, and given their relative novelty, the negotiation of a well-considered conservation covenant agreement might be more, not less, onerous than the negotiation of familiar lease clauses. The objection that leasehold is 'inherently less secure'[13] than freehold might also be challenged: leasehold remains sufficiently secure for ownership of nearly five million leasehold homes in England[14] and for commercial tenants. Being in a position inherently less secure than having freehold ownership is also a characteristic shared both by leaseholders and by those having the benefit of a conservation (or any other) covenant.

A further objection to the sale and leaseback model is that the conservation body's freehold ownership of land after sale may carry with it unwanted responsibilities.[15] Uncertainty in identifying responsibility for the cited examples of occupiers' and council tax liability may result less from the use of leases and more from their specific terms: both liabilities depend not on 'ownership', but on whether a party is respectively an 'occupier' or a 'resident'. The 'occupier' is the party with 'a sufficient degree of control over the premises … to realise that … failure on his part … may result in injury to a person … lawfully there'.[16] Council tax liability depends in large part on the facts and the lease terms.[17] In either case, liability can be determined by the parties; in commercial

[11] Law Commission (n 2) paras 2.71(2) and 2.77–2.78.

[12] C Pulman and N Hopkins, 'The Introduction of Conservation Covenants in English Law' in S Demeyere and V Sagaert (eds), *Contract and Property with an Environmental Perspective* (Cambridge, Intersentia, 2020) 189.

[13] ibid.

[14] Department of Levelling Up, Housing and Communities, 'Official Statistics, Leasehold Dwellings 202=12022', 11 May 2023, www.gov.uk/government/statistics/leasehold-dwellings-2021-to-2022/leasehold-dwellings-2021-to-2022.

[15] Pulman and Hopkins (n 12) 189.

[16] *Wheat v Lacon & Co Ltd* [1966] AC 552, 577.

[17] Local Government Finance Act 1992, s 6.

leases, transfer of business rates liability from the landlord to the tenant is commonplace.

C. Easements

The identified objections to using leaseback arrangements to achieve conservation objectives are therefore open to challenge. The same is less easily said for objections to the use of easements to do so. Conventional easements, which require the accommodation of dominant land and which do not generally require servient owners to maintain servient land, appear unsuitable for the conservation purposes which Part 7 envisages. In 2011, the Law Commission opposed the introduction of easements in gross.[18] It appears to have been influenced by the view that their introduction would 'undoubtedly risk the imposition of heavy additional burdens on servient land'[19] and lead to 'a proliferation of adverse interests in land, unlimited by the needs of … dominant land'.[20]

It is perhaps not immediately obvious why allowing easements in gross would inevitably have either outcome: Analogies might be drawn with public rights of way or with statutory easements conferred on utility companies. Easements granted to conservation bodies to access land, conduct periodic monitoring and gather data would not necessarily impose 'heavy, additional' burdens. Conservation covenants might require the landowner to do significantly more, but in such cases, it is unclear why the objection made so forcefully to introducing easements in gross does not apply with equal force to such agreements.

D. Modification of Existing Covenant Requirements

The Law Commission explicitly identified two characteristics of conventional covenants which impede their use for conservation purposes.[21] First, following *Haywood v Brunswick Permanent Benefit Building Society*,[22] the burden of a positive, as opposed to a restrictive, covenant will not normally bind a subsequent owner of the covenantor's land. Second, the burden of any covenant, whether positive or negative, will only run where the covenantee owns benefiting

[18] Law Commission, *Making Land Work: Easements, Covenants and Profits à Prendre* (Law Com No 327, 2011) para 2.24.

[19] A Lawson, 'Easements' in L Tee (ed) *Land Law: Issues, Debates, Policy* (Cullompton, Willan, 2002) 71.

[20] Law Commission (n 18) para 2.24.

[21] Law Commission, *Conservation Covenants Executive Summary* (Law Com No 349, 2014) (Summary) 2.

[22] *Haywood v Brunswick Permanent Benefit BS* (1881) 8 QBD 403.

land:[23] A covenant by a landowner, for example, to leave a natural habitat undisturbed will bind the original covenantor, but if the covenantee owns no benefiting land, it will not bind the covenantor's successors. The circumstances in which conventional covenants might realistically be used for wider conservation purposes appear restricted to those in which covenantees own nearby land, or artificially created pieces of benefiting land are transferred to, or retained by, them.

Of these two obstacles to the use of conventional covenants for conservation purposes, the differential treatment of positive and negative covenants is perhaps conceptually simpler to address. A statutory provision permitting the burden of positive covenants to run with covenantors' land would address uncertainty as to the validity and purpose of the distinction. Smith[24] notes that whether the ability of the burden of covenants to run in equity established in *Tulk v Moxhay*[25] applied to positive obligations appears to have remained uncertain until *Haywood*,[26] and criticises the basis upon which positive and negative covenants were distinguished in *Rhone v Stephens*.[27]

The requirement that for the burden of a covenant to pass, it must have been imposed to benefit land owned by the covenantee at the time of imposition appears more difficult to address. Its justification is not immediately apparent[28] and has 'a certain opaque quality'.[29] Other requirements, for example, that successors should be bound only if the original covenanting parties intended them to be so and if covenants can, via a notice, be identified before purchase are attractively simple and have more immediately visible rational foundations. The relevance to the binding nature of a covenant of the existence of benefiting land owned by the covenantee is less clear.

Robust removal of the requirement from the covenants regime might resolve this uncertainty. In the circumstances in which they operate, conservation covenants do this. Logically, however, assessing the implications of removing the requirement requires precise identification of its origins and purpose. It appears to be closely aligned with specific historic understandings of what restrictive covenants, and more specifically their capacity to bind successors, are for. Referring to nineteenth-century cases, decided in their contemporary context of rapid urban development, Smith attributes the general rationale for enforcing covenants against successors to a need to protect sellers' retained land

[23] *Renals v Cowlishaw* (1879) 11 Ch D 866; *Formby v Baker* [1903] 2 Ch 539 at 552, per Vaughan Williams LJ.

[24] RJ Smith, *Property Law*, 9th edn (Harlow, Pearson, 2017) 558–59.

[25] *Tulk v Moxhay* (1848) 41 ER 1143.

[26] In *Morland v Cook* (1868) LR6 Eq 252 and *Cooke v Chilcott* (1876) 3 Ch D 694, covenants performing 'public' purposes (the maintenance respectively of a sea wall and a water supply) were held to bind successors.

[27] *Rhone v Stephens* [1994] 2 AC 310.

[28] Smith (n 24) 560.

[29] K Gray and SF Gray, *Elements of Land Law*, 5th edn (Oxford, Oxford University Press, 2009) 268.

when disposals of land for building were in high demand; covenants evolved to encourage disposal by alleviating sellers' fears that uses of the land sold would harm the value of land retained.[30] They fulfilled a dual 'planning function' of encouraging the sale, and limiting the use, of land.[31] Reinforcing this close association of the benefit requirement with the immediate concerns of individual sellers and buyers, Smith argues that enforcement by someone who does not own neighbouring land 'could render them too oppressive'.[32]

Gray and Gray explain the requirement's existence differently, focusing less on the protection of covenantees and more on limitation of the types of obligation to which covenantors' land could become subject. In their view, 'the "benefit" criterion, by excluding substantially personal commitments, silently filters out those contractual undertakings which, *in the public interest* ought not to be imposed as long-term burdens upon any parcel of land'.[33] They argue that the requirement acts as a 'residual legal control over the deleterious social consequences' flowing from an original covenantor's decision to commit to obligations 'which serve merely to gratify some personal interest or whim dear to … the covenantee'.[34]

The existence of statutory exceptions to the benefit requirement under section 8 of the National Trust Act 1937, section 609 of the Housing Act 1985 and section 106(3) (as originally enacted) of the Town and Country Planning Act 1990 might be interpreted as evidence that removing the requirement is inconsequential. Its deliberate exclusion from the conservation covenants regime appears to follow that rationale. But to disapply the requirement too readily may have unintended adverse consequences. It follows neither from the requirement's 'opaque' quality nor from the absence of an immediate or agreed explanation of 'why the requirement should exist'[35] that it has no quality at all or that its existence is unjustified; Gray and Gray and Smith identify (albeit different) advantages conferred by it, which may be lost by its removal. The statutory exemptions also operate in specific and restricted legislative environments, being limited to covenants made with defined covenantees (the National Trust and local housing and planning authorities), both the covenant and the covenantee having specific statutory purposes. By contrast, conservation covenants can be made in favour of a potentially extensive and diverse mix of organisations.

Features of easements and covenants therefore render them wholly or partially unsuitable for parties wishing to create durable conservation obligations, especially where the desired outcome is positive obligations by landowners in favour

[30] Smith (n 24) 557.
[31] ibid 560.
[32] ibid.
[33] Gray and Gray (n 29) 269 (emphasis added).
[34] ibid.
[35] Smith (n 24) 560.

of parties owning no nearby land. Specific legislative provisions allowing easements to exist in gross, and removing the differential treatment of restrictive and positive covenants (as land obligations would) would address those defects. However, the conservation covenant regime takes a different approach: it adopts conventional freehold covenants as a 'starting point', recognises that covenantees are unlikely to meet the normal requirement for the burden to 'run' of owning benefiting land, and removes that requirement. A logical consequence of that removal is the potential imposition on land of 'oppressive'[36] burdens or 'contractual undertakings which, in the public interest, ought not to be imposed as long-term burdens upon any parcel of land'.[37] Whether those consequences can successfully be avoided depends on the robustness of the regime which attempts to operate without the benefit requirement. Determining that robustness requires analysis of the legislation which governs their creation and operation.

III. THE STATUTORY FRAMEWORK

Part 7 regulates the creation and operation of conservation covenants using broadly defined terms. The intention is evidently to allow landowners and responsible bodies to agree provisions appropriate for themselves and the land. However, the implications of inadvertently agreeing provisions which fall outside Part 7 are significant. When viewed alongside conventional covenant requirements, Part 7 has a specific and binary effect: provisions comprising conservation covenants can successfully evade those rules relating to the running of the burden which require that covenants be restrictive and benefit covenantees' land. Those which do not cannot. Accordingly, there is potentially a 'mismatch' between the very specific effect of Part 7 and the broad scope of its operative provisions.

A. Creation and Relationship with Other Obligations

The flexibility inherent in each of the concepts of 'responsible body', 'qualifying kind', 'conservation purpose' and 'public good'[38] which are required for the effective creation of conservation covenants is, depending on the reader's perspective and objectives, either welcome or disconcerting. Landowners wishing to create conservation covenants may welcome flexibility; it will enable bespoke provisions successfully to become conservation covenants, with the consequent exemption from the normal covenant rules. By contrast, their successors (or

[36] Smith (n 24) 560.
[37] Gray and Gray (n 29) 269.
[38] EA 2021, s 117(1)(a).

indeed original covenantors whose priorities have changed) who wish to challenge the validity of what purport to be conservation covenants could use the accompanying uncertainty to argue that one or more of the requirements was unmet when the covenant was created and that the innate capacity of the covenant to bind successors does not apply.

Sections 117 and 118 EA 2021 evidently envisage that a conservation covenant need not exist in isolation, but could be part of a larger agreement. The sections distinguish a 'conservation covenant' from a 'conservation covenant agreement'; the former is part of the latter. Significantly, however, it is the conservation covenant itself, not the wider agreement surrounding it, which binds the covenantor's successors.[39] Under section 118(2)(a) and (b) EA 2021, the conservation covenant is that part of the broader conservation covenant agreement which falls within section 117(1)(a)(i)–(iii) and, significantly, 'provisions ancillary to' that part.

Two issues arise: first, very precise drafting may be necessary to identify which parts of a larger agreement constitute a conservation covenant, and therefore have the capacity, under section 122(2), to bind the covenantor's successors; and, secondly, it is unclear what 'ancillary' means in this context. Butt's recommendation that 'if doubt could arise over the meaning of "ancillary", always clarify' is relevant.[40] To establish whether a provision is properly 'ancillary' to another is perhaps straightforward if what that provision is ancillary *to* (for example, a defined piece of land) is clear. If 'ancillary to' means, in a general sense, 'connected with', Part 7 envisages conferring significant novel effects on provisions which are in some unspecified way 'connected with' other provisions which meet the flexible 'qualifying kind', 'conservation purpose' and 'public good' requirements. The effect appears to be to connect one flexibly defined provision (an 'ancillary' provision) to another (the conservation covenant complying with section 117(1)(a)(i)–(iii)) via the undefined concept of the first provision being 'ancillary to' the second.

This uncertainty as to what is properly an 'ancillary' provision may lead to differential treatment of provisions intended to bind successors. A landowner might covenant with a responsible body to maintain a natural habitat in terms which fall clearly within section 117(1)(a)(i)–(iii). 'Ancillary' obligations might, for example, require the landowner to facilitate the responsible body's monitoring of the conservation activity, data collection and record keeping. If those 'ancillary' obligations were subsequently found not to be sufficiently ancillary to that conservation purpose, they would not bind the covenantor's successors, since they would not fall under section 118(2)(b) and therefore section 122(2). That loss of capacity to bind successors will significantly undermine the effectiveness of the covenant.

[39] ibid s 122(2).

[40] P Butt, *The Lawyer's Style Guide* (Oxford, Hart Publishing, 2021) 49.

B. Responsible Body

Under section 119, only the Secretary of State is automatically a responsible body. Other bodies, including local authorities, wishing to be responsible bodies must apply to be designated by the Secretary of State as such. Perhaps surprisingly, under section 119(3), a local authority may only be a responsible body if the Secretary of State is satisfied that it is 'suitable' to be such. Why they are not responsible bodies automatically is unclear, since they perform a not dissimilar function in relation to section 106 agreements for planning purposes.[41]

Section 119(4) requires bodies other than local authorities not only to demonstrate that they are suitable to be responsible bodies, but also, under section 119(5), that:

> (a) in the case of a public body or charity, *at least some of its main* purposes or functions *relate to* conservation, or
> (b) in any other case, *at least some* of the body's *main* activities *relate to* conservation. (Emphasis added)

Criticisms of the breadth of the terms in section 117(1)(a)(i)–(iii) could equally be applied to the uncertainty inherent in 'at least some' and 'main' and 'relate to' (as opposed to, in the case of the last of these, 'are'). Nor can it be said that the significant further clarity emerges from the definition of 'conservation' for the purposes of section 119(5). Under section 119(9), 'conservation' (in relation to the required purposes or functions of a responsible body) means conservation of:

> (a) the natural environment or natural resources of land
> (b) places of archaeological, architectural, artistic, cultural or historic interest, or
> (c) the setting of land with a natural environment or natural resources or which is a place of archaeological, architectural, artistic, cultural or historic interest.

This explanation, with its emphasis on what is being conserved rather than on what 'conservation' means, could be viewed as essentially an illustration of what conservation 'might look like' rather than as a concrete definition.

Two further features of the requirements applicable to responsible bodies are significant. First, the body need not be not-for-profit. The ability of a responsible body to profit, and the requirement that the covenant made with it be 'intended by the parties to be for the public good', with its implicitly 'not-for-profit' connotations, perhaps conflict. Second, under section 119(7), the criteria to be applied in deciding whether a body is suitable to be or remain a responsible body 'may include criteria relating to the body's connection with the United Kingdom'. A responsible body may evidently be based abroad. It is unclear why the location requirement for responsible bodies is so wide, since under section 117(2)(a)(i), conservation covenants only apply to land

[41] Town and Country Planning Act 1990, s 106.

in England and Wales. In addition, the possibility that the covenantee could be based in another jurisdiction raises significant questions, which current government guidance only partially answers, on the practicality of monitoring and enforcing performance.[42]

C. Qualifying Kind

Section 117(2) defines a provision 'of a qualifying kind' as one requiring the covenantor, or the responsible body, 'to do, or not to do *something*' (emphasis added) on that land. 'Something' is undefined. To place undue emphasis on this uncertainty is perhaps to misunderstand the purpose of the provision; its primary purpose is to emphasise that a conservation covenant may be negative or positive. Nevertheless, the inclusion of 'something' naturally prompts the question of what that 'something' might be, which Part 7 answers only in broad terms.

D. Conservation Purpose

Part 7 maintains a broad approach to defining the components of conservation covenants in its explanation of 'conservation purpose'. The features which a conservation covenant can be designed to conserve mirror those specified in the requirements which an organisation must meet to be a responsible body.[43] It defines 'conserve' only by expanding, rather than clarifying, its natural meaning, providing that 'conserving includes … protecting, restoring or enhancing'.[44] It leaves 'setting' undefined; it appears to differ from the land itself and from its natural environment, but it is unclear to what extent it might extend to land outside that which the covenant is intended to bind.

While much of the other terminology used in section 117 is left open to interpretation, the section does expand on selected meanings; 'natural environment' in relation to land is stated to include its plants, animals and other living organisms, their habitats and the land's geological features.[45] Why 'natural environment' has been defined but 'setting' has not is unclear. Where such clarification is provided, the breadth of the clarificatory wording and the reliance on 'include' tend to broaden, rather than refine, understanding of what the provision is intended to mean.

[42] Government guidance states that a responsible body 'must have an operating base in the UK that allows it to properly carry out its conservation covenant functions'. See Department for Environment, Food and Rural Affairs, 'Guidance – Conservation Covenants: Criteria for Being a Responsible Body', updated 6 February 2024, www.gov.uk/government/publications/conservation-covenants-apply-to-become-a-responsible-body/conservation-covenants-criteria-for-being-a-responsible-body.

[43] EA 2021, s 119(9).

[44] ibid s 117(4).

[45] ibid.

Arguments that highlighting imprecision or unpicking illustrative, rather than definitive, wording amounts to accusatory pedantry, and that instinctive understandings of specific words and phrases render more precise legislative definition unnecessary prompt three responses. First, Part 7 correctly anticipates uncertainty as to what 'natural environment' means; it seeks to clarify it. It is unclear why it does not do likewise in relation to, for example, 'setting'. Second, the innate durability which conservation covenants are intended to have means that a consistent instinctive understanding of these words, or indeed of any other broad terms in Part 7, cannot be relied upon; to the extent that consensus exists on what a word or phrase means now, similar consensus in the future is not inevitable. Third, to argue that such terms will readily be understood perhaps underestimates the inclination of successors in title to challenge them. A future owner may be willing to expend significant time, effort and cost in challenging a conservation covenant, and it is in relation to the precise meaning of these words and phrases that any challenge is likely to be undertaken.

E. Public Good

Perhaps because of its prominence and resonance, the requirement that to be a conservation covenant, a provision must be 'intended by the parties to be for the public good'[46] is significant. The range of human action or inaction which could realistically fall inside or outside the scope of 'for the public good' perhaps presents unanticipated and undesirable opportunities for dispute. The requirement raises questions of what 'for the public good' means and why a conservation covenant must be subjectively '*intended by* the parties' to be such, rather than simply and objectively '*for* the public good'.

A requirement that obligations arising between private landowners and bodies which might be neither public nor charitable must in some way be related to 'the public good' is perhaps surprising; the legislative regime is acknowledged to relate to private voluntary arrangements. Additionally, the concept of a real or imagined collective public sentiment (subjectively or objectively measured) is not routinely found in land law. Direct transposal of the exact phrase 'the public good' from statutory provisions relating to, for example, immigration[47] and obscenity[48] would appear inappropriate. More applicable might be the concepts of the 'public interest' as used in sections 84(1)(aa) and 84(1A)(b) LPA 1925, the 'public benefit' requirement which purposes must serve to qualify as charitable[49] or the 'public conscience', an 'affront' to which has been held to be a foundation of the *ex turpi causa* principle.[50]

[46] ibid s 117(1)(a)(iii).
[47] Immigration Act 1971, s 3(5).
[48] Obscene Publications Act 1959, s 4(1).
[49] Charities Act 2011, s 2(1)(b).
[50] *Euro-Diam Ltd v Bathurst* [1990] 1 QB 1.

The extent, if any, to which the requirement in section 117(1)(a)(iii) resembles of any of these is unclear. Recent government guidance states only that: 'The public good means that the covenant must benefit the public in some way.'[51] Perhaps significantly, there is evidently no requirement that this benefit to the public includes public access: section 118(3) makes a provision for public access an 'ancillary provision' 'if the agreement includes [such a] provision', clearly anticipating that it might not. A utilitarian interpretation might question the extent to which publicly inaccessible private land, perhaps performing no purpose other than being conserved in its current state, is benefiting 'the public'.

The requirement that a conservation covenant must be 'intended by the parties to be for the public good' differs from the Law Commission's recommendations that, first, it should be 'for the public good' and, second, it should become ineffective if that requirement were no longer met. Pulman and Hopkins state that the first change was intended to avoid arguments over 'whether a conservation covenant was ever successfully created by arguing about whether it ever successfully served the public good'.[52] In respect of the second change, they argue that what is now Schedule 18 to the EA 2021 allows the Upper Tribunal to discharge a conservation covenant if it does not serve the public good.

In the absence of any requirement that the parties' subjective intention, while perhaps genuinely held, be objectively determined, it could be formed by personalised, politicised, temporarily fashionable or indeed misplaced understandings, perhaps comprising 'personal interest[s] or whim[s] dear to … the [parties]'[53] of what is for 'the public good'. Historically, covenants against, for example, the production or consumption of alcohol, or, as is common on residential estates, against parking commercial vehicles, conducting business activities or requiring front gardens to be maintained as 'ornamental' have been imposed in a sincere but ultimately 'located in a particular time' belief in what *then* constituted the public good. Such covenants, if perceived as unnecessary and inconvenient restraints reflecting 'past social value', now appear anachronistic.

The ability of a party to apply to modify or discharge a conservation covenant if it objectively *does not* serve the public good appears to be presented as a solution to the uncertainty arising from subjective determination of what the parties *intend* to be for the public good. It might be argued that its effect is merely to make the criteria for the creation of conservation covenants inconsistent with those for their modification or discharge, with two consequences. First, this inconsistent use of 'the public good' requirement might postpone arguments as to what is or is not 'for the public good' from when the covenant is created to when a successor in title, disinclined to comply with it, makes an application under Schedule 18. Second, parties who realise that their subjective intention as

[51] Department for Environment, Food and Rural Affairs, 'Guidance – Getting and Using a Conservation Covenant Agreement', 18 November 2022, last updated 6 February 2024, www.gov.uk/guidance/getting-and-using-a-conservation-covenant-agreement.

[52] Pulman and Hopkins (n 12) 204.

[53] Gray and Gray (n 29) 269.

to what is 'for the public good' will not necessarily determine whether the Upper Tribunal shares their view may be reluctant to create conservation covenants at all; they may perceive that the ease with which, by applying an objective 'public good' measure, their 'good' intentions can be set aside outweighs the effort and cost of creating them.

In addition, the imprecise definitions of 'the public good', and of 'responsible bodies' perhaps cast doubt on the amenability of decisions to create conservation covenants to judicial review. Administrative Court Guidance defines the defendant in judicial review proceedings as 'the *public body* whose conduct is under challenge' (emphasis added).[54] A private body can evidently be treated as public if the nature of the power being exercised has a sufficiently public law character.[55] Whether, for example, powers exercised by small conservation bodies to create conservation covenants over single pieces of land (perhaps inaccessible to the public) would have that character is unclear. In addition, the reference in Part 7 to the subjective intentions of the covenanting parties appears to conflict with the dependence of amenability on *objective* 'consideration of the nature of the power … exercised to see whether the decision has a sufficient public element, flavour or character to bring it within … public law'.[56]

IV. MAKING CONSERVATION COVENANTS BINDING ON FUTURE OWNERS

To be effective, conservation covenants must bind successors to the original covenantor. Hardy et al note that even in Australia, where conservation covenants have existed since 1951,[57] most of the circa 7,500 covenants existing in 2014 had been created since the 1990s. In many such cases, the original covenantor may have owned the land continuously. Drawing on Saunders' observations pertaining to New Zealand, such landowners are perhaps likely to conserve even if they are not legally required to do so. Therefore, it is possible that the capacity of conservation covenants to bind successors, on which their success ultimately depends, remains relatively unexplored and untested.

Section 122(2) EA 2021 explicitly provides that 'an obligation of the owner under a conservation covenant binds … (a) the landowner … and (b) any person who becomes a successor of the landowner'. Reflecting their characterisation as 'voluntary' agreements, it is suggested that successors in title can only be described as assuming commitments made by their predecessors 'voluntarily'

[54] Courts and Tribunals Judiciary, *The Administrative Court Judicial Review Guide*, 7th edn (2022), para 3.2.2.1.

[55] *R v Panel on Take-overs and Mergers ex p Datafin plc* [1987] 1 All ER 564.

[56] *R (Beer) (t/a Hammer Trout Farm) v Hampshire Famers' Markets Ltd* [2003] EWCA Civ 1056, para 16, per Dyson LJ.

[57] MJ Hardy et al, 'Exploring the Permanence of Conservation Covenants' (2017) 10 *Conservation Letters* 221, 222.

if they have been able to discover the covenant before acquisition. Unlike legal easements, or indeed covenants the burden of which is to run to successors, conservation covenants are subject neither to registration nor to entry of a notice on the Land Register. They are local land charges,[58] and override under Schedule 1, paragraph 6 and Schedule 3, paragraph 6 of the Land Registration Act (LRA) 2002. In registered land, they will bind transferees for valuable consideration under section 29 LRA 2002. Donees, assentees and other transferees not for value would be bound by virtue of section 28 LRA 2002.

Two practical issues arise in relation to the likelihood of successors in title discovering the existence of the covenant. Local land charges are identifiable from a local land charges search. Since 2018, the Land Registry's Local Land Charges Programme has been transferring the 331 sets of local land charges data from local authorities to themselves, with the aim of placing these data in 'one accessible place'.[59] By 1 August 2024, less than a third of these sets of data had been transferred. Consequently, the precise searches needed to identify whether conservation covenants exist will vary geographically.

Second, the creation of conservation covenants can be viewed as evidence of covenantors' altruistic intent. Altruistic landowners are perhaps more likely than commercially motivated landowners to transfer ownership by gift or by will rather than by sale. The nature of a disposal determines which searches are conducted: on purchase, particularly with mortgage finance, the purchaser's representative would normally conduct a local land charges search. This is less likely when the acquisition is by gift, assent or other transfer not for value. The likelihood of a donee or assentee receiving the land without knowing of the covenant is therefore likely to rise.

It might be argued that this is merely a technical point: the conservation covenant will override and will bind the successor irrespective of whether they discover it. However, it can reasonably be surmised that the natural inclination of an original covenantor to perform the covenant may not be shared by successors who discover its existence only after acquisition. Hardy et al identify that whether a party expected to comply with a covenant is the original covenantor or their successor 'may be an important predictor of covenant breach or requests for release'.[60]

It might also be asked whether protection as local land charges, as opposed to entry on the land register, correctly recognises the potentially significant burdens which conservation covenants impose. Many local land charges – for example, tree preservation orders, listed building charges, light obstruction notices and planning consents containing conditions – either impose relatively light burdens on land or become effective only if the landowner acts in specific

[58] EA 2021, s 120(1).

[59] HM Land Registry, 'Guidance, Local Land Charges Programme', updated 19th December 2024, www.gov.uk/government/publications/hm-land-registry-local-land-charges-programme, 3.

[60] Hardy et al (n 57) 227.

ways. Conservation covenants can impose significant positive obligations, requiring input of time, effort and expense. The public good which they are intended to serve will only be achieved if successors comply with them, which in turn is likely to require that they know about them before acquisition. Their existence therefore needs to be as visible as possible. The decision to transfer local land charges to the land register can reasonably be viewed as a means of achieving this for local land charges more broadly, by increasing the visibility. Why Part 7 does not similarly emphasise visibility by requiring registration at the Land Registry is unclear.

Discussion of the means used to alert future landowners to the existence of conservation covenants aligns with a broader discussion of where precisely they 'sit' in the different categories of contractual, proprietary and statutory rights pertaining to land. Pratt identifies that they occupy 'an awkward conceptual territory', straddling 'both the public and private sphere'.[61] The Law Commission's view that conservation covenants should be 'statutory burdens' is reflected in Part 7, which does not seek to integrate them into either the registered or unregistered land systems.

On a conceptual level, it might be asked whether the distinction between proprietary interests, in the sense of interests which attach to property, and statutory burdens which bind the future owners of that property, is one which landowners can be expected to appreciate or understand. Their natural question on identifying that conservation covenants affect land they wish to acquire will be whether they must comply with them, to which the distinction appears immaterial. Pulman and Hopkins defend the categorisation of conservation covenants as agreements more closely related to contractual obligations than to proprietary rights on the basis that categorisation of them as the latter would, applying the *nemo dat quod non habet* principle, prohibit the creation of conservation covenants which were inconsistent with existing proprietary rights.[62] They cite the example of land which is already subject to a right of way when a conservation covenant is created. The categorisation of the conservation covenant as proprietary would prohibit its creation in terms inconsistent with those of the existing easement. Applying the principle to subsequent rights, the grant of, for example, a right to park after the creation of a conservation covenant requiring the land to remain undisturbed would likewise breach the conservation covenant.

In defence of the decision to place conservation covenants outside the categories of proprietary rights, they note that the Law Commission did not recommend requiring that the terms of a conservation covenant be consistent with the landowner's proprietary rights; it merely recommended that 'it is a landowner's responsibility to act within the limits of [their] powers and

[61] N Pratt, 'Conservation Covenants: A Proprietary Analysis' [2014] 78 *Conveyancer and Property Lawyer* 328, 328.

[62] Pulman and Hopkins (n 12) 210–14.

legal obligations'.[63] This presupposes that landowners, perhaps unrepresented, will know and understand those powers and obligations. They argue further that categorising conservation covenants as non-proprietary exempts responsible bodies from the need 'to investigate a landowner's legal powers in relation to their land before concluding a valid conservation covenant'.[64] This would appear to envisage circumstances in which neither the landowner nor the responsible body will ascertain, or be required to ascertain, that the landowner can covenant as they purport to. In what might be considered a strictly logical, but perhaps somewhat forced application of the distinction between proprietary and contractual rights, they argue that 'while landowners cannot give what they do not have, they can agree to do what they cannot do'.[65]

While the strict logic of this position cannot be denied, it might be asked if its practical consequence is desirable. The emphasis appears to be on technical validity at the expense of practical utility. Landowners committing to obligations beyond their legal capacity to perform will inevitably fail to meet the intended conservation objectives. In such cases, the obligations are 'valid' only to the extent that they fall within the Act, rather than 'valid' in the sense that the covenantor and its successors will comply with them. Exempting covenanting parties from checking the compatibility of proposed covenants with the title to the burdened land appears to encourage the creation of conservation covenants to be treated as 'standalone' exercises, conducted without reference to prior entitlements. Not ascertaining the compatibility of an intended covenant with those entitlements could expose the landowner to challenges to the existence and performance of the covenant from holders of prior interests – for example, lessees, mortgagees or those benefiting from existing easements, covenants or estate contracts. Consequent disputes to which those third parties, the landowner and the responsible body might all be parties might significantly impede performance of the conservation objective.

Categorising conservation covenants as proprietary interests and integrating them into the existing registered and unregistered land systems would ensure they are discoverable in even the simplest conveyancing transactions. This would not be unduly difficult. Holligan notes that conservation covenants 'have many of the characteristics of a proprietary interest and would not therefore be out of place in the Land Register'.[66] Conventional covenants and contracts, such as options to purchase, are protected by notices on the register, or in unregistered land, by Class D(ii) or C(iv) land charges respectively; if a landowner granted an option to purchase to a conservation organisation or, in the case of that organisation owning benefiting land, created a conventional covenant with that

[63] Law Commission (n 2) para 5.34.
[64] Pulman and Hopkins (n 12) 213.
[65] ibid 214.
[66] B Holligan, 'Narratives of Capital versus Narratives of Community: Conservation Covenants and the Private Regulation of Land Use' (2018) 30 *Journal of Environmental Law* 55, 73.

organisation, either agreement would be protected by a notice on the title. Land obligations, which the Law Commission clearly described as 'rights in or over land',[67] if introduced, would be registrable dispositions in registered land under section 27(2)(d) LRA 2002[68] and would be subject to registration as a new Class G land charge in unregistered land.[69] It is unclear why conservation covenants should be treated differently.

V. CONSERVATION COVENANTS IN BROADER CONTEXTS, INCLUDING BIODIVERSITY NET GAIN

Criticisms of specific words and phrases used in Part 7 might encounter accusations of being characterised by unfairness or purism, and of disregarding the broader objective of effective and durable land conservation, and the wider ambition of EA 2021. Under the Act, conservation covenants are one part of a larger conservation regime. Schedule 14 EA 2021 adds a new Schedule 7A to the Town and Country Planning Act 1990, providing that planning permission for development can be made subject to applicants agreeing to achieve Biodiversity Net Gain (BNG). Conservation covenants are one form which these agreements can take.[70] Some commentators describe conservation covenants in terms which suggest that Part 7 is little more than a procedural or facilitative regime, designed to support the larger and more visible BNG regime.[71] The implication would appear to be that the precise details of Part 7 can justifiably be disregarded, provided the broader ambitions of a successful BNG regime, and in turn a regime for conservation more broadly, are realised.

Yet, to dismiss criticisms of Part 7 on the basis that it is merely a part of a 'bigger conservation picture' may be misplaced. Such criticisms arise not from a personal preference for precision over breadth, but from a suggestion that breadth which landowners, responsible bodies and their advisers cannot easily comprehend, or which they are able easily to exploit, will either discourage the widespread adoption of conservation covenants or present undesirable opportunities for challenge. Either outcome will compromise their effectiveness. Their status as an integral part of a wider legislative regime makes it more, not less, important that landowners and responsible bodies consider them robust and effective. As obligations intended to bind future owners of land, conservation covenants can only succeed by operating effectively alongside existing proprietary estates and interests. To treat them as wholly 'separate' from such

[67] Law Commission (n 18) para 6.6 4.
[68] ibid.
[69] ibid para 6.58.
[70] Town and Country Planning Act 1990, sched 7A, para 9(3)(c).
[71] For example, F Baker and J Charlson, *Environmental Law for Sustainable Construction* (Leeds, Emerald Publishing, 2023) 101.

estates and interests, or for their relationship with them to be left acknowledged or undefined appears to disregard the circumstances in which they must operate.

VI. CONCLUSIONS

Altruism is likely to persist; landowners will continue to conserve land, either voluntarily or using methods to which section II of this chapter refers. Hodge identifies that the range of potential uses for conservation covenants 'depend[s] considerably on the imagination and influence of those … involved with the private conservation organisations and public bodies that might benefit from them'[72] That imagination and influence might productively be applied beyond the use of conservation covenants to the more creative use for conservation purposes of voluntary transfers to conservation bodies, sales and leases back, the introduction of land obligations and even, if permitted, the creation of easements in gross.

Landowners contemplating conservation covenants may be deterred by the broad terms in which they are designed, by the risks posed by that breadth to successful creation, and by their incomplete integration into existing registered and unregistered land systems. They may decline to create binding obligations, or retreat to more familiar devices. This may result in conservation covenants sharing with commonhold the characteristic of being an elaborate statutory mechanism which is rarely used.

Landowners might use conservation covenants only if incentivised or compelled to do so. The current lack of financial incentives to create them (other than as a condition of obtaining planning consent) contrasts with the position in, for example, the US, where, as Reid notes, conservation covenants can attract generous tax status and can constitute charitable gifts, thereby allowing the operation of the cy-près doctrine.[73] If parties are compelled to create conservation covenants to, for example, obtain planning consent, their creation may be motivated more by short-term commercial advantage than by any genuine intention to serve 'the public good'. Successors correctly identifying the apparent incompatibility of this motivation with the wording of Part 7 may be more likely to challenge covenants.

The compulsory creation of conservation covenants may result in their use becoming both routine and indiscriminate. Hodge suggests that they are likely to have most value where the circumstances of the burdened land are characterised by 'irreversibility, uniqueness or extreme rarity, uncertainty and threat'.[74]

[72] I Hodge, 'Conservation Covenants: A Policy Perspective' (2013) 6 *Conveyancer and Property Lawyer*, 490, 500.

[73] C Reid, 'Conservation Covenants' (2013) 3 *Conveyancer and Property Lawyer*, 176, 178.

[74] Hodge (n 72) 491.

This conception of the most advantageous circumstances for their use may not align well with their routine imposition as conditions of planning consent for developments generally. An identifiable 'shift' in their intended purposes away from the altruistic purposes envisaged by the Law Commission and towards the more commercial needs of planning applicants would appear to present a risk that they become a general-purpose conservation 'tool', being used as landowners and local planning authorities wish, and not necessarily for what Parliament, or indeed the Law Commission envisaged.

Perhaps the most significant adverse outcome would be that successors in title, perhaps acquiring land without knowing of existing conservation covenants, will use the breadth of the legislative regime and, in particular, the uncertainty surrounding the meaning of 'the public good' to challenge them. Full integration of conservation covenants into the registered and unregistered land systems would both alleviate the problem of acquisition without knowledge of their existence and resolve uncertainty as to their relationship with prior and subsequent proprietary interests.

Imprecision in the legislative regime governing the creation and operation of conservation covenants can only, it is suggested, be corrected using amending legislation. The opportunities for clarifying the EA 2021 using secondary legislation appear limited. Part 7 contains only two provisions explicitly allowing for such clarification: section 119(7) permits the Secretary of State to determine the criteria for deciding whether a body is suitable to be or remain a responsible body; these need not be published 'by regulation', while section 136(4) allows the Secretary of State 'by regulations [to] make provision about annual returns … by responsible bodies'. Why clarification is limited to these areas, and why one specifies that clarification be by regulations, but the other does not, is unclear. Any argument (perhaps drawing on the uneven and seemingly indiscriminate distribution of such provisions) that the power to make regulations can somehow be 'transplanted' from sections in which it appears to those in which it does not would appear to be misplaced.

Government guidance in the form of, for example, 'Getting and Using a Conservation Covenant Agreement'[75] attempts to assist parties creating conservation covenants. The House of Commons Joint Committee on Statutory Instruments has expressly criticised the use of such non-binding guidance,[76] stating that: 'A key element in the rule of law is for legislation to be clear. Where legislation has been drafted … to leave gaps in the law … guidance … cannot be used to fill those gaps as if it were the law itself.'[77] It acknowledged that primary legislation may expressly permit clarification, but that where enabling powers do not permit it, 'Departments cannot add to the law by referring informally to

[75] Department for Environment, Food & Rural Affairs (n 51).

[76] House of Commons Joint Committee on Statutory Instruments, 'Rule of Law Themes from Covid-19 Regulations', publications.parliament.uk/pa/jt5802/jtselect/jtstatin/57/5707.htm.

[77] ibid para 55.

guidance. Such guidance … has no place in amplifying the law'.[78] It approved practices of Departments which had 'acknowledged that loose or otherwise defective wording cannot be rectified in guidance and should instead be rectified through amending legislation'.[79]

Amending legislation might, perhaps with illustrative examples and non-exhaustive lists of qualifying criteria, expand upon the meanings of 'responsible body' 'qualifying kind' and 'conservation purpose'. 'The public good' might be replaced with a concept more familiar to land law – for example, 'the public interest'. Those drafting the amending legislation might more readily recognise the strength of future motivation to challenge conservation covenants, and the importance of minimising uncertainty which could be exploited as the basis for those challenges. Amending legislation should properly recognise the intricacies of existing proprietary estates and interests, and situate conservation covenants clearly and precisely alongside them. Most importantly, amending legislation should acknowledge that the success of conservation covenants depends not on aspiration, but on the construction of a robust and durable regime for ensuring that they remain binding on multiple successors in title.

[78] ibid para 56.
[79] ibid para 57.

9

Registering Nature

VANESSA CASADO-PÉREZ AND YAEL R LIFSHITZ

I. INTRODUCTION

REGISTRATION IS ONE of the key elements in the arsenal of property tools. It receives much scholarly attention and is often at the centre of policy debates as well. The discussion around registration, especially in English law, tends to focus primarily on land. Yet registration extends beyond land. Milk quotas transaction registries,[1] carbon registries[2] or water allocation registries[3] are but a few examples. Other resources such as art works,[4] woodland carbon capture[5] and bicycles[6] can be partially recorded in other ways.

This chapter explores registries and other data collection frameworks in natural resources, acknowledging how the differences between natural resources and between types of property rights – from Blackstonian-like property rights in land to fish quotas or licences to fish recreationally in a river – impact or should impact the design of the data collection device. This chapter focuses on the aggregate information function these registration mechanisms need to play in order to properly respond to environmental problems.

The first contribution of this chapter is broadening the scope of the discussion by shifting our gaze to natural resources, and the ways in which registration

[1] Real Decreto 754/2005, de 8 de julio, por el que se regula el sistema de cuotas lácteo (BOE núm 160) www.mapa.gob.es/es/ganaderia/temas/produccion-y-mercados-ganaderos/Real%20Decreto%20754_2005%20texto%20consolidado_tcm30-105369.pdf.

[2] California Air Resources Board, 'Offset Project Registries', ww2.arb.ca.gov/our-work/programs/compliance-offset-program/offset-project-registries; see section II below.

[3] Ofwat, 'Licences and Licensees', www.ofwat.gov.uk/regulated-companies/ofwat-industry-overview/licences.

[4] Louvre, 'About the Collections', collections.louvre.fr/en/page/apropos; The Art Loss Register, 'About Us', www.artloss.com/about-us ('The Art Loss Register holds the world's largest private database of lost, stolen and looted art, antiques and collectibles').

[5] Woodland Carbon Code, 'UK Woodland Carbon Code: The Basics', woodlandcarboncode.org.uk/about/the-basics.

[6] A Bell and G Parchomosky, 'Of Property and Information' (2016) 116 *Columbia Law Review* 237, 242.

operates within them. The second contribution of the chapter lies in the novel case study on registration of carbon, a resource which impacts our modern economies, our daily lives and our ability to tackle climate change. The case study serves as a gateway to understanding the registration of natural resources more broadly. Finally, the third contribution of the chapter is underscoring an important, yet understudied function of registration systems: the aggregation of information function.

The analysis here highlights how registration serves an important purpose beyond (and in addition to) facilitating trade and increasing certainty for potential right holders. By aggregating information, registration can serve as a useful tool in addressing some of the complex realities of modern resource management. Registration is particularly useful in this context, we argue, because it enables better resource management, based on more accurate information and more aggregate data. Especially with natural resources which are spread out among so many individuals and entities, gathering the information in one place (via registration) is crucial to facilitating more informed and thoughtful management. Bits of information regarding these natural resources are endlessly dispersed, which prevents both the government and citizens from having the full picture. In a sense, we need to collect data about the trees to be able to govern the forest. The example of curbing carbon emissions to tackle climate change illustrates the significance of registration in this regard.

II. REGISTRATION BEYOND LAND

The registration or recordation of land is a prevalent practice across multiple jurisdictions. It is only natural that the scholarship on registration has focused primarily on *land* registration[7] given the prominent role land plays in our society. It has historical, sociological and economic significance, and while there are other forms of property that are gaining relevance, our legal property system remains land-centric.[8] Land in England and Wales is registered via a system of

[7] For but a few examples, see M Dixon, 'The Land Registration Act 2002: A Risk Assessment' [2003] *Conveyancer and Property Lawyer* 136; E Cooke and P O'Connor, 'Purchaser Liability to Third Parties in the English Land Registration System' (2004) 120 *LQR* 640; M Dixon, 'Proprietary Rights and Rectifying the Effect of Non-registration' [2005] *Conveyancer and Property Lawyer* 447; M Dixon, 'The Future of the Land Registry' [2011] *Conveyancer and Property Lawyer* 1; A Nair, 'Interpreting Section 58 of the Land Registration Act 2002: The Limits of 'Statutory Magic' (2013) 72 *Cambridge Law Journal* 257; A Goymour, 'Mistaken Registrations of Land: Exploding the Myth of "Title by Registration"' [2013] *Cambridge Law Journal* 617; M Dixon, 'Rectification and Priority: Further Skirmishes in the Land Registration War' [2015] *LQR* 207; A Goymour (ed), *New Perspectives on Land Registration: Contemporary Problems and Solutions* (Oxford, Hart Publishing, 2018); A Nair, 'Powers and Incumbrances: The Uncertain Scope of the Land Registration Act 2002 s.26' [2023] *Conveyancer and Property Lawyer* 146.

[8] For a review of the historical significance of land and its continued significance, see 'Sticky Property' (forthcoming, on file with the authors).

constitutive registration.[9] A similar mechanism for land registration is also in place in other jurisdictions, including Scotland,[10] Australia[11] and New Zealand.[12] In many other jurisdictions, land is recorded (though not constitutively registered) – examples include California, New York, France and Italy.[13]

Registration, however, is not limited to land. In fact, registration is both prevalent and useful for a broad range of resources. For example, as the case study below illustrates, carbon rights are registered.[14] Water rights are sometimes registered.[15] Trademarks are registered (but copyrights in the UK generally do not need to be).[16] Data regarding oil and gas rights, in some jurisdictions, is recorded. For example, in Texas, the oil and gas leases are collected and recorded by the Railroad Commission, which is the state's oldest regulatory agency.[17] Sometimes the registration happens through privately organised databases that may even cross jurisdictional borders, as the example of art work registration illustrates.[18]

The claim is not that all resources should be registered, always; indeed, some resources and some instances are less suitable for registration. There are three main reasons why a system of registration is not (or should not) be set up for a particular resource. First, on a functional account, the answer to the question 'to register or not' depends on the costs and benefits of setting up and maintaining such a system. Setting up a register has large, fixed costs (both monetary and social), so it will only make sense to do it if the asset is valuable enough and if

[9] Land Registration Act 2002.

[10] Scottish Law Commission, *Discussion Paper on Land Registration: Void and Voidable Titles* (Scot Law Comm No 125, 2004), 11 (the Land Register of Scotland is a register of title, superseding the earlier deeds-based Register of Sasines).

[11] G Taylor, 'The Emergence of the Torrens System in Australia' in G Brendan (ed), *The Boundaries of Australian Property Law* (Cambridge, Cambridge University Press, 2016) 27–28. See also M Nancarrow et al, *Australian Property Law* (Cambridge, Cambridge University Press, 2022) 171 (the Torrens system accounts for around 99 per cent of interests in private freehold land across all Australian jurisdictions).

[12] Land Information New Zealand, 'The Land Transfer System', www.linz.govt.nz/our-work/property-information-system/land-transfer-system.

[13] Y-C Chang, *Property Law: Comparative, Empirical and Economic Analysis* (Cambridge, Cambridge University Press, 2023) 113, 114.

[14] See section III below.

[15] M Bryan, 'At the End of the Day: Are the West's General Stream Adjudications Relevant to Modern Water Rights Administration' (2015) 15 *WLR* 461.

[16] UK Government, 'How Copyright Protects Your Work', www.gov.uk/copyright#:~:text=There isn't a register,work, including illustration and photography. See also UK Government, 'Intellectual Property and Your Work', https://www.gov.uk/intellectual-property-an-overview/protect-your-intellectual-property.

[17] See, eg, Railroad Commission of Texas, 'Well Records – Online', www.rrc.texas.gov/oil-and-gas/research-and-statistics/obtaining-commission-records/oil-and-gas-well-records-online; D Baird and T Jackson, 'Information, Uncertainty, and the Transfer of Property' (1984) 13 *Journal of Legal Studies* 299, 309–10.

[18] See, eg, Louvre, 'About the Collections', collections.louvre.fr/en/page/apropos; The Art Loss Register, 'About Us', www.artloss.com/about-us.

the benefit of crisply defined rights is large enough,[19] although the set-up and maintenance costs might be lower for those property rights that are created via administrative permits, because the agency granting these rights already has the information necessary. In addition, the nature of these rights allows agencies to impose more reporting requirements on the right holders allowing for more dynamic update of the Register.

Second, the frequency of transfer matters.[20] The intuition here is also one of cost-effectiveness, except not with the value of the resource, but with the frequency of the transaction: when transactions happen every minute, a registration system just wouldn't be able to keep up. However, that calculus might be changing as technological advancements make rapid, and accurate, recordation of transactions increasingly feasible.

Third, certain features of the resource could impact the suitability (and desirability) of a registration system therein.[21] A registry may not be advisable, for instance, for resources that change naturally or can be easily modified, diluting the usefulness of the information in the registry.[22] This could be framed as a matter of durability, where registries are most useful when assets are 'durable'.[23] As Professors Bell and Parchomovsky put it: 'In general, registries are most valuable when there is confidence that the asset as it exists in the real world will continue to match the description in the registry.'[24]

Think, for example, of a single grain of wheat. We don't bother registering, partially because 'a title-based recording system is much harder to organize for a [single] grain in a silo than it is for land'.[25] Similarly, water as a fugitive resource is changing, so a registry needs to adapt to such fugitiveness. When we define property rights over those resources, the measurement challenges translate into less defined property rights. A registry can offer a snapshot of those property rights at their initial allocation. However, the amount of water available and consumed each season may be different. In water registries in the west of the US, for example, annual allocations and consumptions are not recorded. This introduces uncertainty for both regulators and regulated parties. In contrast, with regard to water permits which are administratively granted, as they are in the UK, registries can be designed with a dynamic component. Those with abstraction permits in the UK are required to submit annual 'returns' – that is, report the amount of water they have used.[26]

[19] B Arruñada, *Institutional Foundations of Impersonal Exchange: Theory and Policy of Contractual Registries* (Chicago, University of Chicago Press, 2012) 2.

[20] Baird and Jackson (n 17) 304, 306.

[21] ibid 304.

[22] ibid.

[23] S Shavell, *Foundations of Economic Analysis of Law* (Cambridge, MA, Harvard University Press, 2004) 49–50.

[24] Bell and Parchomosky (n 6) 243–44.

[25] ibid 306.

[26] UK Government, 'Manage Your Water Abstraction Licence Online' (27 March 2018), www.gov.uk/guidance/manage-your-water-abstraction-or-impoundment-licences-online.

This third factor – features of the resource – partially explains the centrality of land in the registration debates; as a permanent, durable and generally consistent resource, it tends to be the paradigmatic case to which registration systems are applied. 'Real property is the paradigm of property for which a filing system of title claims is superior.'[27]

In between a piece of land and a grain of wheat, there are many intermediary cases of different kinds of natural resources and personal property.

Registration of natural resources, to the extent that it exists, is mostly incomplete. Even when land title registries are established, there is a wealth of information that is not included on the registry. Aside from certain right holders (such as beneficial owners), registries of land often also do not include information regarding aspects such as trees, water reserves, in situ minerals, wildlife and more. There is no such thing as a comprehensive land registry that offers a snapshot of all the rights (water, wind, oil, airspace, minerals etc) and who holds them in a particular plot of land. Beyond a land registry, water rights, for example, are defined based on where they are used in many jurisdictions, but their records are usually separated from land.[28]

Relatedly, sometimes even if information is collected, data regarding rights to closely related resources are held by different institutions. For example, closely tied resources, such as vessels and fishing, are kept at different institutions.[29] Technology is ultimately expected to make connecting registries easier and allow people to more readily check their rights and get information about others with a few clicks. But legal barriers will remain, for example, in the form of different governmental levels managing different resources.[30]

Taken together, while not suitable for every resource or situation, registration is usefully applied beyond land, across a broad range of resources. Studying the registration systems in these resources can produce interesting and significant insights.

[27] Baird and Jackson (n 17) 304.

[28] See art 99.1 of the Real Decreto 849/1986, de 11 de abril, por el que se aprueba el Reglamento del Dominio Público Hidráulico, que desarrolla los títulos preliminar I, IV, V, VI y VII de la Ley 29/1985, de 2 de agosto, de Aguas (in Spain, water rights are defined based on place of use); see also Ministerio para latransición ecológica Y el reto demográfico, '¿Que es el Registro de Aguas?' (Vicepresidencia Tercera del gobierno), www.miteco.gob.es/es/agua/temas/concesiones-y-autorizaciones/uso-privativo-del-agua-registro-del-aguas/registros-aguas-desde-1986/que_es_registro_aguas.html# (the water registry is kept at River Basin Organizations and centralised, but there are no ties with the Land Registry); for an analysis of this dichotomy in the US, see M Bryan, 'At the End of the Day: Are the West's General Stream Adjudications Relevant to Modern Water Rights Administration' (2015) 15 *WLR* 461.

[29] UK Government, Centre for Environment, Fisheries and Aquaculture Science, 'Form RW1: Application to Register a Fishery or Cropping Water' (13 August 2014), www.gov.uk/government/publications/application-to-register-a-fishery-or-cropping-water-form-rw1-and-rw2; see also UK Ship Register, 'Register a Boat: The UK Ship Register', www.gov.uk/register-a-boat/the-uk-ship-register.https://www.gov.uk/register-a-boat/the-uk-ship-register.

[30] Baird and Jackson (n 17) 310 (there could be interactions with other public licensing systems – for example, given that cars are already registered by licence plates (state DMVs), there is little need to create an additional registry that tracks ownership).

III. CASE STUDY: CARBON REGISTRATION IN THE UK

Registering carbon serves as an illustrative case for the significance of using registries not only as a tool to facilitate trade, but also as a tool for aggregate data collection and management.

Carbon allowances are essentially entitlements to a specific amount of carbon. In the UK, carbon allowances are recognised as property. In *Armstrong DLW GmbH v Winnington Networks Ltd*,[31] the court was called upon to determine whether carbon allowances under the EU Emissions Trading Scheme (which applied in the UK at the time) are property. The court found that carbon allowances are intangible property at common law.[32] One of the significant points in the court's reasoning had to do with the fact that each allowance is unique and identifiable (based on its unique reference code, like a serial number), which in turn makes the allowances more permanent and stable. This means that allowances are more akin to physical bank notes than to amorphous electronic ledgers. In the wake of *Armstrong*, scholars have also agreed that carbon allowances are best understood as property.[33]

How are carbon rights registered? In the UK, the primary venue for registering carbon rights is tied to the mechanism through which these rights are traded: the UK Emissions Trading Scheme (UK ETS). Before diving into the registration process, a quick primer on the UK ETS is in order.

The UK has taken on a legally binding commitment to reach net zero by 2050.[34] To meet this ambitious goal, the government sets carbon budgets to allocate the amount of carbon which can be emitted within a given period.[35]

[31] *Armstrong DLW GmbH v Winnington Networks Ltd* [2012] EWHC 10 (Ch).

[32] ibid [50]; see also *Gullivair Ltd v Environment Agency* [2023] UKFTT 936 (GRC) 1 November 2023 (where a non-compliance penalty was a proportionate interference on the appellant's property rights due to the public interest of maintaining the integrity of the UK ETS – positive citation of *Armstrong* as a carbon allowance can constitute property); *ABX Air Inc v Environment Agency* [2023] UKFTT 847 (GRC) 13 October 2023 (co-appellant to *Gullivair*, where the imposition of the penalty did not upset the balance between the public interest and the protection of the appellant's property rights – positive citation for *Armstrong* as carbon allowances can constitute property).

[33] B Holligan, 'Commodity or Propriety? Unauthorised Transfer of Intangible Entitlements in the EU Emissions Trading System' (2020) 85 *MLR* 929, 982; 986; 987; see also P Yeoh, 'Is Carbon Finance the Answer to Climate Control?' (2008) 50 *International Journal of Law and Management* 189, 190; Law Commission, *Digital Assets Final Report* (Law Comm No 412, 2023) paras 2.52, 4.67–4.75 (the status of carbon allowances as property was acknowledged which suggested that carbon allowances are recognised as part of their proposed 'third category' of personal property rights).

[34] Climate Change Act 2008, s 1; see also s 4 (a carbon budget is the limit on the amount of greenhouse gases emitted across the UK within a five-year period); s 7(1); s 9(1) (carbon budgets are decided by the government, following independent assessments on emissions targets by the Committee on Climate Change); and s 13 (once a carbon budget has been established, the Climate Change Act places a legal obligation on the government to implement policies that ensure the budget is fulfilled).

[35] *Friends of the Earth v BEIS* [2022] EWHC 1841, [7]–[12] (on the duties of the Secretary of State in setting and meeting the carbon budget) and [32]–[37] (on how the carbon budgets are determined, explaining the carbon budgets mechanism).

One of the mechanisms which is employed to ensure that the carbon budgets are met is an ETS.[36]

The ETS is a 'cap and trade' system.[37] A cap-and-trade system operates by setting a maximum limit on emissions – a 'cap'; allocating the allowances within the cap; and then facilitating trade among the allowance holders.[38] Each allowance is equivalent to one ton of carbon dioxide.[39] Under the UK ETS, covered entities must ensure that their allowances are sufficient to cover emissions.[40] If their emissions exceed allowances, participants must buy additional allowances.[41] Covered entities who fail to comply with their allowances requirement could be subject to civil penalties.[42] Similar cap-and-trade systems are adopted in other jurisdictions. For example, California's cap and trade mechanism[43] sets a statewide limit on emissions[44] and is an example of a carbon market that operates as a crucial competent to meeting overall climate policy objectives.

The UK carbon trading scheme achieves the goal of emissions reduction by decreasing the cap over time. By 2030, the scheme plans to reduce greenhouse gas emissions by at least 68 per cent from 1990 levels, and by 2037, the scheme aims to reduce emissions by at least 77 per cent.[45] Ultimately, the UK ETS aims to achieve net-zero emissions by 2050, in line with the national goal.[46] Because available allowances decrease over time along with maximum emissions, the price

[36] *Armstrong* (n 31) [1]; see also UK Government, 'Guidance: Participating in the UK ETS' (2 January 2024), www.gov.uk/government/publications/participating-in-the-uk-ets/participating-in-the-uk-ets (the UK ETS came into effect on 1 January 2021, through the Greenhouse Gas Emissions Trading Scheme Order 2020; previously, the UK was part of the EU ETS).

[37] Norton Rose Fulbright, 'Eight Things You Need to Know about the UK Emissions Trading Scheme' (July 2023), www.nortonrosefulbright.com/en/knowledge/publications/1f3ecc9e/uk-ets-authority.

[38] For but a few examples, see RB Stewart, 'Privprop, Regprop, and Beyond' (1990) 13 *Harvard Journal of Law & Public Policy* 91, 93; JE Krier, 'Marketable Pollution Allowances' (1994) 25 *University of Toledo Law Review* 379; CM Rose, 'From Local to Global Commons: Private Property, Common Property, and Hybrid Property Regimes: Expanding the Choices for the Global Commons: Comparing Newfangled Tradable Allowance Schemes to Old-Fashioned Common Property Regimes' (1999) 10 *DEL & Policy* 45, 51; J B Wiener, 'Global Environmental Regulation: Instrument Choice in Legal Context' (1999) 108 *Yale LJ* 677, 712–13; J Nash and R Revesz, 'Markets and Geography: Designing Marketable Permit Schemes to Control Local and Regional Pollutants' (2001) 28 *Ecology Law Quarterly* 569 at 571; R Stavins, 'A Meaningful U.S. Cap-and-Trade System to Address Climate Change' (2008) 32 *Harvard Environmental Law Review* 300; DA Farber, 'Pollution Markets and Social Equity: Analyzing the Fairness of Cap and Trade' (2012) 39 *Ecology Law Quarterly* 1, 2.

[39] Norton Rose Fulbright (n 37).

[40] ibid.

[41] ibid.

[42] Greenhouse Gas Emissions Trading Scheme Order 2020.

[43] California AB 32 (Global Warming Solutions Act).

[44] California Environmental Protection Agency, 'Overview of ARB Emissions Trading Program' (2 September 2015), ww2.arb.ca.gov/sites/default/files/cap-and-trade/guidance/cap_trade_overview.pdf; Center for Climate and Energy Solutions, 'California Cap and Trade', www.c2es.org/content/california-cap-and-trade.

[45] International Carbon Action Partnership, 'United Kingdom Factsheet', icapcarbonaction.com/system/files/ets_pdfs/icap-etsmap-factsheet-99.pdf, 4.

[46] ibid 2.

of allowances increases, which encourages participants to decrease emissions.[47] The UK ETS covers the activities of almost 1,000 entities.[48]

How are allowances initially allocated? Through two methods: either freely (which essentially 'grandfathers' in existing uses) or through auctions.[49] First, free allowances are allocated 'to industrial participants at risk of carbon leakage'.[50] New participants also receive free allowances 'based on their activity in the first year of operation, the industry benchmark' as well as the carbon leakage exposure factor.[51] Second, allowances are also allocated by auction, through which participants purchase allowances competitively.[52] Auctions have a £22 (US$27.50) Auction Reserve Price (ARP), below which allowances will not be sold. In 2023, approximately 79 million allowances were allocated through auctioning, raising £4.2 billion (US$5.2 billion).[53]

Once initial allowances are allocated, there is a significant and robust secondary market where the allowances are traded.[54] A 2023 review of the UK ETS secondary market revealed that the secondary market quality is good for a market of the UK ETS' size, as evidenced by continuously improving liquidity and price discovery, and trading activity.[55]

Turning now to the registration of carbon allowances, all allowances issued by the UK ETS are registered on the UK Emissions Trading Registry.[56] The Registry operates as an online platform, which is managed by the Environment Agency.[57] The Registry keeps track of all the allocated allowances; of all transfers

[47] C May et al, 'Review of the UK Emissions Trading Scheme (ETS) and Potential Future' (June 2022), www.nortonrosefulbright.com/en/knowledge/publications/b8b8271f/review-of-the-uk-emissions-trading-scheme-ets-and-potential-future-developments.

[48] International Carbon Action Partnership (n 45) 1. In 2026, the UK ETS will expand to cover new industries and further limit the emission of greenhouse gases. It will cover domestic maritime transport beginning in 2026 and waste in 2028 (ibid).

[49] Norton Rose Fulbright (n 37).

[50] International Carbon Action Partnership (n 45) 3.

[51] ibid 4; see also Natural Resources Wales, 'The UK Emissions Trading Registry and Free Allocation of Allowances' (20 January 2023), naturalresources.wales/permits-and-permissions/carbon-emissions/the-uk-emissions-trading-registry-and-free-allocation-of-allowances/?lang=en; see also the Greenhouse Gas Emissions Trading Scheme (Amendment) Order 2020 (legislation covering free allocation).

[52] International Carbon Action Partnership (n 45) 2–3. For a review of the range of carbon prices in the UK ETS, see Statista, 'UK ETS Carbon Pricing in the United Kingdom 2022–2025', https://www.statista.com/statistics/1322275/carbon-prices-united-kingdom-emission-trading-scheme.

[53] International Carbon Action Partnership (n 45) 2.

[54] UK Government, 'Participating in the UK ETS' (updated 2 January 2024), www.gov.uk/government/publications/participating-in-the-uk-ets/participating-in-the-uk-ets; see also K Bryan 'Traders Place Record Bets Ahead of UK Election on Carbon Credits Price Jump' *Financial Times* (7 June 2024), www.ft.com/content/bdbd165c-c830-43a6-89c1-3ce2bec08b51.

[55] Institute for Sustainable Resources, 'Evaluation of the UK Emissions Trading Scheme: Phase 1 Report – Annex 4' (December 2023), assets.publishing.service.gov.uk/media/657c4fb31c0c2a000d18ce33/evaluation-of-uk-ets-annex-4-secondary-market-data-analysis.pdf.

[56] UK Government (n 54).

[57] International Carbon Action Partnership (n 45) 5; UK Government (n 54) (the registry stores records of 'allowances held in Operator Holding Accounts (OHA), Aircraft Operator Holding Accounts (AOHA), Trading Accounts and Government Accounts'); UK Government, 'UK Emissions Trading Scheme for Installations: How to Comply' (updated 4 September 2023), www.sepa.org.uk/media/594230/how-to-comply-uk-ets-installations.pdf, 7.

of allowances and of all surrendered allowances.[58] It also facilitates trade in allowances under the UK Kyoto Protocol, although these allowances cannot be used to comply with a party's obligations under the UK ETS scheme.[59]

What functions does the carbon registry serve? Registering carbon is essential, first, to establishing property rights in carbon. To participate in the market, an entity must possess a UK registry account.[60] Entities that have obligations under the UK ETS are also obligated to have an account with the UK Emissions Trading Registry.[61] However, anyone who wishes to trade in carbon allowances (and, as mentioned, the secondary trading in allowances is significant and robust) can apply to open an account on the registry,[62] thus enabling broader participation in trade on the registry platform. The registration of carbon is therefore both compulsory and constitutive, in the sense that absent registration, a full transfer of rights cannot occur.

Second, and relatedly, registering carbon facilitates trade among the right holders. As mentioned, absent registration, the trade and transfer of carbon rights cannot take place. Trade in carbon allowances (at least in the UK) can only take place on the platform. Without the facilitating platform, transactions would be very difficult; parties would have to find other mechanisms to ensure that the carbon allowances are legitimate. These mechanisms, such as insurance, will increase transaction costs and so we may not achieve the optimal social solution with reduction of emissions at a lower cost.

Third, importantly, beyond facilitating trade, registration of carbon is also key for the success of the overall programme. Recall that the goal, ultimately, is to curb carbon emissions by adopting a 'cap' on the overall amount of carbon emitted. However, the cap only works if we know how much carbon, overall, has been allocated and used in a given period. Conversely, without the information regarding the overall use of carbon – information which is generated by the Registry – the goal of the programme cannot be met. It is the aggregate perspective – one that tells us, for example, how much carbon was emitted in a given year – that helps us determine whether we will meet our carbon goals.

The carbon registry is also open to the public, which allows the public access to information regarding the carbon rights and the transaction details.[63] The public, a potential new polluter or an administrative agency can

[58] UK Government, 'UK Emissions Trading Registry', view-emissions-trading-registry.service.gov.uk; UK Government (n 36) (the registry tracks 'the movement of allowances between accounts and details of verified emissions and allowances surrendered by operators').

[59] UK Government (n 57) 11.

[60] International Carbon Action Partnership (n 45) 5.

[61] UK Government, 'Documents Required to Register for the UK Emissions Trading Registry' (31 March 2021), www.gov.uk/government/publications/documents-required-to-register-for-the-uk-emissions-trading-registry.

[62] UK Government, 'UK Emission Trading Registry' view-emissions-trading-registry.service.gov.uk/#:~:text=The%20Registry%20is%20a%20secure,Trading%20Accounts%20and%20Government%20Accounts (see 'Apply for access to the registry').

[63] Armstrong (n 31) [16].

get micro-views and macro-views. Anyone can check details about a specific allowance, but also analyse the trends in a particular location, aggregate collective impacts, and project combined effects of potential policies. Without a registry, transparency would decrease, and the effectiveness of cap-and-trade policies would be impaired. Without the data and information aggregated on the Registry, management of greenhouse gas emissions and climate change becomes a guessing game.

The functions of the carbon registry – and especially the overlooked aggregate function – are illustrative of the functions of registration more broadly.

IV. EXPANDING THE FUNCTIONS OF REGISTRATION

Much scholarly attention has been devoted to the question 'why should we register' or what functions a system of registration serves. The two most commonly provided answers are: first, that registration facilitates a market exchange and trade among users; and, second and relatedly, that a system of registration protects the owners' rights and enhances owners' powers. We offer a third, underexplored, function of registries: to serve as key aggregates of data, which is vital to the overall management of the resources which are registered.

A. The Market Facilitation Function

Markets require information. If we want 'things' to be truly alienable and transferable, market participants need to have information about the asset. Particularly, market participants may be hesitant to engage in a transaction if they are uncertain whether their counterpart has rights over the asset. The risk of entering into a transaction with a party who may not own the asset entails larger transaction costs and may discourage some transactions. Conversely, if there is certainty for potential buyers, they will be more willing to enter into transactions and such market transparency will help build trust. Registries help build trust in the transactions and reduce uncertainty, thus facilitating transactions. The facilitating function of registries can also be portrayed as a form of reducing transaction costs by reducing research and information costs because all the information is made more readily available.[64] Reducing such costs will ensure more efficient transactions.[65] Assets will therefore end

[64] LRA 2002, sched 4A; Economic Crime (Transparency & Enforcement) Act 2022, c 10 (the UK recently launched an effort to increase the transparency of its land registry by introducing legislation that compels the beneficial owners to come forward and register); S Douglas and A Layard, 'Ownership Beneath: Transparency of Land Ownership in Times of Economic Crime' (2024) 44(1) *OJLS* 74.

[65] Bell and Parchomosky (n 6) 254.

up in the hands of those who value it more, enhancing the overall efficient use of resources.[66]

This framework dominates the economic literature. Professor Benito Arruñada's work is illustrative of this strand of literature.[67] The main problem with which Arruñada is concerned is asymmetric information between sellers and potential buyers, and the risk of fraudulent transitions.[68] Relatedly, in some cases, one way in which registration facilitates transferability is by establishing the temporal priority of claims.[69] This temporal priority is important specifically to determine who among two competing claimants gets to keep the proprietary rights in the 'thing' in question. Arruñada also specifically emphasises the role of publicly accessible registries in reducing the transaction costs associated with impersonal trade, and the ways in which such publicly accessible registries facilitate such trade (or do so to a greater extent than would otherwise be possible).[70]

Registration, on this account, is a way of conveying information: information about the asset itself (such as its borders); about the right holders; and about the types of entitlements that they hold. The incentives to register are affected by the protection that the legal system offers to those registered or the consequences that can attach to the lack of registration. Legal rules themselves affect the amount of information that is available and hence the amount of risk necessary for the one party or the other to bear.[71] Some have studied the ways in

[66] There is a vast literature on intellectual property law in the context of information. See, eg, C Long, 'Information Costs in Patent and Copyright' (2004) 90 *Virginia Law Review* 465, 468 (emphasising the significance of making observers aware of property rights held by others so they may effectively comply with responsibilities saddled on them by creation of right in question); D Oliar, 'The Copyright–Innovation Tradeoff: Property Rules, Liability Rules, and Intentional Infliction of Harm' (2012) 64 *Stanford Law Review* 951 (investigating the potential for property rules and liability rules to minimise interference between copyright owners and maximise innovators' incentive to invest); MM Render, 'Complexity in Property' (2013) 81 *Tennessee Law Review* 79, 96–118 (providing comprehensive overview of the information-costs thesis propounded by T Merrill and H Smith and important critiques offered in rebuttal); A Kapczynski and T Syed, 'The Continuum of Excludability and the Limits of Patents', (2013) 122 *Yale Law Journal* 1900 (positing excludability in patent rights is asymmetrical for different kinds of information and suggesting alternative approaches to property protection are necessary); G Parchomovsky and A Stein, 'Intellectual Property Defenses' (2013) 113 *Columbia Law Review* 1483 (suggesting ways to expand the binding precedential value of individual patent claims and prevent superfluous litigation from imposing societal costs).

[67] See, eg, Arruñada (n 28) 2–3 (assessing the role of registries in reducing transaction costs of impersonal trade).

[68] B Arruñada, 'Property Titling and Conveyancing' in K Ayotte and H E Smith (eds), *Research Handbook on the Economics of Property Law* (Cheltenham, Edward Elgar, 2011) 237–38 (although Arruñada tends to be concerned more with recordation than registration of title as such).

[69] G McCormack, 'American Private Law Writ Large? The UNCITRAL Secured Transactions Guide' (2011) 60 *ICLQ* 597.

[70] Arruñada (n 19) 11; B Arruñada and N Garoupa, 'The Choice of Titling System in Land' (2005) 48(2) *Journal of Law and Economics* 709.

[71] Baird and Jackson (n 17) 301; note that this concern for the existence and the production of information differs from study of 'information costs' in property, which was developed by T Merrill and H Smith over a series of works. See T Merrill and H Smith, 'Optimal Standardization in the Law of Property: The Numerus Clausus Principle' (2000) 110 *Yale Law Journal* 1; T Merrill and H Smith, 'The Property/Contract Interface' (2001) 101 *Columbia Law Review* 773, 795–96, 801–02; H Smith, 'Property and Property Rules' (2004) 79 *New York University Law Review* 1719, 1753–54.

which particular doctrines, such as adverse possession, serve as a mechanism for incentivising the disclosure of information.[72]

The information is not only useful for subsequent right holders and potential claimants, but also for the public. This insight comes through strongly in a series of works by Professors Henry Smith and Thomas Merrill, who have analysed how the internal design of property itself serves as a means of conveying information to the public.[73] Their analysis shows that information in registries needs to be conveyed not just between subsequent right holders, but also to the general public, as property rights impose limitations and obligations on them as well. The public needs to know to keep off private lawns, even if they are not looking to buy the house.

In sum, registration could potentially be understood as one way of conveying information to the general public as well as to potential claimants.

B. The Owner Powers' Function

Beyond the core function of facilitating trade and transfer, scholars have expanded the functions of registries in two directions. First, in a recent article, Professors Abraham Bell and Gideon Parchomovsky argue that registries can strengthen the power of the owners themselves by playing a role in deterring unwarranted uses or assets.[74] In the UK, a mobile phone database was launched nearly two decades ago.[75] This is thought to have had a significant impact on the number of stolen mobile phones: based on reported theft cases, the number of stolen mobile phones dropped by 20 per cent between 2004 and 2012.[76] 'Knowledge about title to property rights', argue Bell and Parchomovsky, 'is crucial to enjoying their value.'[77] This is true because buyers need the information in order to engage in the transaction (which could benefit the current owner) and, likewise, because the owners themselves need information in order to fully enjoy the resources they hold.[78] Sometimes, it even helps the owner to

[72] TJ Miceli and CF Sirmans, 'An Economic Theory of Adverse Possession' (1995) 15 *International Review of Law and Economics* 161, 164; WC Marra, 'Adverse Possession, Takings, and the State' (2011) 89 *University of Detroit Mercy Law Review* 1, 14–15.

[73] See Merrill and Smith (n 71) 795–96, 801–02 (suggesting that the in rem nature of property rights stems from the need to communicate information to a wider pool of individuals); Smith (n 71) 1753–54 (analysing the advantage of property rules, over liability rules, due to their ability to minimize information costs in certain situations).

[74] Bell and Parchomosky (n 6) 246.

[75] National Mobile Phone Register, thenmpr.com/home (the database also registers other movable items, including computers, bikes and more). See also Immobilise, the UK National Property Register, www.immobilise.com.

[76] Rolfe Winkler, 'Carriers Band to Fight Cellphone Theft' *Wall Street Journal* (9 April 2012), www.wsj.com/articles/SB10001424052702303815404577334152199453024. Other examples include registries of bicycles in Norway: 'Bicycle Theft in Norway' (28 May 2009), www.sykkeltyveri.no/bicycle_theft.html.

[77] Bell and Parchomosky (n 6) 241.

[78] ibid.

know what they actually have. A good example about this latter function is an art registry providing information about works of art that went missing during the Second World War.[79]

The advantages of registration from an owner's perspective can also be linked to the formalisation of title and the increased ability to leverage assets for further economic benefits. Professor de Soto argues that lack of state recognition (which is embodied in the form of registration) diminishes the value of assets.[80] A prime example is the inability of de facto right holders if the favelas in Brazil to leverage their assets in the absence of formal state recognition.[81] However, it is important to note that de Soto's work conflates the creation of formal title and the registration of that title. The benefits which de Soto points to accrue from formalisation, not necessarily from registration.[82] Yet, registration can indeed be the vehicle through which such formalisation happens.[83]

The second way in which scholarship has expanded our understanding of the role of registries recently is by emphasising the role registries can play in creating or promoting market standards. Amnon Lehavi states that they 'may serve as a basis for a future development of regulatory and legal mechanisms';[84] this enables the registries to serve as 'as platforms for future legal innovation'.[85]

C. The Power of Aggregate Information

Importantly, beyond the transactional value and the increase in owner power and information, registries serve a key function by aggregating information and pooling data from across the resource. The power of aggregate data is crucial to our ability to adequately respond to current challenges such as addressing climate change, planning infrastructure or dealing with resource shortages. Tackling these grave challenges requires sound decision-making, which in turn depends on the availability of reliable, aggregate data.

[79] For other examples, see Bell and Parchomosky (n 6) 260 (discussing the examples of Holocaust survivors and Heir Hunters, and the example of orphan works in intellectual property).

[80] H de Soto, *The Mystery of Capital: Why Capitalism Triumphs in the West and Fails Everywhere Else* (New York, Basic Books, 2003) 42–47. However, see also A Bell and G Parchomovsky, 'Property Lost in Translation' (2013) 80 *Columbia Law Review* 515, 570–72 (citing de Soto's work and cautioning that mere recordation of property interests may not necessarily work when localised property norms are at variance with the state-imposed regulatory framework).

[81] De Soto (n 80) 85–86.

[82] The economic literature on registration, spearheaded by Hernando de Soto, Dean Lueck, Gary Libecap and Benito Arruñada, tends to conflate 'titling' and registration. See Bell and Parchomosky (n 6) 247 (providing a review of the economic literature).

[83] Arruñada (n 28) 2 (Arruñada cautions against formality and claims that building universal land titling systems that have high fixed costs may not be the solution for small-value assets or firms).

[84] A Lehavi, 'From Global Databases to Global Norms? The Case of Cultural Property Law' (2023) 44 *University of Pennsylvania Journal of International Law* 359, 374.

[85] ibid 376.

A system of property allocates control over resources to multiple right holders. While a system of property has many benefits, what is lost on the way are the 'bits' of information regarding those allocated resources. How many trees are currently growing in this region? Have the water-based borders in the region changed due to recent rainfall? How much carbon was recently emitted? How much water was used across the entire watershed? Our legal rights over land plots or water rights do not give us direct answers to such questions. Data that are spread across multiple right holders and assets (via a system of property rights) are not otherwise collected, except through some kind of registration or recordation system.

The registry collects two kinds of information: first, information regarding the rights themselves and the identity of the right holders; and, second, while collecting information on the rights, the registries also include information on the resource itself, including borders, quantities, size and location. These 'bits' of information, put together, are invaluable for resource management and governance. In order to get a full picture of what the state of the natural resources is, the data need to be aggregated. In a sense, we need to collect data about the trees to be able to govern the forest.

Aggregate information is important to individuals, to collective or public bodies who seek to manage resources, and to the public.[86] First, aggregate information about natural resources rights is helpful for public agencies. It is hard to manage a natural resource without knowing the demand, the claims, over such a resource.[87] Decisions on whether to expand water supply, for example, by investing in water re-use, desalination or new water diversion infrastructure require accurate information. Similarly, for pollution management, an agency may need to know the aggregate numbers of pollution rights allocated. Indeed, the agency could measure pollution at a given moment in time and react based on that measurement. But that measurement does not give the agency all the information it needs about potential emissions. In addition, given the right aggregate data, agencies could be proactive and, given certain meteorological conditions and expected pollution emissions, order certain polluters to be offline to achieve a pollution concentration level that is healthy for everyone.

To illustrate, this is similar to what some municipalities have done to tackle local air pollution. Vehicles, while significant modes of transport, also significantly contribute to ozone and particulate matter pollution, especially in urban areas. In tackling the issue of pollution created by cars, some cities relied on data from registries: Paris, for example, decided to restrict entry to the city

[86] UK Government (n 57) (the carbon registry makes information about accounts which hold carbon allowances and their holders publicly); see also UK Government, 'UK ETS Public Reports' (UK Emissions Trading Registry), reports.view-emissions-trading-registry.service.gov.uk/ets-reports.html (most registries make much of the information publicly available, such as the UK ETS public records based on the UK ETS Registry).

[87] C Lajaunie, B Schafer and P Mazzega, 'Big Data Enters Environmental Law' (2019) 8 *Transnational Environmental Law* 523, 534.

using granular information based in existing registries.[88] It decided that half of the cars, those with licence plates ending in odd numbers, were not allowed to circulate into the city centre on certain dates. On alternative dates, it was those with even numbered plates that were prevented entry. Later, during a heatwave in 2019, Paris banned more than 60 per cent of its registered fleet from its roads.[89] Barcelona took this a step further. Instead of just using the average car pollution, car registration offers further information about a car such as the manufacturing year, the fuel used or car model. Based on that information, Barcelona labelled cars with 'emissions' grades and those which polluted more had restricted access to the city in days of high pollution, and eventually they will be phased out of the city itself.[90]

Individuals also need aggregate data. Individuals may need to know the broader picture of right holders in the area, as this will impact their own rights. A clear example of this comes from water. In Australia, while each state has different rules, all of them classify water rights at different levels of priority. When there is not enough supply to satisfy the demand of all rights, those with higher priority are more likely to receive water. Thus, in order to plan for low water availability, users need information on who else has a water right and for which type of use. A user needs to know how much water in aggregate is allocated before his or her right would be satisfied.[91] Similarly, in the US, under the Prior Appropriation regime, which allocates water rights based on temporal priority,[92] whether or not a water rights owner will get enough water is dependent on who is ahead of him or her in the priority, as well as the amount of water available.

Aggregate data are important not just for quantity control, but also for quality control. For instance, the quality of water people will receive, everywhere, even assuming full compliance with water pollution regulations, will depend on which types of uses have used the water upstream before that user. Water pollution regulations do not require totally pristine water; rather, they limit the amount of pollutants in our water (up to a certain level). Therefore, to figure out what they actually have, right holders need to know what the other users in the area have as well. Paper mills, farms, an electronics manufacturer and other farmers cause the water that reaches a certain water licensee to have certain pollutants. Thus, the information in a water rights registry is also useful to assess the quality of the water that user will receive, even in countries without a

[88] BBC, 'Car Pollution in Cities: Do Number Plate Schemes Work?' (7 December 2016), www.bbc.co.uk/news/world-europe-38236926.

[89] F Crellin, 'Paris Bans up to 60% of its Cars as Heatwave Worsens Pollution' (*Reuters*, 28 June 2019), www.reuters.com/article/idUSKCN1TT0KU.

[90] Barcelona City Council, 'What is the Barcelona Ring Roads Low Emission Zone?', ajuntament.barcelona.cat/qualitataire/en/low-emission-zone/what-barcelona-ring-roads-low-emission-zone.

[91] Australian Government Murray-Darling Basin Authority, 'Water Entitlements in Basin States' (updated 27 June 2023), www.mdba.gov.au/water-use/allocations/water-entitlements-basin-states.

[92] RD Benson, BW Griggs, and AD Tarlock, *Water Resource Management: A Casebook in Law and Public Policy* (Eagen, MN, Foundation Press, 2021) 132.

priority system.[93] Other resources work similarly to water. Think of wind, which is used for energy production but also plays an important role in the ecosystem, from temperature balancing to seed pollination. One neighbour's wind turbines may leave the neighbouring one without enough wind kinetic energy to power his or her turbines.[94] Wind rights for renewable energy production could work in a similar pattern to water rights, and if registration of wind rights were to take place, the registry could offer similar functions.

Regulatory regimes can impact the incentives to register, thus affecting information availability. In order to get a fishing vessel licence in the UK, you first need to register your vessel. After registering, then you can apply for one of the myriad of types of fishing vessel licences that will allow the vessel to catch fish. However, there are no new licences available given the UK overall quotas, so transfer of licences is essential. Someone who wants to enter the fish industry needs information on who has a fishing vessel licence today in order to target who to approach with a buying offer. Indeed, the bifurcated nature of the process, where there is a registry for vessels and one for fishing vessel licences, could be further improved by centralising the information under one umbrella.[95] But aside from improving the coherence of existing registries, the data collection that takes place in both of the registries is vital.

Even an individual of the public with no claim to the resource may also benefit from more aggregate information. For example, think about a conscientious animal lover who is worried about an endangered fish species, the survival of which depends heavily on the amount of water withdrawals in a stream. In addition, individuals with certain vulnerabilities may want to be more restrictive in their outings when pollution is high or choose areas where businesses do not emit as much particulate matter affecting their respiratory health.

Lastly, facilitating the collection and greater availability of aggregate data also has equitable implications. In brief, those who are already better off are more likely to have other ways to get the information they need. Sophisticated parties, or researchers, may have alternative avenues to obtaining information, for example, through paid, private databases,[96] or through the use of high-tech solutions, such as measuring groundwater via sonars and satellites.[97] Those

[93] United States Environmental Protection Agency, 'Protection of Downstream Waters in Water Quality Standards: Frequently Asked Questions' (June 2014), www.epa.gov/sites/default/files/2018-10/documents/protection-downstream-wqs-faqs.pdf.

[94] Y Lifshitz, 'Gone with the Wind? The Potential Tragedy of the Common Wind' (2010) 28 *UCLA Journal of Environmental Law and Policy* 435, 460–69; Y Lifshitz, 'The Geometry of Property' (2021) 71 *University of Toronto Law Journal* 480, 500–08.

[95] UK Government, 'Registering a Fishing Vessel' (21 April 2021), www.gov.uk/guidance/registering-a-fishing-vessel.

[96] S Jiang et al, 'Mining Point-of-Interest Data from Social Networks for Urban Land Use Classification and Disaggregation' (2015) 53 *Computers, Environment and Urban Systems* 36.

[97] KA Wong, 'Drought Dowsing Goes High-Tech: Sonar Devices Measure Water Hidden Underground', *Cal Alumni Association* (11 August 2014), alumni.berkeley.edu/california-magazine/online/drought-dowsing-goes-high-tech-sonar-devices-measure-water/#.

with lesser means, however, or less sophisticated parties might not be able to access the same information. Likewise, agencies which are sometimes less well resourced may not be able to rely on the information in their decision-making, leaving them at a disadvantage versus more powerful actors.

To be sure, our discussion focuses primarily on registration. But recordation (in its many forms) can also play a similar role in aggregating data from many resources. However, the data pooled under a recordation system may not be as extensive or comprehensive. This could depend on whether the recordation is mandatory or whether sufficient incentives to record exist. The extent to which a system fulfils this aggregate function will depend on the structure of the mechanism and its set-up. But either way, pooling together data is useful and indeed necessary in the complex, ever-changing, natural world.

V. CONCLUDING REMARKS

Collecting data through registration is a key to the functioning of property systems. Land is often the key resource on which the scholars and policy-makers are focused. Yet registration is significant for a broader range of natural resources beyond land. The case of registering carbon illustrates the crucial role registration plays for carbon governance.

Expanding our gaze beyond land registration produces a broader insight on the nature of registration itself. The literature has emphasised the value registries have to facilitate transactions. We underscore a key, and thus far understudied, function: registries are essential to manage resources because they aggregate data. By collecting data on the trees, they allow us to see the forest. In doing so, registries offer regulators, policy-makers and the public both the close-up view of a particular resource, at a particular location, at a particular time, and a chance to get a more holistic 'helicopter view'. Both aspects are indispensable in a complex, changing environment.

To be sure, while registries are essential to the management of complex, dynamic environmental problems we are facing as a society, the claim here is not that registries are always a panacea, both due to exogenous and endogenous causes. Nature is complex, and registries may not be able to capture everything. Ideally, we would capture a perfect, dynamic snapshot of every single slice of earth and its atmosphere, with all the resource attributes and their interconnections. While that perfect picture may someday be technologically feasible, it might still be inefficient and impractical to collect all that data. Regardless, the ways in which legislation defines property rights and how it institutionalises data collection will remain impactful.[98]

[98] For a comparative example, see V Casado-Pérez, 'Inefficient Efficiency: Crying over Spilled Water' (2016) 46 *Environmental Law Reporter* 11046 (water rights in prior appropriation systems in the west of the US are defined, in terms of volume, based on diversion – there is no information about consumption).

Circling back to land, the existing land registries can be further utilised to harness the power of aggregate data for resource management. Where the registries are well established, such as in England, the land registry could be used as a platform for collecting other bits of information regarding other resources. Think, for example, about water supplies and water rights, trees (and the rights therein), minerals, soil stability, flora diversity and more. Given the existing infrastructure and institutional entrenchment of the existing land registration, doing so should not be overly costly or complex. The benefits, on the other hand, could be invaluable to our ability to effectively manage resources in times of drought, floods, storms, changing ecosystems and rising temperatures.

Capturing the richness of data that comes from the diverse natural world is a crucial task, which will be become even more crucial as we face ever more complex environmental challenges. Property already has an important tool that can fill an important information gap: registries. Resource-level and aggregate information can prove to be vital in the face of increasing pressure on our natural resources and a rapidly changing climate.

10

The Metaphysicality of Real Property

JOHN PAGE

I. INTRODUCTION: OF STRANGER THINGS

OUR RELATIONS WITH land are complex, multi-valent and multi-layered. They extend from the transactional to the transcendental, and more besides. Yet, notwithstanding property's reputation as inherently relational,[1] its laws, theories and practices tend to reflect a flatter, more rational, commodity-premised perspective. This has led to much critique. For example, Gregory Alexander describes real property's dominant 'land as commodity' ethos as 'unsatisfying' and 'only half-right'.[2] This chapter is interested in what may lie beyond that one-sided, 'half-right' viewpoint,[3] specifically, those land–people relationalities that defy objective or material metrics, contexts where our lawful relations with land are not always rational or, indeed, of this world. It explores a terrain that dwells alongside a series of fault lines; the contiguous crossovers between the worldly and other-worldly, the ancient and the modern, the sacred and the secular, the 'enchanted' and the 'disenchanted';[4] those liminal spaces where the *physical* and the *metaphysical* in real property abut and sometimes converge.

In sum, this chapter explores how the laws, theories and practices of property in land can reflect this 'strange' positionality, and how they may take the occasional metaphysical turn. While this claim appears surprising, it should

[1] C Clark and J Page, *The Lawful Forest: A Critical History of Property, Protest and Spatial Justice* (Edinburgh, Edinburgh University Press, 2022).

[2] G Alexander, *Commodity & Propriety: Competing Visions of Property in American Legal Thought 1776–1970* (Chicago, University of Chicago Press, 1997).

[3] Alexander's 'other half' explanation of property is 'property as propriety', not the metaphysical.

[4] The term 'disenchantment' was devised by German sociologist Max Weber to explain how late nineteenth and early twentieth-century secularisation had changed the world from one where 'we once believed more fully, was governed more directly and was made more meaningful by faith, by belief in God, by the supernatural, by magic'. A Bashford, *An Intimate History of Evolution: The Story of the Huxley Family* (London, Penguin/Random House UK, 2022) 369.

not be. After all, even orthodox understandings of property are metaphysical in their abstraction and disconnection from the physical world. What *is* surprising, however, is how seamlessly our lawful relations with land spring and shift between these worlds, how abstraction feeds prosaic, transactional, very material outcomes, and equally how proponents of 'law in context' need intangible metrics such as 'belonging' to corroborate their thinking. Yet, none of this should be surprising if we acknowledge, and as this chapter argues, that real property's laws, theories and doctrines possess a stranger 'other-worldliness' that is at least one part of its DNA.

A dictionary definition of 'metaphysics' refers to the 'study of what is outside objective experience'.[5] 'Metaphysical' is cognately defined as 'of, or relating to the transcendent, or to a reality beyond what is perceptible to the senses'.[6] Similes for 'metaphysical' include terms such as 'abstract', 'esoteric', 'spiritual', 'philosophical' and even 'supernatural'. In this chapter, 'metaphysical' or 'metaphysics' are used interchangeably to describe those aspects of real property that do not correspond to measurable, tangible or physically objective metrics. These are the incidents of common law real property that are variously less than rational, at times hauntingly other-worldly, ancient in their origins or 'enchanted' in the (oppositional) sense that 'disenchantment' refers to 'the modern shift away from belief to the knowable, from magic to the provable, from the sacred to the profane'.[7]

Of course, in proposing property's metaphysicality, this chapter does not downplay the 'real-world' side across these fault lines. To argue otherwise would be to ignore property's (and especially land's) integral role in capitalist economic activity, or the 'real-world' implications of its laws of exclusion, where private lines dictate where we belong and where we do not.[8] Academically, it would unpick the hard-won gains of legal geographers and critical property theorists who have compellingly argued for the 'worlded'-ness of the law and its contextual implications.[9] The laws of (private) property serve overwhelmingly instrumentalist ends, which manifest in a 'land as commodity' mindset that fuels national and global economies (on the upside) and provokes real-world crises like housing unaffordability, Indigenous dispossession or the existential climate emergency[10] (very much on the downside). If property is the 'law of things', as Henry Smith posits,[11] this chapter seeks to cast light on the lesser-seen 'things'

[5] www.merriam-webster.com/dictionary/metaphysical.
[6] ibid.
[7] Bashford (n 4) 369.
[8] J Waldron, 'Homelessness and the Issue of Freedom' (1991) 39 *UCLA Law Review* 295.
[9] I Braverman et al, *The Expanding Spaces of Law, A Timely Legal Geography* (Stanford, Stanford University Press, 2014).
[10] N Graham, *Lawscape: Property, Environment, Law* (Abingdon, Routledge, 2011); D Robinson and M Graham, 'Legal Pluralisms, Justice and Spatial Conflicts: New Directions in Legal Geography' (2018) 18 *Geographical Journal* 3.
[11] H Smith, 'Property as the Law of Things' (2012) 125 *Harvard Law Review* 1591.

of metaphysical real property, and to undertake a preliminary stocktake of its inventory. Drawing a loose analogy to the surreal upside-down manifestations of Hawkins, Indiana, depicted in the Netflix series *Stranger Things*, the 'things' of metaphysical property can possess strange, other-worldly incidents, the inverse of the better-recognised 'things' found on its 'normal' rational side. And like *Stranger Things*, there are random 'portals' through which these other 'worlds' may be glimpsed, gateways that lie beneath the thin veneer of everyday legal ordinariness.

It is also important at the outset to signpost what this chapter is not. Despite numerous references to 'other-worldliness', this chapter does not purport to be a work of law and religion, or one of legal philosophy. Rather, its tone tries to be *agnostic* in the way that the inventor of the word, Thomas Henry Huxley, perceived it.[12] This chapter aims to identify both the presence and the extent of metaphysicality in real property's doctrines, theories and practices, and to tentatively catalogue the curious persuasiveness of those 'stranger things' that from time to time characterise our less than rational relations with land. It also explores how insights from legal pluralism and Indigenous laws may enrich these (largely latent) metaphysical attributes and enlists the aid of property theories sympathetic to the *other*; schools of thought that speak of 'property as belonging', or liberal theories of human flourishing or personhood, incommensurable theories that subsist in such shadowlands beyond the full glare of objective material reality.

In seeking to record real property's metaphysical *otherness*, this chapter proposes a sliding scale – from the purportedly 'doctrinal' at one end to (what is tentatively termed) the 'apparitional' at the other. The doctrinal end of the scale is represented by concepts familiar to property scholars, the likes of the feudal estate and related, albeit fantastical abstractions routinely taught to land law students – 'things' that would not normally be considered 'metaphysical', but for the reality that we have become so normalised to their strangeness. Conversely, the 'apparitional' end of the spectrum includes far less 'plausible' concepts, such as the ghost-like hauntings of 'property as belonging'. In between these two ends lies a jurisprudential array of richness: ancient wisdoms of Indigenous laws increasingly recognised in the common law, the emerging personhood of rivers, the fading legacy of natural law and several others.

This chapter is structured as follows. Section II begins at the doctrinal end of the continuum, arguing for the centrality of metaphysics to 'everyday' common law property and practice. As flagged, real property revels in its abstraction and

[12] Bashford (n 4) xxvi–xxvii, 372–75. Agnosticism 'was christened in 1869 at a meeting of the Metaphysical Society … between men scientific and men religious … For Huxley, it all rested on the *method* of making claims from the possibility of evidence. The question was epistemological: what could be known and on what basis? And he turned this knowledge requirement to science itself, as much as religious belief … I think that its essence lies in the determination … not to go beyond the evidence'. ibid 374 (emphasis added).

detachment from context. In so doing, it adopts a language and form that (as the opening definitions imply) often cannot be reached through objective material reality. Consider the fee simple estate, which hovers in the ether above the physical land itself, or the equally fanciful notion of seisin, a construct confected by eleventh-century lawyers to ground this fantastical feudal tale. Section II also touches upon (and enacts) the related role of storytelling in property, a literary device that Carol Rose observes sometimes helps bridge the often-unbridgeable chasm between the implausible and the plausible in doctrinal property by 'teasing out' its underlying narratives, both of this world and beyond it.[13]

Section III likewise remains closer to the doctrinal end of the spectrum, identifying a number of obsolete yet extant real property doctrines or interests with a faith-based or divine derivation. These include the almost forgotten legacy of natural law in real property, the little-considered status of Christian churches as property, and peripheral interests in land like the incorporeal advowson.

Section IV begins the shift towards the 'apparitional', embracing legal pluralism and the ways in which metaphysical concepts from Indigenous traditions are increasingly given voice in settler colonial settings. River personhood is emblematic of this momentum. Forests are another example of something that is both ancient and cutting-edge at the same time. Section V concludes the descriptive work of this chapter by surveying several legal theories that lend credence to or (at least) allow the theoretical oxygen for the metaphysical in real property to subsist. This part sits mostly at the 'apparitional' end of the scale, far removed from prosaic theories, such as law and economics, which have dominated property discourse since the second half of the twentieth century.

Section VI closes with brief reflections on this physical/metaphysical duality. As legal geographer Nicholas Blomley observes, the Anglo-American common law of property has long been on a trajectory to erase the specificities of place and, in so doing, to develop a modern narrative of a detached, universalised, 'go anywhere' legal science, an institution unmoored from its ancient, place-based roots.[14] Property is now largely seen as a series of reductive relations between persons about things, such that the physicalised thing simply becomes the object of property, not its subject.[15] The end product of this paradigm is abstract, yet it is instrumentalist and transactional. The rapid uptake of electronic conveyancing (seen, for example, in Australian jurisdictions) has fed this hyper-abstraction, reducing our already tenuous relations with land to a mere exchange of encrypted algorithms. Conversely, the arguments of critical property theorists to re-*emplace* property have fostered a revival of intangible claims about sense of place and belonging – claims that strike a powerful resonance in

[13] CM Rose, 'Property as Storytelling: Perspectives from Game Theory, Narrative Theory, Feminist Theory' (1990) 2 *Yale Journal of Law & the Humanities* 37.

[14] N Blomley, *Law, Space, and the Geographies of Power* (New York, Guilford Press, 1994).

[15] WJ Hohfield, 'Some Fundamental Legal Conceptions as Applied in Legal Reasoning' (1913) 23 *Yale Law Journal* 16.

this erstwhile age of secularism. It is as if the crucible of physicalised space and place evokes ethereal responses to land, while hyper-abstraction yields an oppositional, very pragmatic, commoditised output.

Property's subjects and objects, like the adolescent, coming-of-age characters in *Stranger Things*, dwell in surprisingly adjacent, constantly dynamic, inherently porous multiverses where, perhaps, such counter-intuitive paradoxes are not so strange. As one 'portal' opens (like river personhood) and another closes (the decline of natural law), the things of real property spring and shift between these two worlds, physical and metaphysical, carrying with them the faint yet discernible upside-down traces of the other.

II. THE METAPHYSICAL IN 'EVERYDAY' REAL PROPERTY

Doctrinal property law has long hinted of the otherworldly, albeit in doctrines less central to everyday practice. Thus, the so-called Modern Rule against Perpetuities relies on 'magic gravel pits' and beyond-rational 'fertile octogenarians' to explain its complex operation. Such fantastical tales also attest to Rose's claim of the significance of 'property as storytelling'. In this vein, this chapter's tale of the metaphysical in 'everyday' real property begins with an anecdote, an unremarkable vignette centred on the freehold sale of a former church in my home village of Clunes in north-eastern New South Wales (NSW), Australia.[16] Beneath its ordinariness, this small-town tale tells a number of core property truths: the abstraction of doctrinal property law, its prevailing 'land as commodity' ethos and, performatively, the importance of storytelling to property's narratives. Specifically, it highlights the precarity of sacred property and the 'property struggles' that arise when 'spiritual needs confront [the] market-driven logic of profit maximization'.[17] But for the plain purposes of this section, it underscores how the metaphysical in 'everyday' real property lies lost to plain sight.

For over a century, the Uniting Church in Clunes has occupied a central place in the human and physical landscape of the village. Built of now rare timbers clear-felled in (what was once) the 'Big Scrub', a vast rainforest reduced to less than 1 per cent of its pre-European footprint, this simple, unadorned structure is typical of the genre of late nineteenth century rural churches in the NSW sub-tropical north. Its humble aesthete belies its placed significance, the *situs* of countless Sunday schools, weddings, funerals and other community gatherings. Despite its ageing congregation, the church exerted an outsized influence in recent (and, as it turns out, its final) years. This was, in part, due to its modest yet

[16] More widely, it attests to the truism that all property is 'local'; see J Orth, *Reappraisals in the Law of Property* (Farnham, Ashgate, 2010).

[17] M Kwan-Chung Yip, J Wai-Yeng Lee and W-S Tang, 'From God's Home to People's House: Property Struggles of Church Redevelopment' (2020) 110 *Geoforum* 14, 15.

imposing physical presence, as one-third of the village's 'civic square' along with the adjoining primary school and Coronation Hall, exemplifying what Maurice Yip et al observe as the 'often forgotten [yet] fundamental character of churches as property in cities'.[18] Beyond its timber walls and iron roof, the church was also important to Clunes' social fabric, a space and place of communal worship, repose and reflection, and a marker of life's milestones. For the village's largely secular, non-churchgoing population, this was also a space of shared sociability, where generations of children played in the churchyard trees while waiting for school buses or parental pick-ups, and parents lingered in conversation. However, in late 2023, the weekly worship sign abruptly disappeared, and the building and its large acreage were advertised for auction. By December, the land was sold. Changing demographics, the opportunity to develop a potentially greenfield site without heritage restrictions and skyrocketing real estate prices transformed a community space known for values of inclusivity and sociability into expensive, exclusive private estates.

This vignette functions at multiple levels. One is societal, the decline of organised religion, and secularism's corresponding rise. Another is institutional, a tale of property's changed values, from those of community[19] to those of commodity. Spatially, it exemplifies at the micro-level yet another loss of community space to the private realm. It also presages a discussion on 'church as property', which is discussed in section III. But running through this everyday account of property is another less obvious thread – that of the metaphysical in real property, a metaphysicality that exists across multiple layers and with multiple storied narratives.

At the surface, the 'obvious' metaphysicality is a doctrinal one, the real estate transaction not of the physical land itself, but of an estate in fee simple held of the Crown. This is the standard mantra of the doctrines of tenure and estates, fictional accounts of interests in land that pointedly do not include, in this case, the volcanic red soils of Clunes. Rather, what is bought and sold is the relationship between the fee simple holder and the Crown, which a new registered proprietor implausibly 'holds' (not owns) through the imaginary medium of seisin, a type of feudal possession that defies easy definition, but which is given practical force through registration of electronic dealings in the NSW Torrens title registry. Estates and tenure are feudal doctrines that have evolved over at least a millennium, and in the case of Australia's legal history, two invasions, one grounded to Country, another inherited.[20] Textbooks argue that feudal tenure has little practical relevance today, but

[18] Yip et al (n 17).

[19] The values of 'community' are well explained in H Dagan, *A Liberal Theory of Property* (Cambridge, Cambridge University Press, 2021) 51–55.

[20] The 'inherited Invasion' is the Norman invasion of 1066, subsumed into Australia's laws through the doctrine of reception into a 'settled colony'; see A Buck, *The Making of Australian Property Law* (Sydney, Federation Press, 2006).

conceptually it continues to frame our relationships with land in ways that remain profoundly 'abstract' and 'esoteric'. Andrew Buck describes this prevailing conceptual relationship as 'the ghost of feudalism',[21] where at the time of colonisation 'the feudal organisation of society in England had long passed into the realm of history, and necessarily never affected this country'.[22] Yet as a defining principle, this ghost still haunts the vast Australian continent. In the landmark native title case of *Mabo (No 2)*, tenure was the pivotal 'skeleton of principle which gives the body of our law its shape and internal consistency', a framework 'too late in the day' to exorcise as the High Court grappled with the conundrum of reconciling native title with the abstractions of tenure.[23]

Doctrinal abstraction is in turn reinforced by the (ever-accelerating) hyper-abstraction of conveyancing practice. Completion of this contract for sale inexorably occurred in yet another parallel ether, the online exchange of encrypted data far removed from ancient practices such as 'feoffment with livery of seisin', the ritualised ceremony wherein the seller symbolically delivered seisin to the buyer. The press of a computer key has superseded transcendental handovers of clumps of soil or turf, and compounds what Sarah Keenan calls 'radical temporal dislocation', a consequence of Torrens title registries 'making land liquid':[24]

> Radical temporal dislocation is … key to the operation of Torrens title registries, which are real, but rely on the fiction that land has no history other than what is represented on the registry entry. Title registries enable their users to take radical temporal journeys, during which they travel at their own unearthly pace, and then safely arrive in new worlds … Once title is registered, it takes on a new temporality, one that is determined only in relation to the registry and its users rather than any reality external to them.[25]

Keenan says that Torrens schemes basically affirm Einstein's relativity of time theorem, such that operators of title registries are modern-day 'time-travellers' who 'move into the future at such a pace that they experience time differently from the unregistered world around them'.[26] The ongoing sophistication of e-transactions exponentially speed up this 'unearthly' pace, transforming the thingness of property into intangible algorithmic data further divorced from the temporalities of what is perceived as external reality. And as Keenan also suggests, the objectification of data 'may further the end of … human

[21] ibid 1.
[22] ibid, citing AD Hargreave and BA Helmore, *An Introduction to the Principles of Land Law (New South Wales)* (Sydney, Law Book Co, 1963) 18.
[23] *Mabo v State of Queensland (No 2)* (1992) 175 CLR 1, per Brennan CJ.
[24] S Keenan, 'From Historical Chains to Derivative Futures: Title Registries as Time Machines' (2019) 20 *Social and Cultural Geography* 283.
[25] ibid 291–92.
[26] ibid 292.

subjectivity by producing a post-human life form'.[27] E-conveyancing has effectively updated one metaphysical account of the fee simple transfer for another, thoroughly modern beyond-human metaphor.

Such 'progress' reinforces the very point of Torrens title, the Australian land titles system routinely described as 'a system of title by registration, not registration of title'.[28] Its efficiency stems from its state-sanctioned erasure, which guarantees a 'blank slate' or 'immediate indefeasibility' each time there is a new dealing with the land. As its founder, Robert Torrens, explained, 'the entire fabric must be razed to the ground and a new super-structure substituted … he [Torrens and, through him, his system] would take a sponge and rub the whole out'.[29]

This simple tale illustrates that the machinations intrinsic to 'everyday' sales and purchases of real property operate in deeply abstract ethers – and indeed across multiversal time zones. But what it also highlights, by omission, are *other* stories lost behind this dominant paradigm,[30] different metaphysical accounts of *relating* to this land. The seething presence/absence of ancient Godwana rainforests, felled for the church's pews, walls and floors, 'ghosts' of forests that live on as palpable memories or as tiny remnants of once vast acreages, forests which legal pluralists argue elsewhere have their own separate agency or legal standing.[31] Or the lawful stories of the Widjabul Wyabul people, traditional owners for millennia who were dispossessed by the violence of colonisation. Or the placed, Protestant rituals of faith consigned to a past age. All lost to plain sight, where one thin abstract tale (the spectre of a time-travelling feudal ghost) conceals *other* metaphysical stories that tell of different ways of relating to this space and place.

Finally, this simple anecdote of an ex-church in rural Australia illustrates Carol Rose's argument that storytelling helps make sense of property.[32] Here, it helps translate the mysteries of property's other-worldliness to everyday, relatable language. Or it helps to tease out its less obvious metaphysical narratives. Rose notes that despite theorists depicting property as a kind of linear legal science, 'their discussions of property at some point take a striking turn towards the narrative or a "diachronic" explanatory mode'.[33] Rose explains this need for post hoc narrative explanation to 'smooth over' inconvenient gaps in property

[27] S Keenan, 'The Transfer of What? Electronic Conveyancing and the Destabilisation of Property' (2023) 5 *Law, Technology and Humans* 11, 21, citing J Kaal, 'The Materiality of Data as Property' (2020) 61 *Harvard International Law Journal Frontiers* 1.

[28] *Breskvar v Wall* (1971) 126 CLR 376, per Barwick CJ.

[29] Robert Torrens, cited in P Butt, *Land Law*, 6th edn (Sydney, Thomson Reuters, 2010) 744.

[30] The wording of the 'for sale' sign emphasises modern property's transactional focus; with the late nineteenth-century de-consecrated church, and greenfield acreage described as potential 'blank slates', with no heritage encumbrances to hinder its re-development. A new owner could incorporate the historic structure, re-locate it or even demolish it.

[31] See section IV.

[32] Rose (n 13).

[33] ibid 38.

theory or 'to paint a plausible picture'[34] of otherwise implausible accounts of property. While Rose was concerned with the failure of classical property theorists to account for co-operative behaviours, the same argument holds true for making sense of the metaphysical in real property, of making its implausibility plausible. Narrative and storied context brings to life the spiritual and relational connections of land, and those landed relationships that came before, whether it is the threadbare yet prevailing fantastical tale of Norman tenure, long-gone ancestral rainforests, or the ongoing lawful stories of Indigenous traditional owners.

III. SACREDNESS, CHRISTIAN SPIRITUALITY AND THE COMMON LAW OF REAL PROPERTY

Another 'portal' through which the physical and metaphysical pass is that which links the sacred and secular via (once) mainstream Christianity – a point of ingress and egress which, as the prior tale of an Australian ex-church shows, appears to be fast closing. Writing in 1998, Stuart Banner argues that the once-widespread maxim 'Christianity is part and parcel of the common law' now occupies 'a dark, barely explored corner of legal history'.[35] This section peers briefly into this near-forgotten 'corner', identifying a number of obsolete, arcane or, at best, peripheral estates or interests that hint of a once-potent, much-lived, connection of faith and land.

The interdisciplinary lens of legal geography provides one insight into faith-based connection through the idea of 'church as property'.[36] Writing of the contested redevelopment of Our Lady of Mount Carmel Catholic Church in Hong Kong, Maurice Yip et al observe that: 'Church is often characterized as sacred space … *but it is fundamentally a property* … It is distinguishable from other properties mainly because the church is functionally used in a different way, which has a spiritual quality as people practice religious rituals.'[37] As such, churches are material examples of real property that sit astride an amorphous fault line, where congregants seamlessly spring and shift between the physical and the metaphysical, a space that is 'not distinctively … sacred or secular … but a hybrid space that is simultaneously [both]'.[38]

The benefit of this propertied/legal geographical lens also reveals churches as 'complex webs of socio-spatial relations in which people [exercise] collective

[34] ibid 53.

[35] S Banner, 'When Christianity was Part of the Common Law' (1998) 16 *Law and History Review* 27, 28.

[36] Consider analogously early Christian monasteries and their hybrid spatial nature as shared common places of this world and beyond it; see J Noeh, *Law, Love and Freedom: From the Sacred to the Secular* (Cambridge, Cambridge University Press, 2019) 102–11.

[37] Yip et al (n 17) 16 (emphasis added).

[38] ibid.

rights to public life and rights of not being excluded from their religious life'.[39] In the case of Clunes, the closure of its last place of Christian worship puts in 'the spotlight this [now lost] spatio-religious hybridity', space which 'serves the spiritual needs and creates a sense of religious belonging',[40] while acting as a buffer against an otherwise universalising 'concern about [private] real estate hegemony'.[41]

Apart from the little-considered notion of 'church as property', there are peripheral property interests that remind us of a once-potent, much-lived, faith-based connection to land. One is the advowson, 'an ancient perpetual property right, which allows [the patron of that right] to present a new incumbent when there is a vacancy in their benefice'.[42] Another is the ecclesiastical easement. Advowsons are incorporeal hereditaments, subsisting at common law and statute.[43] Teresa Sutton says that while a 'relic' and 'irrelevance' to modern practitioners, 'within the Church [of England], they are a matter of everyday use'.[44] Once things of property that were 'hotly traded', advowsons in England can no longer be bought or sold, but they may be 'bequeathed or transferred without value'.[45] The identity of the patron (as the right holder) and their relationship with the parish is critical; in the best case, these are 'genuine, on-going relationships between the patron and the benefice which are supportive of the community and their *faith and mission*'.[46]

As the latter-day advowson shows, sacred rights in land de-centre commodity, since advowsons can no longer be bought and sold. Rather, they encompass lesser-seen property values, the likes of community, sociability and, in the context of this chapter, faith-based connection. Conversely, other once-religious interests in land have lost any lingering semblance of their 'sacredness' or their connection to any metaphysical *other*. Thus, glebes[47] sometimes transform into de facto parks. In the inner Sydney suburb of Camperdown, park users routinely spill over from the Camperdown Memorial Rest Park into the adjoining glebe of St Stephen's Anglican parish, taking with them their picnic blankets, cheese and wine, and playful dogs, seemingly oblivious to their 'trespass'. Parish burial grounds provide another example of enhanced public space, becoming 'sites of local history groups', urban wildlife sanctuaries, 'venues for academic teaching

[39] ibid 23.
[40] ibid 14.
[41] ibid.
[42] T Sutton, 'Advowsons and Private Patronage' (2019) *Ecclesiastical Law Journal* 267.
[43] For example, advowsons are included within the definition of 'land' in s 205(1)(ix) of the Law of Property Act 1925 (UK).
[44] Sutton (n 42) 269. Elsewhere, advowsons remain good law, 'rights analogous to advowsons have from time to time come before Australian courts'; Butt (n 29) 520.
[45] Sutton (n 42) 269.
[46] ibid, emphasis added. At worst, 'patronages are … a remnant of a feudal badge of honour [which] the parish is only reminded of their existence and their rights when it is faced with a vacancy' (ibid 269–70). The advowson remains a valid, albeit rare property right in Australia.
[47] Glebes were income-producing lands that formed part of a clergy's benefice.

and research' or simply 'a place [for residents] to walk their dogs or take their small children, stroll reflectively, or access pubs or coffee shop[s]' at the nearby high street.[48]

Such redundancy of faith-based lands cuts both ways, enlarging public space in the above cases or, conversely, demonstrating the precarity of 'church as property' in booming real estate markets like Hong Kong or even Clunes. The decline of faith-based real property mirrors a commensurate decline of Christian cosmologies in Western society and affirms Joseph Singer's thesis that property is a dynamic institution that conforms to societal contours.[49] Interestingly, however, in parts of the Global South, like the Pacific where Christianity remains vibrant, the metaphysicality of faith has important implications for land, and people's lawful relationality with it. Rebecca Monson writes of the Solomon Islands where the incorporation of Christendom into 'kastom' reflects a post-colonial evolution of nineteenth-century missionary activity[50] into 'reconfigured … idioms, texts, networks and infrastructure',[51] local 'vocabularies and practices' 'crucial to understanding how people come to understand themselves and relate to others as well as their lands and ecosystems'.[52] Monson observes a co-weaving of Christian and Indigenous cosmologies, such that their now-collated stories set the foundation for the norms and regionally diverse practices of landholding in the Solomon Islands. Monson also spots a (metaphysical) gap in the literature:

> With the notable exception of work on Islamic property and inheritance regimes, global scholarship on gender, land and legal pluralities has not yet paid sustained attention to religious norms, practices and institutions, nor to the co-production of religious subjects and places … Yet as we have seen, Christianity is central to Solomon Islands' legal pluralities.[53]

Natural law, and its significance for property as a 'natural right',[54] is another exemplar of metaphysicality's once-significant presence and its latter-day

[48] D McClean and P McClean, 'Shared Burial Grounds' (2022) *Ecclesiastical Law Journal* 293, 308.

[49] JW Singer, 'No Right to Exclude: Public Accommodations and Private Property' (1996) 90 *Northwestern University Law Review* 1283.

[50] R Monson, *Gender, Property and Politics in the Pacific* (Cambridge, Cambridge University Press, 2023) 55.

[51] ibid 229.

[52] ibid 231. Monson also notes that 'detailed discussion of these matters often provoke discomfort, even derision, when they arise in academic settings or in NGO offices outside the region' (ibid).

[53] ibid 227–28.

[54] Stuart Banner ascribes the decision in *Pierson v Post* to natural law, a seminal US property case from the early nineteenth century and cited frequently in property law curricula. In that case, 'New York law had no positive law that could answer the question [as to the ownership of a hunted fox] … The lawyers on both sides accordingly based their arguments on natural law. The judges did the same. The majority determined that chasing the fox was not enough to claim ownership of it, because natural law conferred ownership of the fox on the hunter who first physically possessed it'. S Banner, *The Decline of Natural Law: How American Lawyers Once Used Natural Law and Why They Stopped* (Oxford, Oxford University Press, 2021) 29.

doctrinal decline. This is the thesis behind Stuart Banner's 2021 book *The Decline of Natural Law*, which interrogates why American lawyers 'stopped using natural law'.[55] Banner identifies two once-dominant bodies of law – natural law and positive law – which in previous centuries worked closely in concert with the other. The former was 'found', 'discovered', discerned or indeed divined by judges, an interpretive recognition of a series of pre-existing universal truths that were 'part of the fabric of everyday life'.[56] The latter simply was 'made', filling gaps where natural law was 'silent' or 'indifferent', or else 'supplying the finer-grained rules needed to put [natural law] principles into practice'.[57] Natural law has a distinctly metaphysical provenance, its origins lying in a blend of religion ('the commands of God'),[58] morality[59] and the unstated laws of nature that governed human affairs. Natural law enjoyed pre-eminence, Banner argues, in an era when the boundaries between the empirical and the normative were less distinct, as were the divisions between the realms of science and religion.[60]

Banner charts the decline of natural law in the US from the mid-nineteenth century, citing a combination of factors for its intellectual demise, including the adoption of state written constitutions, the evolving separation of law and religion, and an explosion in law publishing with its 'substitution of precedents for principles'.[61] Banner states that: 'Natural law was almost universally accepted in the legal system in 1870, but it was almost completely gone by the early 20th century'.[62] Lawyers schooled in the natural law tradition lamented its demise, arguing that 'courts [now] have nothing to do with *justice, common sense, right and wrong, or rights*'.[63] Their function was to 'simply administer the law as prescribed by statutes and judicial decisions'.[64] In this new way of thinking about the common law of property, judges were no longer 'law finders', but 'law makers',[65] in the process substituting an institutional mystery in property for an all-consuming, self-referential black letter approach to legal problem solving.

[55] ibid.
[56] ibid 53.
[57] ibid 30.
[58] ibid 33.
[59] 'Traditional biblical hermeneutics posits a fourfold sense of scripture: literal, allegorical, moral and anagogic. According to Dante, the literal operates at the level of sight and sound … the allegorical operates at the level of contemplation, *the moral operates at the level of faith*, and the anagogic operates at the beatific vision that fulfills faith'. J Neoh, *Kaw, Love and Freedom: From the Sacred to the Secular* (Cambridge, Cambridge University Press, 2019) 42 (emphasis added).
[60] Banner (n 54) 35–36.
[61] ibid 128.
[62] ibid 167. Conversely, Banner cites examples of where 'faint echoes' of natural law persist (at 241–49).
[63] ibid 176 (emphasis in original).
[64] ibid.
[65] ibid 249.

IV. LEGAL PLURALISM, INDIGENOUS COSMOLOGIES AND THE RIGHTS OF NATURE

If real property's metaphysicality is hard(er) to discern in orthodox 'Western' property law, it is less so in emerging fields like the rights of nature or, more significantly, in the growing shift to legal pluralism in settler colonial jurisdictions such as Canada, New Zealand and Australia, where Indigenous-based metaphysical accounts of property are increasingly recognised in state law.

In Australia, the 1971 'Aboriginal lands rights' case of *Milirrpum v Nabalco Pty Limited*[66] is instructive in showing how far this shift has come. In *Milirrpum*, bauxite leases granted by the Commonwealth government in favour of the miner Nabalco triggered a judicial exploration of the meaning of 'property' for the purposes of the Australian Constitution (and its 'just terms' acquisition clause).[67] The plaintiffs claimed that their customary 'native' rights and interests in the land had been wrongly acquired by the grant of the mining leases. The court conceded that the 'clans' had an overarching 'subtle and elaborate system of social rules and customs … recognizable as a system of law'. However, their legal relationships with that land, based on 'customs, beliefs and practices', were not sufficiently proprietary for the 1970s common law. The plaintiffs' claims were based on a number of grounds, including a 'mythology' or 'myths of creation' argument, where 'spirit ancestors' since time immemorial had gifted the lands to the 'clans'. The court did not find this line of reasoning 'persuasive'. Blackburn J opined:

> It seemed to me that the ancestral spirits were regarded as having created all things – the land, the clans, the sun, the stars, the animal and vegetable kingdoms, and the sacred ritual, and set them all in their proper relationships … With great respect for the plaintiffs' beliefs, I do not think they help me to decide the issue before me.[68]

In 2023, similar questions[69] over those same lands in *Milirrpum* arose for fresh consideration.[70] In *Yunupingu*[71] the Full Court of the Federal Court[72] took a very different view of 'property' for the purposes of its recognition and compensability in Australian law. The Court's decision was strongly informed by Indigenous worldviews and cosmologies, noting that native title is 'intertwined with and

[66] *Milirrpum and Others v Nabalco Limited and the Commonwealth of Australia* [1971] FLR 141.

[67] Section 109 of the Australian Constitution.

[68] *Milirrpum* (n 66) 270. Blackburn J concluded (at 273): 'In my opinion, therefore, there is so little resemblance between property, as our law, or what I know of any other law, understands that term, and the claims of the plaintiffs for their clans, that I must hold that these claims are not in the nature of proprietary interests.'

[69] Eligibility for compensation for 'past acts' under the Native Title Act 1993.

[70] See also K Galloway and M Castan, 'Comment: Land Rights and the Operation of Public Law: *Yunupingu v Commonwealth*' (2023) 34 *Public Law Review* 175.

[71] *Yunupingu on Behalf of the Gumatj Clan or Estate Group v Commonwealth of Australia* [2023] FCAFC 75.

[72] Leave has been granted to appeal the judgment to the High Court.

un-severable from the spiritual and lived experiences and beliefs of those people who hold it'.[73] Citing with approval an earlier case of *Fortescue Minerals Group v Warrie*,[74] the Court elaborated, 'the very foundation of Aboriginal law and customs … is in the spiritual, and the intermingling of the spiritual with the physical, with people and with land'.[75] It concluded that as 'rights in lands and waters, [such intermingled rights] are in that sense *quintessentially* proprietary in nature'.[76] What had been 'unpersuasive' 50 or so years earlier had now become unequivocally 'quintessential'.

Yunupingu is, at the time of writing, the most recent example of this momentum towards the metaphysical in settler state property law in Australia. Another is the landmark *Timber Creek* case from 2017 that established compensability for the loss of spiritual values when native title is extinguished.[77] There, the High Court majority directly referenced the physical/metaphysical duality, describing 'native title as composed of two distinct bundles of rights in relation to the land', 'the physical and material on the one hand' and 'the cultural and spiritual on the other'.[78]

This metaphysical turn in the Australian common law of property gives belated 'recognition'[79] to ancient, Indigenous understandings of land, or Country. Mary Graham describes Aboriginal relationships with land as holistic, interconnected and indivisible, such that 'the Land is the Law, and the Law is the Land':[80]

> The land is a sacred entity, not property or real estate; it is the great mother of all humanity … The two most important kinds of relationships in life are firstly between land and people, and secondly, those amongst people themselves, the second always contingent on the first. The land, and how we treat it, is what determines our human-ness.[81]

The metaphysical is central to this worldview, derived from narratives of The Dreaming when spirit ancestors or 'Creator Beings helped [proto-humans] to become fully human, teaching them the Laws of custodianship of land, the Laws of kinship, of marriage, of correct ceremonies – they gave them every kind of knowledge they needed to look after the land and to have a stable society'.[82] Once this work was done, these Creator Beings 'went back into the land, where

[73] *Yunupingu* (n 71) [448].

[74] *Fortescue Minerals Group v Warrie* [2019] FCFCA 177, [281]–[288].

[75] *Yunupingu* (n 71) [454].

[76] ibid [444] (emphasis added).

[77] *Northern Territory v Mr A Griffiths (Deceased) and Lorraine Jones on Behalf of the Ngaliwurru and Nungali Peoples* [2019] HCA 7.

[78] ibid [19]–[28].

[79] Compare the 'violence of colonial *recognition*' in I Watson, 'Aboriginal Laws and Colonial Foundation' (2017) 26 *Griffith Law Review* 469.

[80] M Graham, 'Some Thoughts about the Philosophical Underpinnings of Aboriginal Worldviews' (1999) 3 *Worldviews: Environment, Culture, Religion* 105.

[81] ibid 105.

[82] ibid 182.

they all still remain in the same eternal sleep from which they awakened at the beginning of time'.[83]

In Aotearoa New Zealand, the momentum towards legal pluralism arises in markedly different contexts. It is also further advanced. For example, the New Zealand Council for Legal Education, which governs legal education and practitioner admissions in that country, has mandated that principles of tikanga Māori are to be integrated into the content and teaching of core undergraduate law courses from 2025, along with the mandatory teaching of a new, standalone tikanga paper. Māori scholar Claire Browning explains tikanga Māori as a philosophical and legal understanding of 'the right thing to do', a multi-layered, multi-valent customary approach that that often draws on ancestral links and metaphysical realms for the present interpretive purposes. Thus, in interpreting New Zealand's founding constitutional document, Te Tiriti o Waitangi|Treaty of Waitangi, Browning argues that the tikanga principle of tukutuku (a 'back and forth' reciprocity seen in the practice of weaving) is an apt interpretative lens, particularly when construing the Te Reo (Māori language) version of the Treaty. Browning says:

> Tukutuku emulates ancestral connections allegorically: the weavers' relations with one another iterating the constant presence of other realms of the kinship group, and of living ancestrally and metaphysically shadowed and supported by them. Their motions, mirroring one another's moves on either side, recall a 'constant dialogue between the living and their ancestor-gods', each active in metaphysical and present-day tribal domains.[84]

Tikanga thus offers transformative ways of reconceptualising common law jurisprudences in areas as fundamental as constitutional law, contracts, torts, property law and so on.[85] In terms of property, Browning notes that '[t]here are many aspects of land – stories concerning the emergence of humans from the cosmos, the paths ancestors travelled, pre-colonial wars',[86] which should equally and validly inform the development of its evolving pluralist jurisprudence.

Metaphysical concepts have likewise appeared in recent New Zealand statutes. For example, the landed entity (and de-gazetted former national park) Te Urewera is defined in section 3 of the Te Urewera Act 2014 as 'ancient and enduring, a fortress of nature, alive with history; its scenery is abundant with mystery, adventure, and remote beauty',[87] 'a place of spiritual value, with its

[83] ibid 182–83.

[84] C Browning, 'Tukutuku in te Tiriti o Waitangi: A Tikanga Maori Touchstone for Tiriti Interpretation' (2023) 3 *Legalities: The Australian and New Zealand Journal of Law and Society* 163, 172.

[85] This leads to a related argument as to whether tikanga should sit alongside the New Zealand common law as a separate body of law or whether it forms a fused, pluralistic Aotearoan iteration of the common law.

[86] Browning (n 84).

[87] Te Urewera Act 2014, s 3(1).

own mana and mauri',[88] and 'an identity in and of itself, inspiring people to commit to its care'.[89]

More globally well-known is the Whanganui River|Te Awa Tupua,[90] which is established as a separate legal person by section 14 of the Te Awa Tupua (Whanganui River Claims Settlement) Act 2017 and defined in section 12 as 'an indivisible and living whole, comprising the Whanganui River from the mountains to the sea, incorporating all its physical *and metaphysical* elements' (emphasis added).[91] The Whanganui has become the poster child of the global phenomenon of river personhood, thanks to its pioneering legislative imprimatur in 2017.[92] However, the river's link to the rights of nature movement is 'curious', according to Elizabeth Macpherson, 'given that New Zealand law does not recognise environmental rights, let alone the rights of nature within the Constitutional framework'.[93] The Whanganui represents the growing influence of Indigenous cosmologies on settler state law, a worldview where things of the natural world (rivers, forests, mountains) are seen as sacred ancestral beings deserving of legal personhood.[94]

The modern rights of Nature movement had its origins in Christopher Stone's landmark journal article 'Should Trees Have Standing: Towards Legal Rights for Natural Objects',[95] published one year after *Milirrpum*. Like the court in *Milirrpum*, Stone's analysis of the rights of the physical things of the world took no or little account of Indigenous laws or philosophies, signifying that the rights of nature movement can and does stand apart from Indigenous metaphysics. However, as Helen Dancer observes, 'ecosystems have often received greater protection when Indigenous peoples' rights are recognised' and when philosophic premises shift from 'anthropocentric, state-centralist to Earth-centred, and deep legal pluralist approaches'.[96]

[88] ibid s 3(2).

[89] ibid s 3(3).

[90] In te Reo Māori, 'tupua' also has a meaning of 'supernatural … alluding to the living state of the river'. Martuwarra RiverofLife et al, 'Yoongorrookoo: The Emergence of Ancestral Personhood' (2021) 30(3Z) *Griffith Law Review* 505, 514.

[91] When dealing with the river, third parties must interact with the office of Te Pou Tupua, statutorily defined as 'the human face of Te Awa Tupua' (s 18(2)).

[92] E Macpherson, 'Can Western Water Law Become More Relational? A Survey of Comparative Water Laws across Australasia and the Americas' (2022) *Journal of the Royal Society of New Zealand*, DOI: 10.1080/03036758.2022.2143383.

[93] ibid 7–8.

[94] For accounts of the emergence of river personhood as a legal phenomenon, see, for example, C Clark et al, 'Can You Hear The Rivers Sing? Legal Personhood, Ontology, and the Nitty-Gritty of Governance' (2019) 45 *Ecology Law Journal* 787.

[95] CD Stone, 'Should Trees Have Standing? Toward Legal Rights for Natural Objects' (1972) 45 *Southern California Law Review* 450.

[96] H Dancer, 'Harmony with Nature: Towards a New Deep Legal Pluralism' (2021) 53 *Journal of Legal Pluralism and Unofficial Law* 21, 38. However, Dancer also cautions that '[i]n other contexts, states will need to find ways of recognising Nature as a legal subject in a way that decentres the state irrespective of whether Indigenous Peoples' interests are bound with the land in question' (ibid 35).

As foreshadowed, rivers occupy a prominent place in the evolution of the rights of Nature. Alessandro Pelizzon and John Page observe that 'rivers appear to be located at a crucial intersection of [this] acceleration, cast as the main protagonists in a rapidly emerging, and certainly captivating, legal discourse'.[97] The years 2016 and 2017 were especially pivotal, with judicial breakthroughs in Columbia (the Atrata River) and India (the Ganges and Yumuna Rivers, streams and glaciers), and legislatively in New Zealand and Australia (Te Awa Tupua and the Birrarung|Yarra River in Victoria).[98] Distinct generational shifts have been identified as this riverine phenomenon evolves, starting with a rights-based focus, then shifting to a 'legal person/legal subject/living entity' typology[99] and, presently, the 'ancestral' person. The first two iterations have attracted criticism as either importing individualised, anthropocentric frameworks, or colonial discourses that 'divert attention away from the struggle for Indigenous sovereignty and control over natural resources'.[100] Such 'ontological, political, and normative shortcomings'[101] have favoured the ancestral person[102] where Indigenous metaphysics are constitutive. A full discussion of river jurisprudence is beyond this chapter's remit, but suffice to say that its current (and most cogent) iteration is one where legal pluralism weaves Indigenous metaphysicality into modern law through the medium of an ancient, ancestral, beyond-human entity.

Forests are likewise fertile spaces for re-imagining legal pluralism in settler jurisdictions and re-conceptualising land relations through a metaphysical lens. In *The Lawful Forest*[103] Cristy Clark and John Page explore the physical and metaphysical nature of forests as sites for pluralist understandings of property, as both material spaces of trees, but also as a metaphysical idea or metaphor for an ancient, relational understanding of property. In Canada, scholars Kirsten Anker and Estair van Wagner separately consider how forests are portals into other-worldly ways of relating to forested space that disrupt 'settled hegemonic assumptions' about Anglo-Canadian property law. In the forests of urban Montreal, Anker contemplates the metaphor of 'Law as forest. Forest as law'[104] to demonstrate that 'Indigenous forms of deep participation in ecological process suggest that the mythos of storied places is more apt to account for grounded jurisprudence than [their] logos'.[105] On Vancouver Island, vast

[97] J Page and A Pelizzon, 'Of Rivers, Law and Justice in the Anthropocene' (2022) *Geographical Journal*, DOI: 10.1111/geoj.12442, 4.
[98] ibid.
[99] E O'Donnell, 'Rivers as Living Beings: Rights in Law, But No Rights to Water?' (2021) 29 *Griffith Law Review* 643.
[100] Page and Pelizzon (n 97) 5.
[101] ibid.
[102] Page and Pelizzon describe the ancestral person as 'a novel ontological category deeply informed by Indigenous worldviews and yet capable of articulating Indigenous First Law in terms that are recognisable within the colonial legal context' (ibid 7).
[103] Clark and Page (n 1).
[104] ibid 192.
[105] ibid 194.

plantation forests subject to Indigenous legal orders are pluralist legal spaces that disrupt the 'private forest' and plantation owners' rights to exclude. Van Wagner says that 'examining Indigenous forest relations … requires looking beyond the human to explore the agreements and the relationships between humans and the *more-than-human world* of the forest, including the metaphysical realm'.[106] Forests have spiritual and ancestral dimensions where certain places are recognised under Indigenous law as First Ancestors and serve as 'living legal scholars'.[107]

The growing recognition (and enforcement) of Indigenous legal worldviews in settler state jurisdictions reflects a commensurate (re-)taking of a metaphysical turn in the law. Ancient ancestral beings now enjoy state-sanctioned legal standing, and spiritual connections with land have become 'quintessentially proprietorial'. This modern jurisprudential shift is contrasted with a concomitant withering of 'Western' metaphysical legalities canvassed in section III. Both demonstrate in their respective flourishing and quiet decline, the ongoing, shape-shifting presence of the metaphysical in our lawful relations with land.

V. PROPERTY THEORY AND THE TURN TO SECULAR METAPHYSICS

Several property theories, liberal and critical, along with social commentaries which critique property's placeless-ness, leave the door ajar for the metaphysical. Some theories argue that a secularised sense of 'belonging' better explains property's relationships than exclusion-premised theories. Others speak of 'flourishing' or 'well-lived lives' in their appeal to the incommensurable. And yet others directly appropriate the supernatural, as this section will explore.

Liberal theories tend to be more circumspect in their references to property's *other*. Proponents of progressive property theory cite *incommensurable* property values such as 'individual autonomy, personal security, personhood, self-determination, community, and equality'[108] as critical to the enablement of human flourishing. Clearly, such aspirations exceed the strictly instrumentalist or material.[109] Similarly, Hanoch Dagan is concerned with property's capacity to enhance personal autonomy, which he argues is optimised in contexts of structural property plurality.[110] Dagan says that pluralism 'enables property law to

[106] ibid 2 (emphasis added).
[107] ibid 4.
[108] G Alexander, *Property and Human Flourishing* (Cambridge, Cambridge University Press, 2018).
[109] ibid, although Alexander argues that 'human flourishing', unlike 'happiness', is 'objective'.
[110] H Dagan, *A Liberal Theory of Property* (Cambridge, Cambridge University Press, 2021) 4 advocates 'structural pluralism' as representative of property's lived heterogeneity. He also argues that liberal property must be 'autonomy enhancing' and relationally just': 'diverse property relationships tend to enhance rather than detract from belonging. If property relationships are measured by bonds of 'proximity, attachment or connection to proper and rightful place', then explanations of property that speak to sociability or personhood enable entrance to community in ways that commodity's preference for alienation cannot'.

offer varying balances between the different (intrinsic and instrumental) values that property can serve'.[111] Dagan's valorised duality is analogously one that is instrumentalist and *intrinsic*. Personhood is an important value on the intrinsic side of the ledger, a property holding that 'symbolically extends [an owner's] sense of identity beyond the boundaries of their physical bodies'.[112] Margaret Radin's typology of property as either fungible or constitutive similarly speaks to a like dichotomy, where constitutive property extends the propertied relationship beyond the purely prosaic or physical. Yet another prominent liberal theorist, Joseph Singer, blends progressive property tenets with tenets of his faith, exemplifying how a metaphysical dimension amplifies and informs property theory.[113]

By contrast, critical property theories tend to be more explicit as to real property's metaphysical potential. Davina Cooper's refractive lens is that of *belonging*, not exclusion, which she describes as 'central to the formation and assumption of property relationships'.[114] Belonging identifies a 'relationship of proximity, attachment or connection … of proper and rightful place',[115] an affinity based on social relations such as collective identity, community or family history.[116] Cooper's case studies of 'everyday utopias' yield quotidian settings of 'belonging' that 'unsettle' conventional property assumptions, like an owner's right to exclude. The property norms of Summerhill School in Surrey or a Toronto bathhouse only make grounded sense where the 'black box of unofficial property' is opened up. Inside that 'black box' is property's otherness.

In a similar vein, Sarah Keenan sees property as 'a spatially contingent relationship of belonging'.[117] Property is relevant because 'it specifically addresses the subject-space connection'.[118] The subject's body 'belongs to, combines with, and includes time and space',[119] linking the 'here' with the 'there' spatially, and the 'then' with the 'now' temporally. The subject's body passing through space forges these propertied connections, which are both 'physical' and 'exceed the physical'.[120] In particular, it is the *temporal* connections that incorporate the metaphysical, linking the 'then' with the 'now' through the medium of 'ghostly hauntings.' As Keenan explains, '[h]aunting is a way of thinking about how

[111] ibid 7.
[112] ibid 50.
[113] See, for example, JW Singer, *The Edges of the Field: Lessons on the Obligations of Ownership* (Boston, Beacon Press, 2000) 41, 38-56.
[114] D Cooper, *Everyday Utopias: The Conceptual Life of Promising Spaces* (Durham, NC, Duke University Press, 2013) 161.
[115] ibid 163.
[116] D Cooper, 'Opening up Ownership: Community Belonging, Belongings and the Productive Life of Property' (2007) 32 *Law and Social Enquiry* 625, 629.
[117] S Keenan, *Subversive Property: Law and the Production of Spaces of Belonging* (Abingdon, Routledge, 2015) 6.
[118] ibid 151.
[119] ibid 161.
[120] ibid.

"now" is connected to "then"', of 'maintaining a relation of belonging with the place [the ghost] haunts'.[121] Intergenerational inherited property exemplifies the supernatural-like provenance of property as belonging. Think of family farms where title is passed down from generation to generation, and where forebears continue to 'haunt' and shape how present owners relate to that land. Such continuity links 'then' to 'now' through powerful bonds of affinity to place, transforming the current generation's full legal and beneficial title into a kind of cross-generational 'trust' that looks both forwards and backwards.

'Ghostly matters' matter in the theory of 'property as belonging' because they are the glue that link land to the temporal nexus of belonging. Keenan says that haunting is 'a constituent element of modern social life',[122] 'a way of understanding or feeling how the absent is connected to the present – then to now, there to here',[123] and a 'seething presence of something that is absent'.[124] But significantly, haunting also speaks to the dynamics of law and power, and its critical re-evaluation:

> [T]o acknowledge and study ghostly matters is important in recognizing the complex ways that power operates … from state institutions and inescapable meta social structures such as racism and capitalism, through [to] countless, seemingly innocuous everyday things, practices and understandings.[125]

Belonging also has provenance in pre-eighteenth-century understandings of common law property. Consider the relationship that commoners enjoyed with their pre-enclosure rural commons. Jeanette Neeson observes the 'intimate spatiality of the classic commons'[126] where traditional common uses, such as pasturage, were complemented by *other* common rights replete with social meaning and relational implication. Neeson records how 'access to the openness of the commons brought solitude … each usage of common waste created a sense of self; it told commoners who they were, a part of a tribe'.[127] Enclosure not only wrought massive social, economic and demographic disruption, leaving millions placeless and rootless, but it also left a metaphysical legacy, described as '[commoners] moving out of their knowledge'[128] when forcibly dispossessed from their lands.

Although beyond the scope of this chapter, it is plausible to draw a line of sorts from the 'universalizing and totalizing'[129] effects of enclosure to

[121] ibid 169.
[122] ibid 166.
[123] ibid 167.
[124] ibid 168.
[125] ibid 167.
[126] Cited in N Blomley, 'Enclosure, Common Right and the Property of the Poor', (2008) 17 *Social & Legal Studies* 311, 320.
[127] JM Neeson, *Commoners: Common Right, Enclosure, and Social Change in England 1700–1820* (Cambridge, Cambridge University Press, 1993).
[128] ibid.
[129] Blomley (n 14).

contemporary legal and social commentaries that critique modern property's placeless-ness, our consequent 'disenchantment' from place and, in response, a secularised yet also super-naturalised counter-yearning for 'belonging', a search for affinity reliant on spatiality and property.[130] The landscape that succeeded enclosure and replaced property diversity with property monotone[131] persists, especially in those 'geographies of nowhere', the 'sprawlscapes' that characterise many twenty-first-century cities, especially in their suburban and ex-urban peripheries.[132] Critical property scholar Nicole Graham writes of dephysicalised 'lawscapes',[133] while beyond the law, social commentators, including James Howard Kunstler,[134] Rebecca Solnit,[135] Tim Dee,[136] and Suzannah Lessard[137] among others, identify private property's role in shaping these post-commons spaces of 'endlessly repeated form'.[138] It is from these soul-less contexts that a yearning for something else, a quest for 'belonging, finds such resonance.

VI. CONCLUSION

In this (at times stridently) secular age, lawful relations with land can play an unlikely role, one that mediates between this world and worlds beyond it – a role that applies equally for people of faith and for people of none. Land is undoubtedly a core engine room of economic activity, but it may also be a source of 'enchantment' as much (as the preceding section reminds us) of its propensity to 'disenchant'. This chapter has identified several portals, analogous to the fictional gateways of *Stranger Things*, through which real property's strange other-worldliness may be glimpsed and transcended. These are the windows that periodically open and close as the metaphysical in real property springs and shape-shifts in tandem with the ever-changing contours of law and society, and its ever-changing tastes for other-worldliness.

As this chapter also illustrates, the metaphysical things of the common law of real property are a 'broad church', extending from orthodox doctrines such as the variant of tenure transported to the Australian colonies, through to the personhood of ancestral, beyond-human entities. Its wide reach catches

[130] See, for example, WP MacNeil, 'Review: *All of Us Strangers*, 2023, Film', (2024) 4 *Legalities: The Australian and New Zealand Journal of Law and Society* 114.

[131] J Page, *Property Diversity and Its Implications* (Abingdon, Routledge, 2017).

[132] Clark and Page (n 1) 44.

[133] Graham (n 10).

[134] JH Kunstler, *The Geography of Nowhere: The Rise and Decline of America's Man-Made Landscape* (New York. Touchstone, 1993).

[135] R Solnit, *Hollow City: The Siege of San Francisco and the Crisis of American Urbanism* (New York, Verso, 2000).

[136] T Dee, *Ground Work: Writings on Places and People* (London, Jonathan Cape, 2018).

[137] S Lessard, *The Absent Hand: Reimagining our American Landscape* (New York, Counterpoint, 2019).

[138] ibid.

once-potent, now-overlooked doctrines like natural law, along with flourishing Indigenised Christian cosmologies that govern how people relate to and hold land in the South Pacific. In Aotearoa New Zealand, Māori cosmologies put metaphysicality at the centre of tikanga's integration into the common law, a paradigmatic normalisation of metaphysicality where property lies at the vanguard. Meanwhile, Western cosmologies, and their tenuous relations with land, wither. Likewise, the 'turn towards the metaphysical' finds a degree of theoretical oxygen in emerging property theories outside the realms of objective factual materiality, transactional economics or the logic of exclusion.

At the start, the chapter observed the curious phenomenon whereby 'property in context' can feed a turn to other-worldliness, while the law's abstraction yields increasingly material, commoditised outputs. This is a trend that reflects the tensions and unpredictable dynamics of the physical and metaphysical in real property, as well as their proximity and respective porosity. It also reminds us of the institutional mysteries of land, our ancient relations with it, and the sometimes-strange contours of real property law and theory.

Index

[*All references are to page number.*]

www.ingramcontent.com/pod-product-compliance
Ingram Content Group UK Ltd.
Pitfield, Milton Keynes, MK11 3LW, UK
UKHW020816290926
15470UKWH00003B/1184